DICTIONARY OF
RACE AND ETHNIC RELATIONS

By the same author

Rastaman: the Rastafarian Movement in England
Black Youth in Crisis (*with B. Troyna*)
Black Sportsmen
Approaching Social Theory (*with B. Mullan*)
Introduction to Race Relations (*with B. Troyna*)
No Future: Youth and Society
Race

DICTIONARY OF
RACE AND ETHNIC RELATIONS

E. Ellis Cashmore

With contributions from
Michael Banton, Robert Miles,
Barry Troyna and Pierre L. van den Berghe

Routledge & Kegan Paul
London, Boston, Melbourne and Henley

First published in 1984
by Routledge & Kegan Paul plc

14 Leicester Square, London WC2H 7PH, England

9 Park Street, Boston, Mass. 02018, USA

464 St Kilda Road, Melbourne,
Victoria 3004, Australia and

Broadway House, Newtown Road,
Henley-on-Thames, Oxon RG9 1EN, England

Set in Palatino and Helvetica
by Columns of Reading
and printed in Great Britain
by St Edmundsbury Press Ltd
Bury St Edmunds, Suffolk

Library of Congress Cataloging in Publication Data

Cashmore, Ernest Ellis

Dictionary of race and ethnic relations.
Bibliography: p.
Includes index.
1. Great Britain – Race relations – Dictionaries.
2. United States – Race relations – Dictionaries. 3. Great
Britain – Ethnic relations – Dictionaries. 4. United States
– Ethnic relations – Dictionaries. I. Title.
DA125.A1C35 1984 305.8'003'21 84-11730

British Library CIP data available

ISBN 0-7100-9904-5

Contents

Contributors

E. Ellis Cashmore is Senior Research Fellow in Sociology at the University of Aston in Birmingham.

Michael Banton is Professor of Sociology at the University of Bristol.

Robert Miles is Lecturer in Sociology at the University of Glasgow.

Barry Troyna is Research Fellow at the ESRC Research Unit on Ethnic Relations.

Pierre L. van den Berghe is Professor of Sociology at the University of Washington, Seattle.

Introduction

The study of race and ethnic relations has problems. One is that it is becoming so preoccupied with its own theoretical infighting, that it is distancing itself from the world it should seek to change. One of the purposes of this dictionary is to reduce this distance. The idea is to provide a basic source book for use by both practitioners and academics of all levels and varieties and, indeed, for anyone seriously interested in the field of study. I designed it with the object of producing a reference work in which I could spell out as clearly and concisely as possible the meaning of concepts, the significance of important figures, the histories of groups, the current state of research and the contributions of schools of thought. In short, I wanted to cover all the established areas of race and ethnic relations (and some less familiar territory) and make them as comprehensible as I could. In this way dialogue can be encouraged and improved.

The dictionary project started from my belief that the study of race and ethnic relations should concern itself with its central issue. Simply stated, that issue is inequality; specifically, inequality that is constructed, positioned and perpetuated by discrimination. That discrimination may be based on all sorts of convictions, but the common denominator is the belief that the human population is divisible into sets of people, some sets of which are superior to others. Over the centuries, this belief has changed its shape and focus and it has been damaged by facts, scientifically validated facts in many cases, that challenge the premises on which it stands. Yet the basic belief in a fundamentally unequal humanity persists. And this gives rise to situations throughout the world in which some groups are systematically treated as inferior by other groups which believe themselves to be, in some way, superior.

The patterns of behaviour that result from this become what many call 'structured inequality'. In other words, the unequal access to such things as quality housing, adequate educations, good jobs, etc. becomes part of the very structure of society. It becomes institutionalized.

To the groups involved, this may not be a problem. Those believing themselves to be superior often have vested interests in maintaining their positions. Those handed inferior treatment might accept their positions, perhaps also believing in a basic inequality. But the student of race and ethnic relations is committed to a different view: his or her ground assumptions are that such inequalities pose a problem worthy of investigation. The ambition then becomes to understand the beliefs that underlie inequalities, to expose them and to reveal how they fit in with other areas of society. The motivating ideal is to produce the kinds of knowledge that will strike hard at the divisions and, ultimately, destroy the structure of inequality.

There are, of course, all manner of cleavages in modern society, all of which arouse deep emotions. Political, moral, religious, sexual and class divisions all yield patterns of inequality. To these we can add race and ethnic divisions. Concerned as the student of race and ethnic relations may be with other areas, his or her focus is more narrowly defined. On the surface, this may seem straightforward enough; so it is particularly infuriating to observe an unproductive development. While attention should properly be fixed on the removal of structured inequalities, much of the energy of race and ethnic relations study has been diverted to internal disputes. These disputes centre on the nature and range of the field of study, the utility of the conceptual tools of analysis, the status of the knowledge produced, the uses to which that knowledge should be put and the motivations of the practitioners involved.

It could be argued that these types of disputes lead to vigorous and often fruitful discussions and that any discipline that wishes to remain reflective has, by its nature, got to entertain continual self-criticism. Race and ethnic relations is no exception: it should and must eye itself critically. This stated, it must also be reaffirmed that the object of the field of study lies not within the discipline but outside it.

I remember sitting next to a West Indian friend at a

seminar on racism where the discussion gravitated toward a dispute between two interpretations of a marxian perspective. What began as general exposition of the origins of the racism issue turned into a highly abstract and semantic quibble. My friend, a nonacademic, listened intently as the discussion built around the question of whether the speaker had conflated Marx's concept of dialectical materialism with historical materialism. My friend was incredulous. 'What's all this got to do with Asians getting bad housing or blacks not getting jobs?' he asked.

Well, there is an answer and I tried to go through it point-by-point as logically as I could, linking the wider theoretical problem to the specific instances. 'I see the point – just,' he eventually replied, 'But surely they should be trying to relate what they're saying to the "real" world.' His remarks have to be taken seriously, for they suggest a gulf that is growing between practitioners and academics. We can agree that changes have to be made. So research must be directed towards those changes and theories must be oriented to exposing the ways in which the changes might come about. But if academics can't even agree on the nature of the world they wish to change, how do they begin?

Nonacademics who are interested and involved in the field of race and ethnic relations are geared to solving problems, often everyday manifestations of wider social divisions. They grow intolerant of many academics who produce theoretical damnations of them and the system in which they operate (and support). Who can blame them? One can further appreciate their intolerance when one considers the language employed by academics when making their pronouncements. Going back to the seminar, I recall the smiles on the faces of some attendant social workers as the academic protagonists couched their argument in such terms as 'hegemonic control', 'endogenous political-economic forces', 'authoritarian statism', 'cultural reproductions' and 'macro-determinants of ideology'. Much of the theoretical infighting has become so impenetrable that the whole field of study is in danger of becoming a pure, insular academic discipline. This is not its purpose and, in a way, this dictionary is an attempt to open up and clarify the whole field. The priority is to give people usable working definitions so that they may find some of the theoretical contributions illuminating rather than obscuring and the practical contributions constructive rather than destructive.

It would have been misleading had I collapsed all the entries so that, collectively, the dictionary read as if race and ethnic relations constitutes a coherent, unified sphere of study. It does not: there are a great many disagreements and I have, accordingly, given full expression to conflicting and divergent views, in some instances, providing two totally separate perspectives on the same term (see 'race relations', for instance). This is a necessary feature of the dictionary, as it is not meant to cover up the internal disputes; it merely seeks to make them understandable.

In this sense, the dictionary is a companion to *Introduction to Race Relations*, in which Barry Troyna and myself set out the limits of the field of study, the history of its development and the key issues within it. We argued for a new approach to race relations studies and a fresh recognition of what we felt were becoming increasingly fuzzy intellectual boundaries. Reception of the book (first published in late 1983) was generally positive, though two reviews in particular illustrate perfectly the appreciable disagreements within the field of race and ethnic relations.

The book, though concentrating on the UK, constantly uses evidence from the USA, either to substantiate or refute arguments. Juliet Cheetham, writing for the *Times Educational Supplement* (4 November 1983), found this agreeable: 'The focus is largely on Britain but helpful parallels are drawn with the United States.' On the other hand, Michael Banton in *New Society* (13 October 1983) was irritated by what he termed 'the unsystematic and superficial comparisons with the United States'.

This was not the only point on which Cheetham and Banton disagreed. Cheetham, a specialist in social policy, thought the book's chapter on education 'the weakest in the book', while Banton, a professor of sociology, found this one of the strongest where 'Cashmore and Troyna look fairly carefully at what the evidence can actually substantiate'. But Banton objected to the more general theory of the book, which he summarized thus: 'that the causes of all the trouble lie in the way capitalist interests and the colonial mentality feed upon and reinforce each other. . . . Such a scheme leaves no place for the moral responsibility of individuals.' Cheetham found this theoretical canvas 'refreshingly broad': 'By insisting that race relations must be examined in their social, political and historical contexts the authors avoid oversimplifying the problems, their origins or solutions.'

On this last point, Banton again took issue, arguing that, by analysing the problems and their solutions as part of a complex social system, 'Cashmore and Troyna contribute to the vicious circle they set out to describe.' But Cheetham saw the opposite potential in the conclusions, noting how there were implications for reforms rather than total transformations: 'Cashmore and Troyna are critical of those for whom radical change is the only one worth contemplating.'

Even on the book's style, there was no common ground. Cheetham: 'Like many ambitious books, *Introduction to Race Relations* is a hard and at times confusing read, not made easier by an irritating folksy style.' Banton: 'Some readers will warm to this book for its direct and breezy approach.'

Quite obviously, different reviewers will have different views. But, such is the disparity between these two on several central issues that one is bound to wonder how any kind of vague consensus is possible within the discipline. Cheetham and Banton are both experienced, respected and rational thinkers and neither is prone to extremisms; yet they disagree at almost every turn in their appraisals. The two reviews make an exemplary case study of the internal disagreements that can bedevil race and ethnic relations study.

Disputes and even controversies can be stimulating for any discipline if they are informed, logical and backed by reasoned argument. Where these factors are missing, they can be harmful and retrogressive. This dictionary may supply at least the basis for more informed, logical and reasoned debate. It can be a source of agreement on the actual terms used when constructing debates, if nothing else.

As I stated before, there are several contentious terms in a dictionary, and, where relevant, I have allowed full expression to the various divergent arguments both in my own contributions and those of my specialist contributors whom I instructed to give balanced accounts whilst airing their own personal views. In order to embrace the full complexity of many of the terms used in race and ethnic relations, I allowed the entries to run to essay length: most items are substantial articles; some are concise definitions. Schools of thought, important figures, theories, fundamental concepts and empirical studies are treated in depth – as, of course, they should be in a work of this nature.

The dictionary is fully cross-referenced and every entry is appended with suggested further reading so that the reader wishing greater detail can pursue his or her studies. This said, I am mindful that the work might well suffer from the same problem as any other dictionary: omissions. I tried to be as comprehensive as possible and include all the important terms used in the field of race and ethnic relations – and even included some unusual ones. As a safety net, I sent the full lists of items to my commissioned contributors (and one also to Robert Blauner) for their comments. They all responded by making additions and thus my catalogue was extended. All the additional items were handled by myself or members of the contributing team, except the entries written by Gita Jairaj and Carl Bagley.

E. Cashmore

Affirmative action Often used synonymously with positive discrimination, this broad social policy is directed towards reversing historical trends that have consigned minority groups to positions of disadvantage, particularly in education and work. Basically, the policy involves actively encouraging educational institutions and sectors of industry to grant access and give promotion to members of groups which have suffered multiple disadvantages, So, whereas in history, certain groups have been negatively discriminated against (for example, denied access or promotion because of their origins, colour or even beliefs), the more modern trend, especially in parts of the USA, is to assist positive discrimination by singling out members of those groups for benefits.

Positive (or 'reverse') discrimination is inspired by the motive to create equality of opportunity. It seeks to provide facilities for those who might be disprivileged in other spheres to 'catch up' in education or at work. The concept as expressed by the British Commission for Racial Equality, is that, 'even if racial discrimination were stopped overnight', some groups would still not be able to compete for jobs because of the past effects of racialism and disadvantage. By giving preferential treatment to groups which are deprived in terms of housing, material wealth and social services, it is intended that they may be provided with sufficient scope to develop their potential and aspire to occupational equality.

US governments, since the 1964 Civil Rights Act, have encouraged programmes implemented with this kind of objective. This Act forced the issue of discrimination in places of public accommodation and gave the attorney the right to act against such discrimination. In the 1970s, however, it was recognized that centuries of inequality could not simply be undone with a piece of legislation. The Equal Employment Opportunity Commission (EEOC) established by the federal government to combat discrimination in employment, grew more strident, insisting that 'affirmative action' be taken by businesses and public employers which were contracted federally. Employers were instructed to make ethnic background a key factor in hiring and promoting – not so that blacks and Spanish-named Americans could be excluded and kept down, but so that they could be included and raised up.

Despite these developments, it was in education that positive discrimination first became the basis for controversy. Marco DeFunis, a Jewish candidate for a place at the University of Washington Law School, was the first rejected applicant to sue an institution that had a programme favouring the admission of minority groups. But it was legal action of Allan Bakke that pointed up the ethical dilemmas of positive discrimination. After his application for a medical school place was turned down by the University of California at Davis, Bakke challenged the decision. In 1978, he had his claim supported by the US Supreme Court, which took the view that the limits of positive discrimination should be set in such a way so as not to work against the interests of whites by requiring their discharge and replacement by minority group members. Nor should the policy serve as a bar to the advancement of whites. It was a complex decision favouring Bakke and one which raised many moral problems.

These problems have formed the core of a debate, two protagonists of which have been Ronald Dworkin and Nathan Glazer. Dworkin defends positive discrimination by arguing that programmes aimed at the achievement of important social goals should not negated by the interests of individuals. Rejected majority group members, like Bakke, may possess greater paper qualifications and thus be harshly dealt with; but this is seen as 'a cost that must be paid for a greater gain'. The gain in this instance would be a long-term one benefiting the whole society rather than isolated indviduals. Dworkin holds the view that a more equal society is the ultimate reward for positive discrimination programmes.

Glazer opposes this on three points: (1) some improvements in the positions of minorities in the USA have been made and, where those improvements have not happened, it is unclear whether discrimination has been the sole cause of the lack of improvement; (2) positive discrimination programmes tend to benefit the skilled and better-qualified minorities rather than the chronically poor; (3) by constructing categories of people to be singled out for preferential treatment, governments formally divide populations into groups with different rights and privileges. The final point raises visions of Orwell's *Animal Farm* in which 'all animals are equal, but some animals are more equal than others.' An additional clause to this argument might be that new divisions could be created by sustained positive discrimination policies: new resentments could be generated, leading to the possibility of a strong white backlash.

Whether one believes the practical benefits of positive discrimination are balanced out by its moral undesirability is a matter of opinion rather than fact. It is certainly an effective instrument for balancing out inequalities; yet there remains the danger that, in establishing groups for preferential treatment, governments may isolate those groups and deepen divisions. There is also the broader critique of positive discrimination that states that it is merely a façade: a method of giving the illusion that the conditions of some minority groups can be improved whilst leaving the basic structure of inequality in fact, with whites firmly in control of all the positions of power.

Read:

Discrimination and Disadvantage in Employment edited by Peter Braham *et al* (Harper & Row, 1981), contains a section on 'Equality opportunity in employment' with extracts from, amongst others, Dworkin and Glazer.

Bakke, DeFunis and Minority Admissions by Allan P. Sindler (Longman, 1978), subtitled 'the quest for equal opportunity' this is one of the more general texts on positive discrimination and its effects.

Introduction to Race Relations by E. Cashmore and B. Troyna (Routledge & Kegan Paul, 1983), has a chapter on 'Work-class-inequality' that sets out the key areas of disadvantage in employments and assesses the means of ameliorating them.

See *Anti-discrimination laws (UK and USA); Equality; Institutional racism; Racism*

Ellis Cashmore

AFRICA

Africa The history of race and ethnic relations in Africa antedates the European colonial conquest by several millennia. The continent has been swept by numerous waves of migration and countless indigenous states conquered multiethnic empires. Indeed, the first European colonialism in Africa is over 2000 years old: it began on a large scale with the defeat of Carthage by Rome in 146 BC. Christianity entered Ethiopia in the fourth century; the Arabs conquered North Africa in the seventh, and Islam crossed the Sahara in the early years of the second millennium. The entire coast of East Africa has been in trade contact with Arabia, India, Indonesia, and China for at least 3000 years. In the interior, a succession of large multiethnic empires rose and fell in the Sudan belt from Senegal to Ethiopia.

The states of central, eastern, and southern Africa were on the whole smaller, somewhat more recent and more ethnically homogenous, yet a number of them were also ethnically stratified as a result of conquest. Some of them developed indigenous forms of racism, for example the kingdoms of Rwanda and Burundi where a Tuzi minority of some 15 per cent of the population dominated Hutu peasants and Twa serfs. The Tuzi claim to superiority was based in good part on their towering stature.

The second half of the fifteenth century marks the Portuguese expansion along the coasts of Africa. The Portuguese were followed in the sixteenth and seventeenth centuries by every other maritime power of Western Europe, principally the English, French, Spaniards, Dutch, and Danes. The Dutch settlement at the Cape of Good Hope in 1652 marks the first sizable European colony in sub-Saharan Africa and was the embryo of contemporary South Africa.

During the 1500 to 1850 period, Europe's relationship to Africa was dominated by the slave trade, in order to supply with labour the European colonies of the New World. Contrary to common belief, the slave trade generally pitted Africans against Africans, and Europeans against Europeans, rather than Africans against Europeans. It was mostly Africans who waged war against their neighbours in order to enslave them, or to avoid being themselves enslaved, and then traded peacefully with European slavers on the coast. The Europeans, on their side, fiercely competed with each other for access to profitable markets and for control of the seas. In all, perhaps some 15 million

Africans crossed the Atlantic in chains, coming principally from West Africa, but also from the Zaire-Angola area, and, in the nineteenth century, increasingly from East Africa. The East African slave trade was centered in Zanzibar, and was largely the product of Arab entrepreneurship. The most massive trading took place during the last century of the traffic (1750–1850), with annual totals often exceeding 50,000.

After the abolition of slavery, the relationship between Africa and Europe entered a new phase. 'Legitimate' trade continued, while the interior was gradually penetrated by 'explorers', missionaries, and military expeditions. France conquered Algeria in 1830; the Boers and the British greatly extended their territorial encroachments in South Africa in the 1830s and 1840s. By the 1870s, the scramble was on; it consisted of a preemptive set of moves by competing colonizers (mostly the French, British, Belgians, and Portuguese, and belatedly the Germans and Italians), to claim vast stretches of African real estate as theirs. The Berlin Conference of 1884–5 divided the spoils and established the ground rules for fighting over the African carcass. It was not until the First World War, however, that European colonial rule was well entrenched over most of Africa (except for Ethiopia, Liberia, and Egypt). When one considers that the Second World War marked the beginning of the end of European colonialism, the ephemeral nature of European political domination over Africa is evident: it only achieved a measure of solidity for one generation.

Much has been written of the differences between the colonial policies of the various powers. The British and the Belgians were probably more racist and less assimilationist than the French and the Portuguese. The French, Portuguese, and Belgians had more centralized colonial administrations based on more direct rule, while the British favoured indirect rule at least where they encountered large indigenous states as in Northern Nigeria and Uganda. However, the similarities between the European colonizers overshadow the differences. The basic ideology of colonialism was paternalism and the reality was domination and exploitation.

A distinction was often made between colonies of settlement and colonies of exploitation. The former (such as Algeria, South Africa, Zimbabwe, the Kenya highlands, and the Angolan plateau) were opened for European rural settlement and were anticipated to have a substantial contingent of permanent European settlers. (The less tropical areas of the continent were preferred for that purpose.) Today, only South Africa retains a substantial population of European settlers. Colonies of exploitation, on the other hand, were meant to be administered by a rotating cadre of European administrators and managers exploiting native labour for the production of minerals and tropical crops (such as cotton, coffee, and cocoa). The economic exchange between metropole and colony was based on unequal terms of trade: dear European finished products against cheap African raw materials (mostly in mining, agriculture, and forestry).

The winds of change brought about by the Second World War affected the colonial relationship in Asia first (principally in India, Indochina, and Indonesia), but by the 1950s, the rumblings of independence were beginning to be heard in Algeria, Ghana, Kenya, Guinea, and elsewhere. The Mau Mau movement in Kenya and the Algerian war of independence were the violent exceptions to a largely peaceful process of political evolution of power leading to the great wave of independence of 1960.

By the mid-1960s, only the southern third of Africa remained under colonial or white-settler rule. The independence struggle in the south took a violent turn as it became clear that independence was not going to be granted through peaceful negotiations. Angola and Mozambique had to fight the Portuguese for 15 years before achieving their independence in 1975. In Zimbabwe, too, the struggle was violent, and freedom had to wait until 1981. In Namibia, the fight is still on, and in South Africa it has yet to break out on a more than sporadic basis.

Since independence, African states have developed different relationships to Europe. Some ruling elites of African states have maintained close economic, political, cultural, and educational ties with Europe in general, and their former colonial power in particular, a relationship often characterized as neo-colonialism. Countries like the Ivory Coast, Senegal, and Kenya are examples. Others have taken a more militant course, and have sought to break their colonial ties, or, at least, to multilateralize their dependency. Tanzania, Guinea, Congo-Brazzaville, Ghana, and Nigeria might be put in that category. Some have sought alliance with communist states to achieve independence, only to fall into another form of dependency: Angola, Ethiopia, and Mozambique are cases in point.

Another interesting shift with independence has been one from race to ethnic relations. The accident of pigmentation differences between colonizer and colonized made the independence struggle to some extent a white-black conflict, even though many of the liberation movements stressed their non-racial and antiracist character. After independence, however, the racial issue receded into irrelevance, except for the expression of hostility against certain 'middleman minorities' such as Asians in East Africa. (Uganda, under Idi Amin, forcibly expelled its Asians, for instance.)

On the other hand, conflicts between indigenous groups for the spoils of independence quickly surfaced in many parts of Africa. Stigmatized as tribalistic, these movements were often, in fact, genuinely nationalist or irredentist. In some cases, ethnic conflicts led to open wars and massacres, as in the Sudan, Ethiopia, Rwanda, Burundi, and Nigeria. In other countries, the game of ethnic politics, while a constant reality, has remained relatively peaceful.

Terminological confusion reigns supreme in the analysis of ethnic relations in Africa. What is called nationalism in Africa is nothing like what the term has conventionally meant elsewhere. How can the concept of nationalism be applied to such multinational states as Senegal, Nigeria, or Zaire? Conversely, what is called tribalism in Africa is often genuine nationalism. The real nations of Africa are the Ibo, the Kikuyu, and the Ewe, not Nigeria, Kenya, and Togo. Only a few of these nations, like the Somali and the Swazi, have their state; the overwhelmingly majority are part of multinational states, or, even worse, are split between several states. It serves, of course, the interests of the ruling elites of these multinational states to stigmatize demands for national self-determination as tribalist, thereby also conforming to the old colonialist view of Africa as congeries of tribes.

Few African states show concrete signs of moving toward the creation of new nations coinciding with their geographical boundaries. Indigenous traditions and languages remain vigorous, and the official languages (French, English, Portuguese) remain tools of convenience of the ruling class, not the basis for the emergence of new national languages. Only Tanzania, with the effective spread of Swahili as a true national language, shows clear progress toward welding a multiplicity of ethnic groups into what may in time become a genuine new nation.

Read:

The African Slave Trade, by Basil Davidson (Little Brown, 1961), a fascinating account of the African-European partnership in slaving, by a radical British scholar.

Race and Ethnicity in Africa, edited by Pierre L. van den Berghe (East African Publishing House, 1975), a collection of articles on North, West, East, and Southern Africa, with several general analytical pieces.

Africa, the Politics of Independence, by Immanuel Wallerstein (Vintage, 1961), a brief treatment of the transition from colonialism to independence by a sympathetic American scholar.

See *Apartheid; Colonialism; Pluralism; Racism; Slavery; Zimbabwe*

Pierre L. van den Berghe

Afro-Caribbeans in the UK The post Second World War movement of Afro-Caribbeans from their countries of origin to the UK, their routine experience of racism and discrimination in the metropolitan centre and their eventual location at the subordinate levels of the UK's class-stratified society are phenomena of colonialism, the system geared towards the open exploitation of human labour and natural resources. Not only was this system secured and justified by the belief in racial inferiority and inequality, a belief which has remained firmly embedded in the collective consciousness of the indigenous white UK population, it also had enormous and far-reaching implications for the economies of the metropolis and periphery and, crucially, for the economic and social relations between them. A. Sivanandan has emphasized this point in his argument that: 'colonialism perverts the economy of the colonies to its own ends, drains their wealth into the coffers of the metropolitan country and leaves them at independence with a large labour force and no capital with which to make that labour productive' (1982).

At the end of the Second World War, the UK and other western capitalist nations embarked on a process of rapid economic growth which necessitated the import of migrant labour. This labour demand was only partially satisfied by the influx of workers from Poland and other parts of Europe and it was at this juncture that the UK, almost in desperation, turned to its colonies and ex-colonies in Africa, India and the Caribbean.

Now, migration from the Caribbean, especially Jamaica and Barbados, had been a fairly routine experience – a conventional means of escape from the twin problems of overpopulation and under/unemployment, phenomena which had been determined by colonial exploitation. Until 1952, the migrants, for a variety of economic and social reasons, had generally headed for the USA; however, the enactment of restrictive immigration legislation by the US government in that year effectively blocked this route. All in all, then, the UK found a vast reservoir of cheap and alternative labour in the Caribbean which could more easily than ever be attracted to the metropolitan centre. These migrants, along with those who later arrived from India (and after 1947, Pakistan) collectively came to be known as 'a reserve army of labour' to the British economy.

The nature of the work they were put to in the metropolitan centre was also predetermined by the colonial legacy: in a period of full employment, white indigenous workers inevitably moved into the higher echelons of the labour market. The vacancies which remained at the 'cellar level' of the market were filled by the migrants: these were the low-status, often unskilled positions in the textile and clothing industries, engineering and foundry works, hotels, hospital and transport services. Native workers' perceptions of blacks as inferior, fit only for menial tasks, had originated in the colonial era; but their experiences of black migrants in the metropolitan centre reinforced these stereotypes. In short, because blacks were compelled to accept 'shit work' in the UK, and were seen to demonstrate the veracity of colonial stereotypes about them, they were inevitably caught in the most vicious of vicious circles.

In profile, the migrants formed a fraction of the working class: they occupied similar positions in relation to the means of production and supplied labour not capital. Nevertheless, though their interests were basically those of the broad working class, the migrants were often seen as unwelcome competitors and, as the post-World War economic boom began to recede in the late 1950s, hostility towards them increased. The outbreak of violence between blacks and whites in 1958 in the Notting Hill district of London and in Nottingham exemplified this growing trend. The increasing demands for selective immigration control, primarily to curtail the entry of non-white colonial and ex-colonial migrants, can also be understood from this perspective.

It is difficult to establish with any precision the collective response of the Afro-Caribbean migrants to these circumstances, though research does indicate that there was widespread disillusion with life in the 'Mother Country'. After all, they had not expected to compete with native workers for jobs, nor had they anticipated the hostility and discrimination which they habitually experienced in their day-to-day lives. Nor were they completely unmoved by these experiences: the manifestation of racial violence in 1958 highlighted the need for greater organization and militancy within the communities and set the scene for the publication of journals such as the *West Indian Gazette* and the establishment of the Standing Conference of West Indian Organizations in the UK. Despite these sporadic gestures of defiance, however, it is difficult to disagree with the view that the energies of the Afro-Caribbean migrants were primarily geared to a process of social involution: the cultivation of separateness from the hostile society and the emergence of group solidarity and community-togetherness. The enormous growth of the Pentecostalist movement in the UK testified to the extent of this withdrawal process. In 1970 it was estimated, for instance, that one branch of this sectarian movement alone had a following of nearly 11,000 people.

This tendency to eschew more militant postures against the daily iniquities of British hostility derived from a variety of factors: some Afro-Caribbeans adhered to what has been termed 'the migrant ideology'; in other words, because their presence in the UK was based purely and simply on economic grounds, they saw themselves as transient workers who would return to their countries of origin once they had accumulated sufficient money. As such, they were prepared to tolerate conditions in UK, because they regarded their stay as temporary. Others put up with what Nancy Foner called 'the pain of being black in Britain' largely because they believed that their children, born and brought up in the UK and therefore not encumbered with an immigrant culture, would not experience the debilitating effects of racial discrimination; they would, in effect, compete on an equal footing with their white counterparts in the UK's meritocratic education system.

The persistence of the colonial legacy ensured that this was false optimism, however. The disadvantages experienced by the Afro-Caribbean migrants in the UK were only tenuously related to their newness in the society; they were unlikely to diminish with the passage of time. It is precisely because their disadvantaged positions were likely to be reproduced in the life patterns of their children that distinguishes colonial migrants from the experiences of other migrant workers. The result: children of Afro-Caribbean origin continue to occupy subordinate positions in the labour market, tend to earn less than white indigenous workers and are more vulnerable to the risk of unemployment. Nor is this trend attributable in any significant measure to their apparent 'under-achievement' at school. The proposition that, even in the midst of a severe recession, school leavers of equal merit stand an equal chance of getting a job simply cannot be sustained. Young unemployed blacks tend to be better qualified than their white unemployed peers.

Though there is always a risk of oversimplifying the issue, the eruption of disorders in many multiracial areas in 1981 gives clues to the response of black youngsters to their situation. The recognition that their life chances are often determined not by their possession of educational qualifications but by their skin colour has generated the adoption of a more militant posture than their parents were willing to assume. Of course, black youths do not constitute an homogeneous or undifferentiated social category: many black youngsters openly reject the oppositional stance taken in 1981 as well as the ideology and practices of the Rastafarian movement. At the same time, many of the youths involved in the disorders and/or in the Rasta subculture retain a commitment to the work ethic and other features of UK society. To characterize black youth as an alienated social group is simplistic and misconceived. At the same time, it is difficult to deny that they display a far greater and more overt resistance to racism and discrimination than their parents did.

In the continued absence of a coherent and politically unified movement in the UK, comparable to, say the civil rights movement in the USA, Afro-Caribbean resistance is likely to take the form of episodes such as those witnessed in 1981. Though these may generate short-term, ameliorative action, they are unlikely to bring about any substantial improvement in the life opportunities of the Afro-Caribbean communities.

Read:

A Different Hunger by A. Sivanandan (Pluto Press, 1982), a series of polemical essays on black resistance in the UK.

Colonial Immigrants in a British City by John Rex and Sally Tomlinson (Routledge & Kegan Paul, 1979), a sociological analysis based on an empirical investigation of the experiences of colonial migrants in the housing and labour markets and educational system in the major UK city of Birmingham.

Labour and Racism by Annie Phizacklea and Robert Miles (Routledge & Kegan Paul, 1980), explores key issues in the relationship between colonial migrants and white indigenous workers in a developing area of North-West London.

See *Colonialism; Immigration laws (UK); Migrant ideology; Migration; Pentecostalism; Rastafarian movement*

Barry Troyna

American dilemma, the See *Myrdal, Gunnar*

Anti-discrimination laws: UK The development of anti-discrimination laws in the UK has to be considered, first and foremost, against a background of increasingly Draconian measures designed initially to reduce the number of black and brown migrants entering the country, and subsequently to eliminate this process entirely. By invoking the principle, 'keeping numbers down is good for race relations', both major political parties have presented anti-discrimination laws as a complementary aspect of their policy initiatives on this issue. The imperative for these laws has been to secure equality of opportunity for all people in the UK, irrespective of ascribed features such as skin colour. The reality of the situation, however, suggests that they are seen as little more than a token gesture by the nonwhite populations of the UK whose confidence in central government's commitment to 'harmonious race relations' has been irrevocably undermined by the obsession with the numbers question, the development of external and internal immigration controls, the division of family units, and so on. These constitute the thrust of government policy and formally legitimate the second-class status of the nonwhite communities in the UK. In short, the avowed intention to create a society in which 'every citizen shares an equal right to the same freedoms, the same responsibilities, the same opportunities (and) the same benefits' is no nearer its realization in the 1980s than it was when it was first declared in 1968 by the Labour government's Home Secretary, James Callaghan.

The commitment to ensure equal opportunity for the nonwhite communities in the UK has most often been translated into practice by the Labour party, but it was not until 1965 that the move towards an exclusionist immigration policy was accompanied by any action to improve the lot of these communities. In that year, the Labour government introduced its White Paper, *Immigration from the Commonwealth*, which tried to sweeten the pill of further immigration restrictions by introducing protective laws to combat racial discrimination. Compared to similar initiatives in Canada and the USA, the 1965 Race Relations Bill was very limited in scope. It outlawed racial discrimination in 'places of public resort' such as restaurants, hotels, places of entertainment and on public transport, and set up the Race Relations Board which was charged with the responsibility of dealing with complaints of discrimination and resolving them through conciliation.

But, quite apart from its practical limitations – it failed to protect nonwhites from discriminatory practices in housing and work spheres, for instance – the 1965 Bill was also logically incoherent. On the one hand, it insisted that the black and brown migrants were not depriving whites of jobs, did not have lower health and sanitation standards, and were not scrounging off the welfare state; but, having denounced racialism and dissociated itself from racialist practices, the Labour government then proceeded to orchestrate and support racist views by implementing immigration policies which deliberately excluded nonwhites.

The limited practical use of the anti-discrimination laws included in the Bill was highlighted by the findings of the PEP investigation two years later. This revealed the extent of discrimination along colour lines in employment and housing. The need for an extension to the 1965 measures was further underlined by the eruption of violence in Watts and elsewhere in the USA around this time. It was precisely the systematic denial of equal opportunity which had precipitated the volatile reaction of blacks in the US. Fearful of a similar occurrence in the UK, the Labour government initiated new legislation in 1968, the Race Relations Act. This enlarged the scope of the law to the important spheres of employment and housing. But, crucially, the powers of the Race Relations Board were not extended; it remained a reactive body, permitted to respond to complaints rather than to initiate investigations into racialist practices. Quite obviously, a law which required proof of deliberate acts of racial discrimination could have only a limited effect on the more widespread patterns of inequality between whites and nonwhites; after all, it could do nothing to cope with the more subtle, less visible and conspicuous expressions of racial discrimination.

The veracity of this argument was demonstrated in the next PEP investigation which reported its findings in the mid-1970s. It showed that the proscription by law of racialism in housing and employment had led to a substantial decrease in its incidence; at the same time, this apparent success of the 1968 Race Relations Act may have been mitigated by the replacement of overt racialist practices by less conspicuous and detectable forms of its operation. What is more, the PEP study showed that discrimination along colour lines remained common and that many nonwhites who had been discriminated against had failed to inform the Race Relations Board.

The PEP survey provided the main stimulus, once again, for legislation and in 1976 the Labour government introduced a new Race Relations Act. This totally restructured the machinery dealing with anti-discrimination and integrated the functions of the Race Relations Board and the Community Relations Commission (which had been established in 1968 to promote 'harmonious community relations') into a new body, the Commission for Racial Equality (CRE). Unlike its predecessor, the CRE has been empowered to initiate investigations where it suspects discrimination has taken place and, where its investigations prove positive, to issue non-discrimination notices.

Since its inception, the CRE has been assailed on all sides;

in 1981, for instance, a team from the Home Affairs Sub-Committee on Race Relations and Immigration was severely critical of the CRE's lack of direction, its incohesiveness and consequently, its ineffectual attempts at eliminating racial discrimination.

It is difficult to deny the legitimacy of these and other criticisms of the CRE. At the same time, it needs to be recognized that the CRE functions in a political climate which is not only indifferent to a co-ordinated policy on race relations but is wholly antagonistic to such a policy. Regardless of the internal faults of the CRE, any organisation integrated into the state machinery is unlikely to be effective either in combating racial discrimination or assuaging the anxieties of the nonwhite communities in the UK. How can the CRE or the range of anti-discrimination measures be effective when they are linked to governments which are resolutely determined to prevent black and brown settlement in the UK and to sanction the low status of these communities? In this context, policies to combat racial discrimination, however determined and well organized, can never be sufficient to ensure equality between white and nonwhite citizens in the UK.

Read:

'The contradictions of the sixties race relations legislation' by John Lea, in *Permissiveness and Control* (Macmillan, 1980), edited by the National Deviancy Conference, places the attempts to provide protective laws against racial discrimination in their proper context: a political climate designed to emasculate the rights of nonwhites in the UK.

'The politics of race in Britain, 1962–1979: a review of the major trends and major debates' by Gideon Ben-Tovim and John Gabriel in *'Race' in Britain: Continuity and Change* (Hutchinson University Library, 1982) edited by Charles Husband, a marxian analysis of the politicization of race in the UK since the early 1960s.

Immigration and Social Policy in Britain by Catherine Jones (Tavistock, 1977), deals with the main thrusts of social policy initiatives including anti-discrimination measures.

See *Affirmative action, Anti-discrimination laws (USA); Discrimination; Institutional racism*

Barry Troyna

Anti-discrimination laws: USA Apart from the brief period immediately after the Civil War, American legislation up to 1938 had the effect of maintaining discrimination against blacks and other minority groups. Reconstruction was an exception to the general pattern which denied blacks civil rights such as voting, access to education and so on. The 1866 Civil Rights Act signalled the end of *de jure* discrimination (that is legal racialism), but various federal actions had worked to diminish racialism in various sectors before that time.

In 1938, for example, the Supreme Court ruled that the University of Missouri should admit a black applicant to law school because the state had no comparable institution open to blacks (*Missouri ex. rel.* v. *Canada*). Four years later, governmental agencies were instructed to end discrimination in employment; and, in 1946, segregated interstate travel was made illegal. Segregated transport was generally more widespread in southern states than in the north, though *de facto* segregation was rife throughout America, with public facilities having allwhite and allblack areas.

In housing, blacks were prevented from buying certain properties by restrictive housing covenants (a provision attached to a deed in which the buyer must agree not to sell or rent to a member of a particular group, such as blacks, Jews or Chicanos). In 1948, the Supreme Court in the *Shelly* v. *Kraemer* case ruled that the restrictive covenants were not enforceable by the states any longer. This did not eliminate the covenants, however: it simply meant that they were no longer enforceable. The 1968 Act eventually banned them.

Perhaps the single most important piece of legislation in regard to race relations came in 1954 with the famous case of *Brown* v. *Board of Education*. The Supreme Court overturned the 'separate but equal' principle established in 1896 by the *Plessy* v. *Ferguson* case in which it was established that different facilities should be made available to blacks. In the area of education, black institutions were truly separate but rarely equal to their white equivalents. The 1954 decision ended this and made segregation in schools illegal. The decision's importance was magnified by the fact that many believed that the whole issue of equality hinged on integrated schooling. The National Association for the Advancement of Colored People (NAACP) precipitated the 1954 ruling by arguing the case of Oliver Brown, whose daughter had been forced to travel by bus to an allblack school even though she lived close to an allwhite institution. The NAACP insisted that school segregation was unconstitutional and the Supreme Court agreed, the presiding Chief Justice Warren concluding: 'In the field of public education, the doctrine of "separate but equal" has no place.'

Between 1957 and 1960, Civil Rights legislation introduced enforcement powers through a Civil Rights Division of the US Department of Justice. But, the critical period in anti-discrimination legislation came over the following four years. Pressure from Martin Luther King's movement resulted in the strengthening of voting rights for blacks (1960) and the banning of discrimination (including sex discrimination) in employment and trade union membership as well as in access to privately owned accommodation, like hotels, restaurants and theatres. Enforcement of provisions against discrimination in education was also given more weight.

Constitutionally, the Civil Rights Act of 1964 was something of a watershed in US race relations, extending federal powers to eliminate discrimination in places of public accommodation and the desegregation of all public facilities maintained by public organizations. In addition, public education was desegregated and the Civil Rights Commission granted new powers. Discrimination in employment on the grounds of 'race, color, sex or national origin' was illegalized. The Equal Employment Opportunities Commission was established to investigate and monitor complaints pertaining to this.

The most widespread requirement limiting minority voting was the literacy test that existed in various forms in numerous states in the south, west and northeast. This tended to reduce voting opportunities for black, Hispanic and North American Indian groups, because these groups suffered extensive educational discrimination and, therefore, did not always match up to the literacy test requirements (in some cases, this was compounded by the fact that more stringent demands were made of minorities than of whites). The Voting Rights Act of 1965 largely ended the tests. Discrimination of sorts continued with some states operating policies that governed voter registration that made voting easier for whites; but the 1965 Act made discrimination in access to the ballot box considerably more difficult.

In terms of legislation, the US government could claim

quite legitimately that it has sharpened its instruments against discrimination so as to make the law a formidable weapon (certainly more so that its UK equivalent). However, to legislate against a practice perpetuating inequality does not necessarily negate that inequality. A useful metaphor comes from John Farley, who writes of a twenty-mile race organized by the government: 'The race is started with one of the runners required to wear a ten-pound weight on each foot. Halfway through the race, the organizer decides that this is not fair and decides to remove the weights. By now, however, the runner with the weights is exhausted and far behind but the organizer says that he must nonetheless continue the race from his present position. Because the weights are gone, says the organizer, there is no more discrimination.' But, of course, 50 years of partial anti-discrimination laws do not necessarily make up for 200 years of discrimination.

Read:

An American Dilemma by Gunnar Myrdal (Harper & Row, 1944), the classic statement on racism in the USA, now dated, but useful for its analysis of the legal situation before the advent of civil rights.

Majority-Minority Relations by John Farley (Prentice-Hall, 1982), has a chapter on 'The American political and legal system and majority-minority relations' which is very clear and systematic.

American Ethnicity by H. Bahr, M. Bruce, A. Chadwick and J. Strauss (Heath, 1979), looks at segregation policy and its effects in the school system.

See *Affirmative action: Anti-discrimination laws (UK); Civil rights movement; Equality; Jim Crow; Segregation*

Ellis Cashmore

Apartheid The system used in South Africa to segregate whites from nonwhites. Apartheid means 'apartness' or total separation in all spheres of life, private and public. It involves the belief in white racial purity and *baasscap*, a Dutch-African (Afrikan) word meaning white supremacy.

The system has its roots in the white master/black slave relationships of the seventeenth-century colonialism. The Dutch developed a small slave colony in Cape Town (on the Atlantic coast) in the 1650s and began to supply fresh produce to ships sailing from Europe to Asia. In the eighteenth and nineteenth centuries, Dutch settlers known as Boers (farmers) moved into the inner regions of Southern Africa. The Boer's incursions brought them into severe conflict with native peoples, such as the Khoikhoi (Hottentots, as they were called by the Boers) from the Cape and Bantu tribes from the southeast. The black native peoples were suppressed by the 1870s and the Boers constructed a series of allwhite republics in the Orange Free State and the Transvaal.

The British interest in the areas grew after the discovery of gold in Johannesburg and confrontation erupted into the Anglo-Boer War, 1899–1902. Britain emerged victorious and established the area as a colony, the Union of South Africa. This was declared a self-governing state, or white dominion, in 1910, with blacks being excluded from all areas of political influence.

The division between blacks and whites was continued by the United Party under the leaderships of Smuts and Herzog from 1934 onwards (with South Africa a member of the Commonwealth) and was fully institutionalized in 1948 when the Afrikaner Nationalist Party won the election. Verwoerd's ascendancy in 1958 gave further impetus to the division as Verwoerd himself believed that the system of apartheid was an enactment of the will of God.

The first plots of land for native peoples, called Bantu reserves, were officially set up in the Transkei in 1962. The South African stated policy was that separate self-governing black states should be created with a view to their eventually becoming independent (a native reserve system had been started in the 1840s designed to restrict the native's rural land to 13 per cent of the total area of the country). Blacks comprise about 70 per cent of the total population of nearly 30 million; they were allocated 12 per cent of the land. Whites constitute about 17 per cent of the population (the remainder being composed of 'coloureds' and Asians).

In order to sustain the economy, the system had to allow blacks to migrate temporarily to white urban areas, or zones. Blacks were issued with pass books and required to carry them at all times; they were made to produce them on demand by the police; failure to carry or produce was made a punishable offence. Blacks, it was determined, were allowed to enter white areas only for the specific purpose of working; basically, they were needed to do menial jobs that whites refused to do. Thus a dual labour market was operated with whites sometimes earning as much as twelve times as much as nonwhites.

After working, blacks were legally required to return to their reserves. This arrangement had actually started in the nineteenth century, when a solution had to be found to the problem of maintaining a supply of cheap labour (then for the mines) without disrupting the essential white-black division. Black workers were made to stay in austere barracks for the length of their contract of labour, then forced to return to their reserves. Overstaying was made punishable by long prison sentences.

Certain other elements of apartheid, such as the illegalization of sexual relations between whites and nonwhites were in effect before 1948, but the implementation of the system served to cement the segregation legally and totally. To complement the whole system, blacks were denied any effective political rights. So the whole thrust of the apartheid system is to: (1) ensure legally strict geographical and social segregation in all spheres of life; and (2) maintain a rigid pattern of inequality in which blacks are effectively kept powerless and without wealth.

Needless to say, such a harsh system has experienced periodic challenges, two of the most important coming from black organizations in 1960 (at Sharpeville) and 1976 (at Soweto). Both attempted coups were suppressed after horrific bloodshed. The South African army and police have, over the years, equipped themselves thoroughly to deal with uprisings, one of the common tactics being to torture and even kill suspected seditionaries (as the death of Steve Biko in 1977 amply demonstrates). There are signs that the system of apartheid will eventually collapse whether through external or internal pressure, but for the moment it remains and keeps nonwhites locked into positions of nonprivilege and powerlessness.

Read:

Living Under Apartheid by David M. Smith (Allen & Unwin, 1983), a collection of general chapters on the society, economy and polity of South Africa and case studies about the problems of work, housing, civil disorder, etc.

Apartheid: Power and Historical Falsification by Marianne Cornevin (Unesco, 1980), a recent critical account of the modern situation in South Africa which is complemented by a chapter called 'Caste' in

Pierre van den Berghe's *The Ethnic Phenomenon* (Elsevier, 1981), which gives a neat summary of the main dimensions of apartheid.

The Psychology of Apartheid by Peter Lambley (Secker & Warburg, 1980), an unusual perspective on the negative effects of apartheid on the minds of those who live amidst it.

See *Institutional racism, Verwoerd, Smuts, Zimbabwe, Africa*

Ellis Cashmore

Aryan A Sanskrit word meaning noble (but apparently in earlier use as a national name), which was used in English primarily to denote the family of Indo-European languages related to Sanskrit. The word acquired greater currency when it was used in the 1850s and 1860s by Gobineau and Max Müller to identify a group of people who produced a particular, and higher, civilization. Gobineau maintained that there was a hierarchy of languages in strict correspondence with the hierarchy of races. He wrote: 'Human history is like an immense tapestry. . . . The two most inferior varieties of the human species, the black and yellow races, are the crude foundation, the cotton and wool, which the secondary families of the white race make supple by adding their silk; while the Aryan group, circling its finer threads through the noble generations, designs on its surface a dazzling masterpiece of arabesques in silver and gold . . .' Most of the authors, who in the late nineteenth century dilated upon the history of the Aryans, wrote less elegantly than this but often in almost equally general terms. Max Miller came to regret the extension in the use of the word and complained 'To me an ethnologist who speaks of an Aryan race, Aryan blood, Aryan eyes and hair, is as great a sinner as a linguist who speaks of a dolichocephalic dictionary or a brachycephalic grammar . . . We have made our own terminology for the classification of languages; let ethnologists make their own for the classification of skulls, and hair, and blood.'

Read:

The Aryan Myth by Leon Poliakov (Chatto, 1974), a comprehensive account of the concept.

Race: The History of an Idea in America by Thomas F. Gossett (Schocken Books, 1965), a briefer treatment.

See *Chamberlain; Fascism; Gobineau; Holocaust; Race; Volk*

Michael Banton

ASIANS IN THE UK

Asians in the UK The concept of 'Asian' is widely used in everyday discourse but is, analytically, a potentially confusing term insofar as it groups together a number of populations which are historically and culturally distinct. In everyday discourse, it is employed to refer to migrants, and their British-born children, who originate from what is now India, Pakistan and Bangladesh. It also includes those political refugees from Kenya and Uganda who are themselves the descendants of an earlier migration from India to East Africa. It is not normally used to refer to Chinese migrants, and their British-born children, although strictly these also originate from the Asian continent. Some writers have used the notion of South Asian to avoid confusion on this point. Others have moved to referring to migrants from the Indian subcontinent and distinguishing these from the later arrival in Britain of the political refugees from East Africa.

Viewed historically, the Asian presence in the UK predates the labour migration of the post-Second World War period. Asian seamen have been employed by British (and other) shipping companies and Asian soldiers have fought in British armies for more than a century, and this has provided the basis for a small Asian presence in Britain. There is also evidence of the presence of predominantly Sikh travelling salesmen from the 1930s, wandering the full length of Britain selling mainly textile goods. Britain has also, in the twentieth century, been a location for military and professional training of individuals who now constitute the dominant class in the Indian subcontinent. These groups have not been the focus of either academic or political attention.

Rather, this attention has focused, first, on the larger migration from India and Pakistan, beginning in the late 1950s. The importance of labour demand in Britain as the stimulus to this migration of, initially, single males has been well-established, as has the secondary importance of declining economic resources and a tradition of migration in the areas from which the migrants came. State racism in the form of immigration controls played an important part in turning this intended temporary migration in search of wage labour into a more permanent settlement, which, in turn, induced the migration of wives, children and fiancées.

These migrants originated neither from just one area of

the Indian subcontinent, nor equally from all parts of the subcontinent. Rather, they came from a small number of areas, mainly but not only rural, whose populations are characterized by a wide cultural diversity. This is evident in religious, linguistic, gastronomic and other cultural differences. However, what is shared between these culturally diverse groups is a common historical experience of a particular form of colonialism and, consequently, a particular tradition of resistance to colonial exploitation. It is in the matrix of this cultural diversity and common experience of colonialism that one must assess the political and cultural practice of these migrants and their British-born children. The evidence shows that both migrants and children wish to maintain religious and other cultural characteristics in Britain, although there is evidence of cultural change at the interface with the British culture. This process of cultural negotiation is, on occasion, highly politicised, as demonstrated in the struggle of Sikhs in Britain to wear the turban and maintain their adherence to other religious symbols and practices. Parallels can be found in the case of Muslims whose religious beliefs clash with a co-educational system of education and work practices if accommodation is not made.

The vast majority of Asian men and a significant minority of Asian women are employed as wage labourers in British industry, often but not solely in low-skilled, low-paid jobs. They are also over-represented in jobs involving shift work. However, a small but significant proportion of migrants have established themselves in small-scale businesses, ranging from newsagents, through retailing to manufacturing (especially clothing). A very small proportion of this petit bourgeoisie has accumulated sufficient capital to now constitute a part of the British bourgeoisie, with trading links both within and outside Britain.

The labour migration from the Indian subcontinent is characteristically confused, analytically, with the subsequent arrival in Britain of, in 1967/68, Kenyan Asians and, in 1972/73, Ugandan Asians as political refugees. These two migrations were prompted not by the demand for labour in the British economy, but by political developments in East Africa following the decolonization settlement of the early 1960s. The presence in East Africa of a population originating from the Indian subcontinent was a result of the use of Indian indentured labour to build the East African railway network in the early twentieth century. A proportion of those indentured labourers remained in East Africa, to be joined by later migrants, and they came to constitute a petit bourgeoisie with interests in trade and manufacuring. The decolonization settlement allowed them to opt for British citizenship and, when political developments encouraged them to migrate to Britain, those rights of citizenship were withdrawn. Within Britain, their entry into Britain was interpreted not in terms of their status as political refugees but within the ideological (ie. racist) framework established in response to the earlier labour migration.

Both these groups of migrants have become, in effect, settlers (but often with economic and certainly with cultural interests in the Indian subcontinent) and their British-born children will remain in Britain. These children are currently negotiating a cultural and political position within a framework which has the cultural inheritance of their parents and their experience of racism and discrimination as two of the primary constituent elements. It is in the resistance to racism that community organization takes on a specifically political dimension. This has happened in a number of industrial disputes involving Asian workers and, for example, in Southall in 1979 when the police attempted to prevent the local community from organizing a demonstration to protest against a National Front meeting by launching an assault upon those who had attempted to demonstrate, in the course of which a demonstrator, Blair Peach, was murdered.

Read:

The Myth of Return, by M. Anwar (Heinemann Educational Books, 1979), for an example of an essentially anthropological account of the Pakistani presence in Britain.

Finding a Voice: Asian Women in Britain, by A. Wilson (Virago, 1978), for an account of the experience and reactions of Asian women to British society.

'The Sikhs: The Development of South Asian Settlements in Britain', by R. and C. Ballard, in *Between the Cultures* edited by J.L. Watson (Basil Blackwell, 1977), for an analysis of the migration and settlement process as experienced by Indian Sikhs.

See *Migrant ideology; Migration; Myth of return; National Front; Skinheads*

Robert Miles

Assimilation The process of becoming similar. The primary sense of this word has been overlaid in sociology by one of its subsidiary meanings, that which denotes the absorption of nutriment by a living organism – as the body is said to assimilate food. The popularity of the organic analogy in early twentieth-century sociology increased the tendency to give assimilation this secondary meaning. So did the concern in the United States at that time about the influx of immigrants from Eastern Europe and the Mediterranean countries: these were suspected of being of inferior stock and less easily assimilable than immigrants from north-western Europe. Thus under the pressures of the age, assimilation came to be equated with Americanization just as in Britain in the 1960s it was identified with Anglicization.

The confusions in this oversimplification were exposed by Milton M. Gordon who distinguished several different models employed in the United States. One he called Anglo-conformity; this was the process by which immigrants were brought – or should be brought – to conform to the practices of the dominant Anglo-Saxon group. The second was the 'Melting Pot', in which all groups pooled their characteristics and produced a new amalgam. The third model comprised two versions of pluralism: cultural and structural, according to whether the minority, while resembling the majority in many respects, retained elements of distinctive culture or could be distinguished by the way its members continued to associate with one another.

For sociological purposes, further distinctions are necessary. Assimilation can be seen as one kind of ethnic change in which people become similar, and contrasted with differentiation in which groups stress their distinctiveness, for example by observing food taboos or displaying distinctive signs and symbols. Members of a group who differentiate themselves in one respect (as, say, Sikhs wear turbans) may assimilate in another (like language use). So in discussing ethnic change it is necessary to specify particular items of culture and to examine the direction in which change occurs and the speed with which it takes place. Moreover, ethnic change at the local level may in the short term run in a direction opposite to that at the nation level. A group which is a numerical minority in the country may be in a majority locally, so that people belonging to the national majority may be under pressure to change towards the group which is the local majority. For example in parts of British cities where there are substantial numbers of black children it is not uncommon for white and Asian children to interest themselves in black music and adopt black speech patterns. In the 1960s, there were neighbourhoods in which most black families came from Jamaica. Black children whose parents came from other countries tended to adopt forms of the Jamaican dialect and that dialect contributed more than others to the new black speech patterns.

Some minorities consciously adopt practices designed to resist the pressures towards assimilation that are generated within the national society, such as the advertising of consumer goods. Religious groups establish their own schools, while gypsies and travellers keep their children away from state schools if they fear that these threaten their family ties. In other circumstances, members of the majority may impede assimilation by withholding social acceptance, as white Americans have discriminated against black Americans although the latter were culturally much more Americanized than recent white immigrants. Sociologists should therefore be on their guard against the simple view of assimilation as a unitary process on the group level which assumes that the minority will conform to majority ways and that the majority, in absorbing them, will not itself change. The processes of assimilation are much more complex. They need to be studied on the individual and the group levels, with the focus on specific forms of behaviour seen in their full political and social context.

Read:

Assimilation in American Life by Milton M. Gordon (Oxford, 1964), for a general discussion.

Racial and Ethnic Competition by Michael Banton (Cambridge, 1983); chapter 7 discusses the interrelation of processes at the individual and group levels.

Ethnic Change, edited by Charles F. Keyes (University of Washington Press, Seattle, 1981), a collection of essays analysing the processes of change in a variety of situations.

See *Boas; Ethnicity; Integration; Pluralism; Social Darwinism*

Michael Banton

Authoritarian personality, the See *Prejudice*

Black Muslims See *Nation of Islam*

Black Power The Civil Rights Act of 1964 was a major achievement of Martin Luther King's organization and seemed to attest to the success of nonviolent tactics in the pursuit of equality. Essentially, King's campaign was mounted on limited objectives: desegregation in a number of key social institutions and the elimination of overt discrimination.

But, throughout the King campaign, there had been a continuous white reaction: virtually each success in the legislature was paid for with the lives of civil rights campaigners. For blacks in the south, the atrocities of white reactionaries were counterbalanced by the tangible improvements in their lives; but for many blacks in the north and the east, the changes in the legal system merely highlighted the more general phenomenon of inequality. The actual improvements in their immediate material lives were negligible.

Accordingly, they found new modes of responding to their conditions, new ways of articulating their discontent. Disillusioned by what they regarded as the limitations of King's approach, more militant blacks like Huey P. Newton, Stokely Carmichael and Malcolm X began to point to the futility of working inside the system. For them, the political and economic system itself was inherently wrong. In this system, whites held the key to power; for blacks to improve their conditions, they needed to acquire positions of power. In short, what was needed was *Black Power*.

Black Power became a slogan and the collective name for the broad social response of people frustrated by King's approach and desperate to find an alternative. As many blacks questioned the viability of nonviolence, many more demonstrated the value of wholesale violence in forcing their protests to the highest levels of public visibility. In the period 1965–8, riots in such places as Watts, Newark and Detroit signalled the increasing alienation of blacks from a political system they felt denied them a full participation in society. As whites prided themselves on their liberalism in granting blacks a greater measure of equality, sections of the black community issued a strong notice of their total discontent.

In effect, Black Power developed not in an atmosphere of depression and despair, but in one of heightened expectations when blacks were beginning to sense some improvements. The impressive shows of solidarity in Watts and elsewhere convinced blacks that they would challenge the white establishment. Lewis Killian wrote of the riots: 'They did reflect the basic truth that Negroes, mobilized in ghettos to an extent never before experienced and, made confident by earlier victories, were no longer afraid of white power. Within a few months after Watts, they would begin to proclaim their faith in Black Power.'

At one extreme, there was the Nation of Islam (Black Muslims), preaching a strong black nationalist philosophy based on physical separatism. One of its prominent ministers, Malcolm X, left after an internal disagreement, and formulated his own revolutionary programme for blacks, involving a complete overthrow of extant 'political and economic institutions as as prerequisite for the liberation of black Americans'. Further, his tactics did 'not exclude the use of violence'.

This programme was adopted by Stokely Carmichael and H. Rap Brown and used as the philosophy for the Black Panthers in the middle 1960s. Malcolm X was assassinated in 1965 and in the years that followed, many other Black Power leaders were killed and many more imprisoned for their activities.

The shift from the peaceful resistance of King's movement to the violent manifestations of Black Power was a response to a what William Wilson calls 'the sudden gap between expectations and emotional gratification caused by mounting white violence – an intolerable gap preceded by several years of rising expectations and rising gratifications associated with improving black competitive and (political) pressure resources.' As important was the persuasive argument put forward by some leaders that the reactionary white society had a high capacity to absorb protests such as King's and respond violently; blacks therefore could only achieve improvements by fighting 'fire with fire' – actually intensifying the violent protest.

Black Power surfaced in sport at the Mexico Olympic Games in 1968 when two black American athletes, John Carlos and Thommie Smith, demonstrated on the victory rostrum after receiving their medals. They donned black berets, dropped their heads as if in shame and held their black-gloved fists defiantly upwards as the American national anthem played. In fact, the whole business was not as spontaneous as some first thought, for it was part of an orchestrated plan to bring the efforts of Black Power to the attention of the world via the Olympic coverage. Both athletes were immediately banned from representing the US national side.

The notoriety of Black Power generally and the Black Panthers in particular was relatively short-lived: by 1972 the Panthers had announced a retreat from what they called 'the rhetoric of the gun' and sought advancement through more conventional political channels. Given Wilson's theory, it could be suggested that the advent of the Nixon administration in 1968 had the effect of depressing expectations: blacks expected little improvement and had their expectations met.

In the UK, Black Power surfaced briefly in the 1960s, principally through two organizations, the Racial Adjustment Action Society and the Universal Coloured People's Association. Like their American counterparts, the UK groups were influenced by revolutionary black nationalist philosophies and inspired by the desire to be self-governing and have internally generated resources. Carmichael visited London in 1967 and addressed a meeting, after which he was deported. Four others were arrested for inciting racial hatred.

A leader of one of the UK organizations, Obi Egbuna, summed up one of the general doctrines of Black Power when he stated 'Integration is beautiful . . . but it's a mirage. You just can't achieve it.' The response to this view captures the whole Black Power movement: it wanted to cut itself away from any dependence on white-controlled organizations or agencies that had white representatives. In so doing, it would eliminate blacks' reliance on whites for their improvement and place the control in their own hands. Blacks could be responsible for their own destiny; they would not need to listen to empty promises about integration, less still assimilation.

Ultimately, Black Power failed to enact significant political changes on either side of the Atlantic, yet the impulse that gave rise to it has never quite been subdued and the rejection of integration as a mere 'mirage' rather than a meaningful route to equality has manifested itself in a variety of groups ever since.

Read:

The Impossible Revolution? Black Power and the American Dream by Lewis M. Killian (Random House, 1968), written in the immediate aftermath of the 1960s riots, an appraisal of the rise, of Black Power in its social context.

Soul on Ice by Eldridge Cleaver (McGraw-Hill, 1968), perhaps the most articulate, subjective statement on the meaning of Black Power.

Power, Racism and Privilege by William J. Wilson (Free Press, 1973), part two of this book looks at the various modes of black protest since slave days.

See *Ethiopianism, Civil rights movement, Garvey, Nation of Islam, Rastafarian movement*

Ellis Cashmore

Blues A style of music originating in the southern states of the US in the 1910s, the blues expressed the feelings of despondency and bitterness prevalent amongst blacks at the time. Black singers and musicians drew their main musical inspiration from slave gospel songs (which were in turn influenced by African music) but based most of their work on a twelve bar structure to emphasize rhythmic power rather than harmony and chorus. In contrast to gospel, lyrics reflected the changing orientations of blacks: away from exhortations to God and toward secular expressions of poverty, racialism and multiple deprivation.

At first, blues was performed by and listened to almost exclusively by southern blacks, who were frequently without any musical training or access to conventional instruments; thus they evolved a distinctive empirical musical form. In the 1920s and 1930s, blues attracted a white following and its popularity spread north. Chicago became known as the main blues centre. Its structure was used as the basis for the improvisation that eventually became known as jazz. An uptempo variation developed into rhythm and blues (r and b) and this gained popularity in the Second Word War. Both these offshoots were played by both blacks and whites and drew mixed audiences.

R and b played down the more depressing social commentary of pure blues and introduced a more popular dimension. This, in turn, was taken up by white musicians who fused it with country and western (a sort of American southern whites' folk music) to produce rock 'n' roll.

With reggae, blues is one of the two most inspirational musical forms to be created and accepted by blacks.

A second meaning of blues is that developed by black youths in the UK in the late 1970s and early 1980s. In this context, it refers to a particular style of house party at which liquor is illegally sold, marihuana usually (and, again, illegally) consumed and reggae music played loudly. 'Going blues' was an integral part of black youths' cultural habits. 'Shebeen' was another name given to the house party.

Read:

The Roots of Blues by Samuel Charters (Quartet Books, 1983), an exploration of the origins of this influential music which traces them back to Africa.

Black Culture and Black Consciousness by Lawrence W. Levine (Oxford University Press, 1977), digs back deeply into black American folklore and analyses the lyrics, symbolism and logic of the slave folk music that was the predecessor of blues.

The Devil's Music by Giles Oakley (Ariel Books, 1983), a revised publication tied in with a television series of the same name, this careful account of the development of blues plots its sources in late nineteenth century Mississippi and traces its changes to Chicago in the 1920s and throughout the USA from the 1930s; compilation of social history, biography and song lyrics and interviews with special attention paid to how blacks' social conditions influenced the style and content of their music.

See *Reggae, Creole*

Ellis Cashmore

Boas, Franz (1858–1942) A United States anthropologist who was born and educated (in physics and geography) in

Germany. His research on racial variation illustrates the transition from the pre-Darwinian concern with morphology to the statistically based approach later established in population genetics. Boas's study of 'Changes in the Bodily form of Descendants of Immigrants' (1912), carried out on behalf of the immigration authorities, attracted particular attention. In it the stature, weight and head-shape of 18,000 individuals were measured, comparing United States-born children with their European-born parents and with children born to such parents prior to immigration. He found that the round-headed ('brachycephalic') East European Jewish children became more long-headed ('dolichocephalic') in the United States, whereas the long-headed South Italians became more round-headed. Both were approaching a uniform type. Moreover the apparent influence of the American environment made itself felt with increasing intensity the longer the time elapsed between the immigration of the mother and the birth of her child. Boas was puzzled by his findings. They were measures of phenotypical variation and anthropologists at this time were ignorant of the causes of the variation which had to be sought in the genotype.

The physical changes Boas documented were not of great magnitude but they brought into question the assumption to which most anthropologists were then committed, that the cephalic index (the ratio of the breadth to the length of the skull when seen from above) was a stable measure of genetic history. Boas was an influential teacher, respected for his industry and devotion to objective analysis, who was willing publicly to challenge the racial doctrines propagated by the anti-immigration compaigners. Thomas F. Gossett, a historian of racial thought, was so impressed by Boas's record that he concluded 'what chiefly happened in the 1920s to stem the tide of racism was that one man, Franz Boas, who was an authority in several fields which had been the strongest sources of racism, quietly asked for proof that race determines mentality and temperament.'

Read:

Race, Language and Culture by Franz Boas (Macmillan, 1912), the classic text.

The Anthropology of Franz Boas, edited by Walter R. Goldschmidt (American Anthropological Association Memoir 89, 1959), an appraisal of Boas's work.

Race: The History of an Idea in America by Thomas F. Gossett (Shocken Books, 1963), has sections on Boas's analyses and his overall contribution to the field of research.

See *Assimilation; Culture; Genotype; Phenotype*

Michael Banton

Brazil The arrival of the Portuguese in 1500 marks the historical beginning of Brazilian race relations. The most salient characteristic of that history is the gradual elimination of Brazil's indigenous populations, both physically and culturally, and their replacement by populations of African and European origin.

The Portuguese encountered 'Indian' groups of thinly settled, small-scale, semi-nomadic, stateless, classless, tropical horticulturists. These native societies, numbering, in most cases, only a few hundred to a few thousand individuals each, were not only organizationally and technologically unable to resist the encroachments of the colonizers; their lack of immunity to diseases imported from Europe (especially measles, smallpox, and influenza) made them vulnerable to disastrous pandemics.

Attempts to enslave the Indians proved mostly abortive, as they either withdrew into the less accessible parts of the interior, died of disease, or escaped. This secular process of retreat into the Amazonian jungle continues to this day, as the Brazilian frontier gradually encroaches over the last pockets of Indian populations. The latter now number well under 1 per cent of Brazil's 120 million people, although perhaps 5 to 10 per cent of Brazilians have some Indian ancestry, especially in the interior states. (People of mixed Indian-European descent are often referred to as *caboclos*.)

This process of displacement of Amerindians in Brazil has sometimes been called genocidal. There has, of course, been sporadic frontier warfare between Indians and colonists, resulting sometimes in small-scale massacres, and there have been numerous allegations of deliberate spreading of epidemics through sale or distribution of contaminated blankets. It is untrue, or at least unproven, that the Brazilian government in this century has deliberately sought to exterminate Indians, although the effects of policies of frontier development and Indian resettlement have often been disastrous for the Indians, and continue to be so. As autonomous cultures, Amazonian Indians are fast disappearing, although surviving individuals become assimilated and interbreed with the encroaching settlers. The clash is more an ecological one between incompatible modes of subsistence than a 'racial' one, and the process is better described as one of gradual 'ethnocide' rather than as genocide.

The other main feature of Brazilian race relations is, of course, the relationship between people of European and African descent. Extensive interbreeding between them, particularly during the period of slavery, has created a continuum of phenotypes, described by an elaborate nomenclature of racial terms. Conspicuously absent from Brazilian society, however, are distinct, self-conscious racial groups. Nobody can say where 'white' ends and 'black' begins, and indeed, social descriptions of individuals vary regionally, situationally, and according to socio-economic criteria, as well as phenotype. In Brazil as a whole, perhaps 40 per cent of the population is of partly African descent and might be classified as 'black' in, say, the United States. In northeastern Brazil, the heart of the sugar plantation economy, and hence of slavery, perhaps as many as 70 to 80 per cent of the population is distinctly of African descent.

Much discussion has centered on how racially tolerant Brazil is. Brazilian slavery has been described as more humane than in the United States or the British Caribbean, and the Catholic church has been seen as mitigating the harshness of the owners. It is probably true that the Portuguese were less racist and more relaxed and easygoing in their relations with blacks, and thus created a less rigid, caste-bound society than did the British and North Americans in their slave colonies. Thus, emancipation was more frequent and easier, and freedmen were probably freer than their counterparts in the US south, for example. On the other hand, the physical treatment of Brazilian slaves was undoubtedly inferior to that meted out to slaves in the United States. Mortality rates were extremely high, especially in the mines, which, next to the sugar plantations, were the main destination of Brazilian slaves.

A century after their emancipation, Afro-Brazilians continue to be overrepresented at the bottom of the class pyramid, but substantial numbers are found in the middle class, and conversely, many white Brazilians, expecially first and second-generation European immigrants, are also quite poor. Afro-Brazilians have never been subjected to the institutionalized racism, segregation, and discrimination characteristic of, say, South Africa, or the United States. They do not constitute a self-conscious group, because Brazilians do not classify themselves into racial groups. This is not to say that they are not race conscious. Indeed, they are often very conscious of racial phenotypes, so much so that they commonly use a score or more of racial labels to describe all the combinations and permutations of skin colour, hair texture, and facial features. Indeed, racial taxonomies are so refined that members of the same family may well be referred to by different racial terms.

Paradoxical as it sounds, it was probably this high degree of racial consciousness at the level of the individual phenotype which, combined with a high level of marital and extra-marital interbreeding, prevented the formation of self-conscious, rigidly bounded racial groups in Brazil. To be sure, blackness has pejorative connotations, but more in an aesthetic than in a social or intellectual sense. Courtesy calls for ignoring an individual's darkness, using mitigating euphemisms (such as *moreno*, 'brown'), and 'promoting' a person racially if his or her class status warrants it. 'Money bleaches' goes a Brazilian aphorism. Thus, it is certainly not true that Brazil is free of racial prejudice, but it is relatively free of *categorical discrimination* based on racial group membership.

To be sure, class and race overlap to some extent, but there are no *institutional* racial barriers against upward mobility for blacks. Intermarriage between the extremes of the colour spectrum are infrequent, but not between adjacent phenotypes. Race, or better, phenotype, is definitely a component of a person's status and attractiveness, but often not the most salient one. In many situations, class is more important. Indeed, race relations at the working-class level are relatively free and uninhibited, compared to the United States, for example, and residential and school segregation is based almost entirely on class rather than race.

In short, Brazil may be described as a society where class distinctions are marked and profound, where class and colour overlap but do no coincide, where class often takes precedence over colour, and where 'race' is a matter of individual description and personal attractiveness rather than of group membership. Brazil is definitely a race conscious, but not a racial caste society. It is not a racial paradise, but neither is it a racially obsessed society like South Africa or the United States.

Read:

The Masters and the Slaves, by Gilberto Freyre (Knopf, 1964), the classic account of Brazilian slavery by a distinguished Brazilian scholar of psychoanalytic orientation.

Race and Class in Rural Brazil, edited by Charles Wagley (UNESCO, 1952), a collection of articles on race relations in several regions of Brazil.

Race and Racism, by Pierre L. van den Berghe (Wiley, 1978), especially Chapter 3, a summary of Brazilian relations.

See *Caste; Colour line; Discrimination; Ethnicity; Phenotype; Race*

Pierre L. van den Berghe

British Movement During the 1950s and throughout the 1960s, Colin Jordan was amongst the most vigorous and prominent of the UK's young fascists. His commitment to racism and antisemitism was extreme and unassailable. In 1957, with financial assistance from Arnold Leese's widow, he established the White Defence League, an organisation which played an important part in exacerbating tensions between black and white residents in the Notting Hill district of London which resulted in the eruption of violence there in the summer of 1958. In 1960, Jordan's organisation amalgamated with the National Labour Party to become the British National Party. But, frustrated by his attempts to impose a more explicitly Nazi character on the BNP, Jordan, along with John Tyndall, soon left and on 20 April 1963 – Hitler's birthday – they formed the National Socialist Movement, 'an imitation Nazi party', according to one commentator.

Tyndall resigned from the NSM within a couple of years but Jordan remained with what amounted to about 150 members, and in 1968 changed the name of his party to the British Movement (BM). Despite the change in name, it fared no better under Jordan. In 1975 the BM reached its nadir when Jordan resigned after being found guilty of shoplifting from a departmental store. Active membership at this time hovered around 50 and the party had little money to produce leaflets or pamphlets. Jordan was replaced by

Michael McLaughlin and under his leadership the party was invigorated; by 1981, membership had reached around 3,000. This was largely due to the demise and gradual disintegration of the National Front after its humiliating performance in the 1979 general election and the BM's successful exploitation of potential fascist support created by the subsequent vacuum.

Unlike the National Front, the BM had never seriously entertained the notion of securing support through the ballot box; instead, its members saw their role as operating along National Socialist lines, employing the politics of intimidation and agitation. Survey after survey in the 1970s had shown that actual and potential support for the National Front was extensive amongst the young but, apart from launching its youth wing, the Young National Front, in June 1977 and producing one or two leaflets aimed at those under 18, the NF did not fully exploit this source of support, at least until after the 1979 débâcle. By then, the BM had made its intentions clear: it entirely eschewed notions of electoral respectability, preferring instead to mount a strategy aimed at recruiting young white working-class males. Its primary target was the reborn skinhead cult which little more than a decade before had terrorized Asians in the UK during the wave of 'paki-bashing' episodes. The settings for the BM's recruitment strategy were the traditional leisure-time arenas for these youths where racial abuse and violence could be expressed almost with impunity: football grounds, rock concerts, inner city streets and so on.

It is generally agreed that the 'politics' of the BM (and NF) have probably provided little more than a legitimating framework for the expression of the skinheads' existing chauvinistic and racist attitudes and actions. Nevertheless, in an atmosphere of rising youth unemployment and the BM's simplistic identification of blacks and Asians as direct competitors for jobs, the BM/skinhead link has presaged a dramatic rise in the incidence and severity of physical attacks on these perceived 'outsiders'. The current wave of racial violence thus supersedes the 'paki-bashing' incidents of the late 1960s and early 1970s.

Read:

'Skinheads: the cult of trouble' by Ian Walker in *New Society*, (26 June 1980), discussions with skinheads about their political commitments, generally, their involvement in the BM, their aspirations and their beliefs.

'The far right fragments' by Stan Taylor in *New Society* (26 March 1981), chronicles the demise of the NF after the 1979 general election and the emergence of the BM as its most prominent and notorious successor.

Football and the Fascists (January 1981); *Nazis in the Playground* (May 1981); *Rock and the Right* (August 1981), all produced by the Centre for Contemporary Studies, they consider the three most important dimensions of the fascists' intrusion into youth culture spheres.

See *Fascism; National Front; Politics and 'race'; Skinheads*

Barry Troyna

Busing In 1954, in the *Brown* v. *Board of Education*, Topeka, Kansas case, the US Supreme Court ruled that segregated education was unconstitutional and in violation of the 14th Amendment. By this ruling, schools had to be desegregated and specially laid-on buses were to transport black, Chicano and other Latin American students to schools in the suburbs. There, they would receive the same educational provision as white students. It was contended that the process of desegregation, or busing, would ensure that students would be treated first and foremost as individuals and not as members of a caste. Desegregation would equalize educational opportunities, counteract the historically divisive nature of perceived racial difference and facilitate the emergence of a more tolerant society. It was conceived as a liberal practice and its opponents, and their arguments, were generally characterised as racist.

Nine years after the Brown decision, a similar attempt was made in the UK to ensure a greater ethnic mix in schools. This, however, provoked the opposite reaction. Busing was seen as racist, a denial of equality of opportunity to colonial migrants and their children. Black and white liberals up and down the country vehemently opposed both its principle and practice. How do we account for these contrasting reactions?

In the USA, legally sanctioned school segregation embodied 'a persisting badge of slavery', as David Kirp has put it (1982). Schools in black neighbourhoods were generally old and run-down and tended to be the last repaired, worst funded and understaffed. Because education is conventionally viewed from the liberal democratic perspective as the gateway to social and occupational advancement, the provision of inferior education to black students was seen as a legally sanctioned instrument which endorsed and perpetuated black subordination in the USA. Not surprisingly, then, the initiative for desegregation derived from the black American communities.

In the UK, on the other hand, there was no clear educational justification for the introduction of busing. The initiative had come from a group of white parents in the Southall district of London who had complained to the Minister of Education, Edward Boyle, that the educational progress of their children was being inhibited in those schools containing large numbers of nonwhite, mainly south Asian, students. Boyle subsequently recommended to government that the proportion of immigrant children should not exceed 30 per cent in any one school. In 1965, 'Boyle's law', as it came to be called, received official backing from the Department of Education and Science. As a result, a few local education authorities followed the steps already taken in Southall and West Bromwich and formally implemented busing procedures.

The main imperative for this action was clear: to assuage the anxieties of white parents. The fact that skin colour was used as the sole criterion for deciding which students were to be bused vividly demonstrated this point. But, as opponents of busing pointed out, these fears were largely unfounded in any case. Research carried out in primary schools in London, for instance, had shown that the ethnic mix of a school had a minimal influence on the level of reading ability attained by pupils. Opponents also insisted that busing was premised on the racist assumption that schools with a large proportion of nonwhite students are inherently inferior to those in which white students are the majority.

By the late 1970s, most of the local education authorities which had introduced busing had been persuaded by the efficacy of these arguments and abandoned the procedure. In the USA, the slow process of desegregation continues despite the contention that it has encouraged 'white flight' and has only slightly, if at all, led to educational or interpersonal benefits. Nevertheless, the different reactions to busing of the black and other nonwhite communities in the USA and UK highlight its symbolic importance. One side of the Atlantic, it is seen as a catalyst for equality of opportunity; on the other, it is an instrument designed to undermine that notion.

Read:

Just Schools, by David Kirp (University of California Press, 1982), after a brief but critical discussion of the relationship between the Brown decree and equality of opportunity, Kirp considers the experiences of five Bay Area communities in the twenty-five years since the introduction of desegregation.

School Desegregation, edited by Walter Stephan and Joe Fagan (Plenum Press, 1980), contains articles dealing with the historical background to the Brown decree, the legal issues and public attitudes related to desegregation and the implementation of the procedure.

'School Busing in Britain' by Lewis Killian in *Harvard Educational Review* (vol. 49, no. 2, 1979), details the busing controversy in the UK and compares this with perceptions of the process in the USA.

See *Anti-discrimination laws (UK and USA); Dispersal; Civil rights movement*

Barry Troyna

C

Capitalism This refers to a particular type of socio-economic structure bounded by a particular historical period. However, there are substantial disagreements between marxists and nonmarxists, and between various strands of marxism over the defining features of the socio-economic structure and historical period.

Nonmarxists tend to define capitalism in one of the following ways. First, it is conceived as any society characterized by the presence of exchange or market relations. Thus, the defining characteristic is individuals bartering or exchanging products for money. Second, as any society in which production occurs for the purpose of profit. Thus, the defining characteristic is the intention on the part of a group of people to organize the production and distribution of goods in order to realize more money at the end of the process than the sum they started with. Third, as any society in which production is carried out by means of industry. In this instance, it is the specific use of power-driven machinery that is identified as the defining characteristic of capitalism.

The first two definitions imply that capitalism has existed over very large areas of the world since the earliest times of human activity. Proponents of these positions often also argue that this demonstrates that capitalism is a natural and inevitable form of socio-economic organization. This conclusion is less likely to be accepted by some advocates of the market as the defining characteristic if they then wish to draw a distinction between market and nonmarket forms of socio-economic organization (the latter being defined as some form of state socialist society). The third is more historically specific, locating the development of capitalism in the later eighteenth century in Europe from where it has spread to characterize large areas of the world in the twentieth century.

Of these various positions, the most influential within sociology in the past two decades has been the identification of capitalism with the existence of market relations, as in the work of Max Weber. It is upon this tradition of theorizing that much of the sociology of 'race relations' has drawn in its attempts to analyse 'race relations' in some form of historical and structural context.

Similarly, within marxism, there is a long-established debate over the origin and nature of capitalism. There are two main positions, although both are premised on the acceptance of Marx's method and labour theory of value. Thus, both accept that all previously existing societies are characterized by class exploitation which takes the form of one class living off the surplus product produced by another class. Despite other similarities with nonmarxist analyses, the acceptance of this claim makes the following two positions quite distinct.

The first position identifies capitalism with a system of production for the market which is motivated by profit. Thus, for advocates of this position, the appearance of markets and the development of trade, particularly international trade, marks the origin of capitalism in Europe in the fourteenth and fifteenth centuries. This position has been developed to the point that capitalism is seen to be synonymous with the development of a world market of exchange relations, in which Europe stands at the centre of a series of dominant/subordinate relations with South America, the Caribbean, India, Africa and Southeast Asia. These analysts typically employ the following dualisms: centre/periphery, metropolis/satellite, development/underdevelopment. It is argued that the development of the centre/metropolis is both product and cause of the underdevelopment of the periphery/satellite. In its most extreme form, it is claimed that capitalism refers to this system of international relations rather than to any national unit or units which participate in those relations.

The second position identifies capitalism as a mode of production sharing the following characteristics: (1) generalized commodity production, whereby most production occurs for the purpose of exchange rather than for direct use; (2) labour power has itself become a commodity which is bought and sold for a wage. On the basis of these characteristics, the origin of capitalism is located in England in the seventeenth century, from where it has spread out beyond Europe as nation-states have formed themselves around generalized commodity production utilizing wage labour. Advocates of this position place primary emphasis upon the character of the production process, to which the process of exchange is viewed as secondary. It accepts that the origin of capitalism lies partly in the accumulation of capital by means of colonial exploitation, but adds that this only led to capitalist production once a class of free wage labourers had been formed.

Both marxist positions maintain that capitalism developed out of feudalism and that the development marked the beginning of a world division of labour and a world process of uneven development. They therefore suggest a determinant relationship between capitalism and colonialism and this forms the backdrop to various marxist accounts of historical and contemporary 'race relations'.

Read:

General Economic History by Max Weber (Transaction, 1981), a general account of Weber's analysis of the nature and origins of capitalism.

Capital, vol. 1 by Karl Marx (Penguin 1976), especially Parts 2, 3, 5, 7 and 8, for Marx's analysis of the nature and origins of capitalism.

The Transition from Feudalism to Capitalism edited by Rodney Hilton (Verso, 1978), for an outline of the essentially contested issues in the debate over the origin and nature of capitalism amongst marxists.

See *Colonialism; Exploitation; Labour; Marxism and race relations*

Robert Miles

Caste The concept of 'caste' has been applied to a wide variety of social institutions, both human and nonhuman. Entomologists have used it to describe the functionally and anatomically discrete morphs (workers, soldiers, etc.) of many species of eusocial insects, especially ants, bees and termites. Social scientists have spoken of castes in societies as different as those of Spanish Amerian colonies until the nineteenth century, the Indian subcontinent, twentieth-century South Africa and the United States, and precolonial West Africa.

CASTE

In the social sciences, there have been two main traditions in the use of the term caste. There have been those, mainly Indianists, who have reserved the term to describe the stratification systems of the societies influenced by Hinduism on the Indian subcontinent. The other tradition has extended the term to many other societies that lacked some of the features of the Hindu caste system, but nevertheless had groups possessing the following three characteristics:

(1) endogamy, ie. compulsory marriage within the group;

(2) ascriptive membership by birth and for life, and, hence, hereditary status;

(3) ranking in a hierarchy in relation to other such groups.

These three characteristics have been called the minimal definition of caste, and such a definition has been extensively applied by Lloyd Warner, Gunnar Myrdal and many others to white-black relations in the United States and in other societies, like South Africa, with a rigid racial hierarchy.

There is a double irony in the position of those who want to reserve the term for India and related societies. First, caste is not a term indigenous to India at all; it is a Spanish and Portuguese word (*casta*), first applied to racial groupings, mostly in the Spanish American colonies. The *casta* system of the Spanish colonies, however, was not a caste system in either the Indian or the extended sense. There was little group endogamy, and extensive racial mixtures gave rise to a proliferation of 'half-caste' categories like *mestizos, mulatos* and *zambos*. As a result, *casta* membership became rather flexible, negotiable and subject to situational redefinitions based on wealth and prestige.

Second, the term 'caste', far from helping to understand the Indian situation, actually confuses it. It has been applied, often indiscriminately, to refer to two very different groupings: *varna* and *jati*. The four *varnas* (brahmins, kshatriyas, vaishyas and sudras) are broad groupings subdivided into a multiplicity of *jati*. The effective social group in most situations is the *jati* rather than the *varna*. Yet most Hindu scriptural references are to *varnas*. Little seems gained by using a single exotic term such as 'caste', to refer to two such different types of groups.

Beyond use of the term caste in Indian society and in racially stratified countries such as South Africa and the United States, the word has also been applied to certain specialized occupational groups, especially low-status endogamous pariah or outcaste groups in a range of other societies. For example the Eta or Burakumin of Japan, and the blacksmiths and praise-singers of many African societies have been called castes.

There is little question that the Hindu caste system has a number of unique characteristics, but that is no reason to restrict to India the use of the concept to designate rigid ascriptive, stratified and endogamous groups. A useful distinction should be made, however, between genuine caste societies where the whole population is divided into such groups, and societies with some caste groups, where only a minority of the people belong to pariah groups. Perhaps only India and South Africa, each in its own special way, could be described as caste societies, while many more societies, both past and present, have endogamous groups of pariahs and outcastes.

Read:

Homo Hierarchicus, by Louis Dumont (Weidenfeld & Nicholson, 1970), probably the best recent account of the Hindu caste system.

Caste and Race, edited by Anthony de Reuck (Little Brown, 1967), a collection of essays by leading authorities, covering many societies.

The Ethnic Phenomenon, by Pierre L. van den Berghe (Elsevier, 1981), especially Chapter 8, which gives a more extensive discussion of the issues above.

See *Cox; Myrdal; Race*

Pierre L. van den Berghe

Caucasian A name introduced by J.F. Blumenbach in 1795 to designate one of the 'five principal varieties of mankind'. Europeans were classified as Caucasians. This name was chosen because Blumenbach believed the neighbourhood of Mount Caucasus, and especially its southern slope, produced the most beautiful race of men, and was probably the home of the first men. He thought they were probably white in complexion since it was easier for white to degenerate into brown than for a dark colour to become white. The other four 'principal varieties' were the Mongolian, Ethiopian, American and Malay races.

Caucasian has continued to be used as a designation for white people into the twentieth century though there is no longer any scientific justification for the practice. The distinctive characteristics of white populations need nowadays to be expressed statistically in terms of the frequency of particular genes, blood groupings, etc. Apparent similarities in appearance may be the basis for social classifications but are of little use for biological purposes.

Read:

The Idea of Race by Michael Banton (Tavistock, 1977), has notes on interpretations of the concept by Cuvies, Kingsley, Nott *et al.*

The Anthropological Treatises of Johann Friedrich Blumenbach edited by Thomas Bendyshe (Longman, Green, 1865), for the original source.

See *Aryan; Ku Klux Klan; Phenotype; Race*

Michael Banton

Chamberlain, Houston Stewart (1855–1927) 'The Nazi Prophet', as he came to be called, was the son of a British naval admiral, who studied zoology under Carl Vogt in Geneva. He later moved to Dresden where he developed a theory that would influence world history. Published in 1899, Chamberlain's work was a gigantic exploration of what he called *The Foundations of the Nineteenth Century*. He traced them back to the ancient Israelites, locating the critical year as 1200, the beginning of the Middle Ages, when the *Germanen* emerged 'as the founders of an entirely new civilization and an entirely new culture'.

A large section of the work was intended to downplay the parts played by Jews, Romans and Greeks in the development of European culture. Yet Chamberlain was careful to note the increasing influence of Jews in the spheres of government, literature and art.

Inspired by the older theories of Gobineau and the newer work of Darwin, Chamberlain speculated that the indiscriminate hybridization, or mixing of races, was undesirable, though he remained convinced that the strongest and fittest race could, at any moment, be able to assume its dominance and impose its superiority and thus curb the degeneration process caused by racial mixing.

For Chamberlain, that race derived from the original peoples of Germany, created 'physiologically by characteristic mixture of blood, followed by interbreeding; psychically by the influence that long-continued historical-geographical circumstances produce on that particular, specific physiological disposition.' Interestingly, however, he was rather imprecise on the exact definition of race. The term *Germanen* referred to a mixture of northern and western European populations which were said to form a 'family', the essence of which is the *Germane*.

Chamberlain's importance was not so much in his adding new knowledge to the concept of race itself, as in his general argument about the inherent superiority of one group over all others. There was a clear complementarity between Chamberlain's version of history and, indeed, the future and what was to become National Socialist philosophy.

Although he played no active part in the rise of Nazism (he died in 1927 before the Nazis came to power in Germany) his work was used selectively to support theoretically many of the atrocities that accompanied the Nazi development.

Read:

The Foundations of the Nineteenth Century, 2 vols, by Houston Stewart Chamberlain (Fertig, 1968), the infamous work translated by John Lee from the 1910 edition, but with a new introduction by George Mosse.

Race by John R. Baker (Oxford University Press, 1974), explores many aspects of the concept of race, and gives close attention to Chamberlain's treatment.

Race: A Study in Superstition by Jacques Barzun (Harcourt, Brace & Co., 1937), a relatively early, but significant, overview of the concept of race and its often bewildering uses.

See *Fascism; Gobineau; Race; Racism; Volk*

Ellis Cashmore

Chávez, César See *Chicanos*

Chicanos There are over 8 million people of Mexican origin or descent living in the USA (and this probably an underestimate considering the massive illegal immigration). About 90 per cent live in the southwestern states that were seized from Mexico in the nineteenth century. For years, these people had no uniform identity, often basing associations on region rather than common culture and material position. In the 1960s, however, an old word, *Chicano,* was enlivened and given new relevance by groups of Mexican descent. Despite being regarded as a pejorative term by some, the word gained acceptance to describe the shared identity of Mexican-Americans. Chicanismo – the attempt to restore Mexican dignity and culture – became a watchword, signifying Chicanos' rejection of assimilation and their wanting to use their origins as a point of unity for organizing political struggle

Before going further, a profile of Mexican-Americans might be useful. About 85 per cent are born in the USA (approximately half of these being born to American parents). The vast majority are under thirty. Most speak Spanish as well as English and belong to the Roman Catholic church. Since the 1950s, there has been a fairly rapid movement from rural areas into the cities, though this geographical mobility has not been accompanied by any upward social mobility.

Educationally, there have been improvements from one generation to the next, but the average Mexican-American child has less education than his or her white American counterpart and tends to achieve less. Thus, the children demonstrate little evidence for predicting an improvement in status and material conditions and remain a predominantly poor people with limited education.

During the 1950s, Mexican-American war veterans founded the GI Forum which became quite an important force in fighting discrimination against them, but out of the social upheavals of the 1960s, grew the Chicano movement which was committed to changing the impoverished circumstances of Mexican-Americans. The idea was to promote economic changes through uniting people. And the unity was achieved through the restoration of Mexican culture by making people of Mexican origins recognise the commonness of their background and current conditions; it was hoped to mobilize them for political action, and thus produce constructive change.

In the early 1960s, Chicano political activity came through the 'viva Kennedy' campaign which sought to involve Mexican-Americans in a political process they had for long regarded as remote and unconnected with their own interests. The liberal Kennedy-Johnson administrations in this period benefited from the support of both black and Chicano minorities.

As King had adopted Gandhi's nonviolent civil disobedience as a means of furthering the struggle of blacks, so César Chávez (1927–) did with Chicanos. Chávez became synonymous with the Chicano movement: his principal achievement was the creation of the United Farm Workers' Union (UFW) which attracted a considerable proportion of California's agricultural labour force and led to improvements in wages and working conditions for Chicanos.

UFW tactics were modelled on King's boycotts, strikes, mass demonstrations and pushing for new legislation. When violence did threaten to upset his tactics, Chávez, like Gandhi, went on an extended fast in protest.

Chávez had many obstacles to overcome, including the apathy of many Mexican-Americans, the resistance of agricultural businesses and their influential supporters and also the opposition of the formidable Teamsters' Union which, until 1976, challenged the UFW's right to represent Californian farm workers. Though his main success came in California, Chávez spread his efforts to unionizing agricultural workers elsewhere and became the single most important figure in the whole Chicano movement.

Beside Chávez, other Chicano leaders emerged in the period, some, like Jerry Apodaca and Raul Castro, opting for party politics. José Anger Gutiérrez in 1970 founded the Partido de la Raza Unida organization in south Texas and successfully fought school board, city council and county elections.

In addition to the visible successes of Chávez in employment, Chicano groups have striven with some success for important educational objectives such as the reduction of school dropout rates, the improvement of educational attainment, the integration of Spanish language and Mexican culture classes into curricula, the training of more Chicano teachers and administrators and the prevention of the busing of Chicano schoolchildren.

After the impetus of the 1960s, Chicanos became more fiercely ethnic, establishing their own colleges and universities, churches, youth movements. More recently, the movement has spawned Chicano feminist organizations. A further development came in 1967 with the Brown Berets, a militant group fashioned after the Black Panthers. As the Panthers reacted to the nonviolent working-the-system approach of King *et al*, so the Berets reacted to the Chicano resistance as led by Chávez. This wing of the Chicano movement was perhaps inspired by the incident in New Mexico in 1967, when, led by Reies Lopez Tijerina, Chicanos occupied Forest Service land and took hostage several Forest Service Rangers. Tijerina and others were arrested, but escaped after an armed raid on a New Mexico courthouse. Several hundred state troopers and national guardsmen were needed to round them up.

Although the Chicano movement does not reflect the general experience of Mexican-Americans, it demonstrates the effectiveness of militant ethnicity in the attempt to secure advancement. Chávez, in particular, created a broad base of support from a consciousness of belonging to a distinct ethnic group that was consistently disadvantaged, and thus pointed up the importance of ethnicity as a factor in forcing social change.

Read:

The Mexican-American People by Leo Grebler, Joan W. Moore and Ralph C. Guzman (Free Press, 1970), the most comprehensive source on the whole subject.

The Chicanos: A History of Mexican Americans by Matt S. Meier and Feliciano Rivera (Hill & Wang, 1972), traces Chicano history and developments through the 1960s.

Race and Class in the South-west by Mario Barrera (University of Notre Dame Press, 1979), an economic approach to the Mexican presence in the USA.

See *Black Power; Civil rights movement; Ethnicity; Migrant ideology; Puerto Ricans in the USA*

Ellis Cashmore

Civil rights movement On 1 December 1955, Rosa Parks, a black seamstress, refused to give up her seat to a white man on a bus in Montgomery, Alabama. Her action was to prompt changes of monumental proportions in the condition of blacks in the USA. It provided the impetus for the most influential social movement in the history of North American race and ethnic relations.

Six months before the incident, the US Supreme Court had, in the *Brown* v. *Board of Education* case, reversed the 58-year-old doctrine of 'separate but equal' after a campaign of sustained pressure from the National Association for the Advancement of Colored People (NAACP) which believed the issue of social equality rested on desegregating schooling.

Parks's refusal to surrender her seat resulted in her arrest and this brought protest from black organizations in the South. The immediate reaction to the arrest was a black boycott of buses in Montgomery. So impressive was this action that it led to the formation of the Southern Christian Leadership Conference in 1957. This loosely federated alliance of ministers was the central vehicle for what became known collectively as the Civil Rights Movement, or sometimes just 'the movement'. It was led by the Reverend Dr Martin Luther King (1929–68), a graduate of Boston University, who became drawn to the nonviolent civil disobedience philosophies of Gandhi. King was able to mobilize grassroots black protest by organizing a series of bus boycotts similar to the one in Montgomery which had eventually resulted in a Supreme Court ban on segregated public transportation.

Securing desegregation in education and obtaining black franchises, however, were more difficult and King was made to mount a sustained campaign of black protest. Two laws in 1957 and 1960 aimed at ensuring blacks' right to vote in federal elections were largely negated by the opposition of southern states which actually made moves to reduce the number of black registered voters. Legal actions to desegregate schools were also foundering at state level as federal executive power was not widely available to enforce the law. By 1964 (ten years after the *Brown* case), less than 2 per cent of the South's black students attended integrated schools.

At this point, King's movement was in full swing: boycotts were augmented with sit-ins (in streets and jails) and mass street rallies. As the campaign gained momentum, so did the Southern white backlash and civil rights leaders and their followers were attacked and many killed. By now John F. Kennedy was president, elected in 1960 with substantial black support. The first two years of his administration brought circumspect changes, but in 1963 Kennedy threw his support behind the civil rights movement calling for comprehensive legislation to: (1) end segregation in public educational institutions; (2) protect the rights of blacks to vote; (3) stop discrimination in all public facilities. A show of support for the proposed legislation came on 28 August 1963, with a demonstration staged by some 200,000 blacks and whites. It was at this demonstration that King delivered his famous 'I have a dream . . .' speech.

CIVIL RIGHTS MOVEMENT

The movement's campaign saw its efforts translated into results in the two years that followed. Following Kennedy's assassination, President Lyndon B. Johnson's administration passed acts in 1964 that extended the powers of the attorney general to enforce the prohibition of discrimination in public facilities and in 1965 to guarantee the right to vote (regardless of literacy or any other potentially discriminatory criteria). The latter piece of legislation significantly enlarged the black vote in the South and, in the process, altered the whole structure of political power, especially in southern states. But it was the former, the 1964 Civil Rights Act that marked a dividing point in the US race relations. Amongst its conditions were: (1) the enlargement of federal powers to stop discrimination in places of public accommodation; (2) the desegregation of all facilities maintained by public organizations (again with executive power to enforce this); (3) the desegregation of public education; (4) the extension of the powers of the Civil Rights Commission; (5) the prohibition of discrimination in any federally assisted programme; (6) the total illegalization of discrimination in employment on the grounds of race, colour, sex, or national origin; (7) the establishment of an Equal Employment Opportunities Commission to investigate and monitor complaints.

The Act was a comprehensive legal reformulation of race and ethnic relations and was due, in large part, to the sustained, nonviolent campaigns of the civil rights movement and the ability of King to negotiate the highest political levels. The leader's assassination in Memphis on 4 April 1968, symbolized the end of the era of the civil rights movement, though, in fact, there had been a different mood of protest emerging in the years immediately after the 1964 Act. Whereas King and his movement brought, through peaceful means, tangible gains and a heightening of self-respect for blacks, the new movement was based on the view that no significant long-term improvements could be produced through working peacefully within the political system – as King had done. The alternative was to react violently to the system. For many, Black Power replaced civil rights as the goal to be aimed for.

Read:

King: A Biography by David C. Lewis (University of Illinois Press,

1978), a comprehensive account of the life of the man and the movement he led.

Martin Luther King by Kenneth Slack (SCM Press, 1970), another biographical account.

Chaos or Community? by Martin Luther King (Hodder & Stoughton, 1968), originally entitled 'Where do we go from here?' this is a statement of King's progress and his visions of the future.

See *Anti-discrimination laws (USA); Black Power; Gandhi; Jim Crow*

Ellis Cashmore

Colonialism It is impossible to understand the complexities of modern race and ethnic relations without considering the historical aspects of colonialism, for many contemporary race relations situations are the eventual results of the conquest and exploitation of poor and relatively weak countries by technologically advanced nations. Colonialism involved the domination of one group over the other, culturally unrelated groups which lived in distant territories and had few defences against the conquering powers.

Following conquest, new forms of production were introduced, new systems of power and authority relations were imposed and new patterns of inequality, involving people of different backgrounds, languages, beliefs and, often, skin colour, were established. These patterns of inequality persisted for generation after generation.

In the colonial system, the more powerful, conquering groups operating from the metropolitan centre (home society), were able to extract wealth from the colonized territories at the periphery of the system by appropriating lands and securing the labour of peoples living in those territories. In extreme instances, this took the form of slavery, though there were what John Rex calls 'degrees of unfreedom' less severe than slavery.

Empire is the term usually applied to the total colonial structure: it refers to the countries involved and the relationships of political dominion and absolute control. The colonized countries were tied to the metropolitan centre to the extent that their overall social, political and economic developments were determined by the colonial power's requirements.

It was characteristic of colonialism that the conquering powers regarded the colonized peoples as totally unrelated to themselves. Their assumption was that the colonized were so different in physical appearance and culture that they shared nothing. Racist beliefs were invoked to justify the open exploitation, the reasoning being that natives were part of a subhuman species and could not expect to be treated in any way similar to their masters. Even the less racist colonizers, such as Spain and France, held that, although the natives were human, they were so far down the ladder of civilization, that it would take them generations to catch up. Racism, therefore, was highly complementary to colonialism (though it should be stressed that there are instances of racism existing independently of colonialism and vice versa, so there is no causal relationship between the two).

Colonization, the process of taking the lands and resources for exploitation, has a long history. The great imperial powers (the countries acquiring colonies) were, from the sixteenth century, Spain, Portugal, Britain and France and, to a much lesser extent, Holland and Denmark. These were quite advanced in navigation, agricultural techniques, the use of wind and water power and the development of technology, so they had the resources necessary for conquest.

By 1750, all of South and Central America and half of North America were divided amongst these powers, with Britain the paramount force in North America. Britain's military might enabled it to conquer vast portions of India also, making its empire supreme; its conquests were successfully completed by white men with supposedly Christian ideals.

The interior of Africa remained for several hundred years untouched by the European empires because of the control of its northern coast, including Egypt, by dependencies of the Turkish empire and because of the prevalence of tropical diseases such as malaria in the centre and south of the continent. The more accessible west coast of Africa, however, was comprehensively exploited, with western Europeans establishing forts for slave trading right from Dakar to the Cape (Arabs had done similarly on the eastern coast). There was a triangular trade route involving Europe, West Africa and the Americas (including Caribbean islands), so that a slave population was introduced to the Americas to supplement or even replace native Indian labour. An estimated 15 million Africans were exported to the Americas, mostly from West Africa, but some from the east, in the late nineteenth century when the continent was divided up amongst France (which controlled 3.87 million square miles), Britain (2 million square miles), Belgium, Germany (both 900,000 square miles), Italy (200,000 square miles), Spain (80,000 square miles) and Holland (whose republic of Transvaal was subsumed by 1902 in British South Africa, leaving a mere 400,000 square miles of uncolonized territory.

European domination extended also to Australasia. The French, Portuguese, Spanish and, especially, the Dutch made incursions in the sixteenth and seventeenth centuries and the voyages of Captain Cook in the 1770s led to the British occupation of Australia, New Zealand and Tasmania. Later, the Pacific islands of Fiji, Tonga and Gilbert were absorbed in the British empire; other islands were taken by France and Germany, with some of Samoa, Guam and Hawaii later being taken by the USA.

By about 1910, the 'Europeanization' of much of the world was complete, with colonial rule extending over most of the globe – Russia held territories in Central and East Asia. Outside the zones of direct European control, the Turkish and Chinese empires were inhabited by paternalist European officials and merchants. Only Japan, Nepal, Thailand, Ethiopia, Liberia and the rebel Caribbean island of Haiti were without European political direction.

The colonial structures of empire were maintained as they had been established: by military might. Despite this, it would be wise to recognize the pivotal parts played by missionaries in disseminating Christian ideas that were highly conducive to domination; for example, the basic concept of salvation encouraged colonized peoples to accept and withstand their domination and deprivation in the hope of a deliverance in the afterlife, thus cultivating a passive rather than rebellious posture. This is not to suggest that the missionaries or their commissioning churches were deliberately engaging in some vast conspiracy. They were guided by the idea of a civilizing mission to uplift backward, heathen peoples and 'save' them with Christianity. This was, indeed, as Kipling called it the 'white man's burden'. Colonialism operated at many levels, crucially at the level of consciousness.

The 1914–18 war did little to break the European's colonial

grip: Germany lost its African and other colonies, but to other European powers. After the Second World War, however, the empires began to break up with an increasing number of colonies being granted independence, either total or partial. Britain's empire evolved into a Commonwealth comprising a network of self-governing nations formerly of the empire; social and economic links were maintained, sometimes with indirect rules by Britain via 'puppet' governments.

Colonialism worked to the severe cost of the populations colonized. For all the benefits they might have received in terms of new crops, technologies, medicine, commerce and education, they inevitably suffered: human loss in the process of conquest was inestimable; self-sufficient economies were obliterated and new relationships of dependence were introduced; ancient traditions, customs, political systems and religions were destroyed. In particular, Islam suffered inordinately: the military conquests of Africa simultaneously undermined the efficacy of the Islamic faith.

(The great imperial power of modern times is Russia: the Soviet area of control, whether through direct or indirect means, has spread under communism to encompass countries in Eastern Europe, Cuba and Afghanistan. Soviet systems do not, of course, operate slavery, but evidence suggests that their regimes are extremely repressive. The manipulation of consciousness, or 'thought control', so integral to earlier colonial domination is equally as accentuated in Soviet systems.)

The basic assumption of human inequality that underlay the whole colonial enterprise has survived in the popular imagination and manifests in what has been called the 'colonial mentality' (see *Introduction to Race Relations*, Chapter 1). The belief in the inferiority of some groups designated 'races' has been passed down from one generation to the next and remains beneath modern race relations situations. The colonial mentality which structures people's perceptions of others is a remnant of colonialism, but is constantly being given fresh relevance by changing social conditions.

Read:

Introduction to Race Relations by E. Cashmore and B. Troyna (Routledge & Kegan Paul, 1983), is an approach to the subject area that emphasizes the historical importance of colonialism and the persistence of the colonial mentality.

Race Relations by Philip Mason (Oxford University Press, 1970), is a shorter interpretation of the author's main thesis, *Patterns of Dominance* (Oxford University Press, 1970), which chronicles the imperial expansions and the resulting race relations situations.

An Unfinished History of the World by Hugh Thomas (Pan, 1979), has a chapter called 'Empires' which provides a readable, historical account of the European conquests.

See *Internal colonialism; Politics and 'race'; Power; Pluralism; Racism; Slavery; Third world*

Ellis Cashmore

Colour and citizenship This was the title of a report which has its origin in the activities of the Institute of Race Relations which, throughout the 1950s, had been concerned primarily with the political and ideological consequences of decolonization. The violent attacks on West Indians and their property in 1958 forced a new attention upon the British situation and in 1962 an approach was made to the Nuffield Foundation to fund a wide-ranging survey of what was defined as British 'Race Relations'. The funds having been obtained, 19 major and 22 minor research projects were commissioned or assisted to provide a wealth of raw material on the 'coloured immigrants' and the reaction of 'British society' towards them. The project was substantial and seemed unlikely to produce a single final report in that decade, until the events of 1967/68 when state racism was intensified by the hasty passage of the 1968 Commonwealth Immigrants Act through Parliament. The political context for this legislation prompted those responsible for the Survey to assemble and publish what findings were then to hand. The result was a massive, 800-page report, titled *Colour and Citizenship* and published in 1969. It was hastily followed by an abridged version in the following year.

This report is now primarily of historical interest. This is because the British political situation of the later 1960s which prompted this essentially liberal concern over the experiences of 'coloured immigrants' in Britain has significantly changed. Whereas in the second half of the decade, state racism was still in the making, in the early 1980s, it was fully formulated in law and put into practice, supported by the virtual political endorsement of views and policies consistently articulated by the neo-fascists. There is no longer the political space for such a lengthy and detailed liberal definition of 'British race relations'.

The very scale and detail of the report bespoke authority and precision. Given the context of the period, with only a small academic literature, it represented a major contribution to what was known about 'coloured immigrants' in Britain. Any assessment of the report must begin with this fact. But, second, it must also take account of its self-conscious model, the publication of *An American Dilemma* by Gunnar Myrdal. Both Myrdal's book and the Institute of Race Relations Survey assumed some sort of contradiction between a tradition of fair play and equality and the experience of 'coloured people' in the United States and Britain, characterized as it was by discrimination and racial prejudice. The hope was to reveal the true facts about this experience and, in so doing, certain determinant features of British society, with the intention of making a series of recommendations to improve 'race relations' in Britain. In this respect, the report has been a failure.

One of the keys to this failure lay in the Survey's liberal assumptions and analysis which played down the significance of colonialism to the development of British capitalism and society. In so doing, the significance of racism was also bypassed, to the extent that the very concept was replaced by that of racial prejudice. The shift in concept marked a move from an analysis of the historical relationship between colonialism and the institutionalized practice of racist ideas at various levels of British society to an analysis of the idea of individuals. This conceptual shift was mirrored by the claimed research finding that the majority of the British population are 'tolerantly inclined'. Insofar as a problem was identified, it was the small minority of the population whose personality type gave rise to intense prejudice.

This conclusion was controversial and stimulated a major political and academic debate, in the course of which the Survey's analysis was criticized as a meaningless statistical artifact. It is now clear that the analysis of the interview data obtained from British-born persons was arbitrary and misleading to say the least. Moreover, the emphasis upon prejudice and personality type bypassed the fact that 'hostile views' can be learnt in the process of socialization, from parents, books, teachers and television. The process of reproducing such ideas is not an individual but a social one and so the focus of analysis must shift from individual prejudice to the social reproduction of racism. That this is now well recognized in the academic literature is a measure of the limitations of the liberal contribution of the 1960s, of which *Colour and Citizenship* is the archetypal example.

Read:

Colour and Citizenship by E.H. Rose, et al. (Oxford University Press, 1969), the text itself.

Colour, Citizenship and British Society by Nicholas Deakin (Panther, 1970) for a shortened and updated version of the original report.

Black Migrants: White Natives by Daniel Lawrence (Cambridge University Press, 1974) for a critique in Chapter 3 of the findings of the original report on 'racial prejudice'.

See *Anti-discrimination laws (UK and USA); Assimilation; Discrimination; Race relations*

Robert Miles

Colour line The colour line is that symbolic division between 'racial' groups in societies where skin pigmentation is a criterion of social status. It is, of course, most clearly and rigidly defined in the most racist societies, that is in societies which ascribed different rights and privileges to members of different racial groups. If access to social resources (such as schooling, housing, employment, and the like) is contingent on race, racial classification must be maintained and racial membership must be kept as unambiguous as possible. This is true even when racial discrimination is supposedly benign as with affirmative action in the United States, for instance.

The simplest systems of racial stratification are the dichotomous ones, in which one is classified as either white or black, white or nonwhite, white or coloured. An example is the United States, where any African ancestry puts one in the social category of 'Negro', 'Black', 'Coloured', or 'Afro-American' (to use different labels applied at different times to the same people). More complex systems have three groups, as do some Caribbean societies, with distinctions drawn between whites, mulattoes, and blacks. South Africa officially recognizes four racial groups (whites, coloureds, Indians, and blacks), but often lumps the three subordinate groups into the blanket category nonwhite.

The colour line may be more or less rigid. In some countries like some states of the United States until 1967, interracial marriage was forbidden by law. In South Africa, both intermarriage and sexual relations between whites and nonwhites are criminal offences subject to stiff penalties (up to seven years of imprisonment). To prevent 'passing' (ie. the surreptitious crossing of the colour line), the South African government passed the Population Registration Act, providing for the issuance of racial identity cards, and the permanent racial classification of the entire population.

Especially in societies that are virulently racist and attempt to maintain a rigid colour line, the incentives for 'passing' are great enough to encourage those whose phenotype is sufficiently like that of the dominant group to cross the colour line. Even extensive 'passing' does not necessarily undermine the colour line. Indeed, 'passing', far from defying the racial hierarchy, is a self-serving act of individual *evasion* of the colour line. The very evasion implies acceptance of the system, a reason why 'passing' is often resented more by members of the subordinate group to whom the option is not available, than by members of the dominant group who are being infiltrated by racial 'upstarts'.

At the other end of the spectrum are societies where racial boundaries are so ambiguous and flexible that, even though they exhibit a good deal of racial consciousness, one may not properly speak of a colour line. Brazil is an example of a country lacking any sharp breaking points in the continuum of colour. Nobody is quite sure where whiteness ends and blackness begins.

Read:

Race Relations, by Michael Banton (Tavistock, 1967), a classic text on the subject, from a comparative sociological perspective.

Race Relations, by Philip Mason (Oxford University Press, 1970), a shorter account from a more historical point of view.

South Africa: A Study in Conflict, by Pierre L. van den Berghe (University of California Press, 1967), a detailed account of apartheid in South Africa.

See *Apartheid; Brazil; Discrimination; Phenotype; Race; Racism; Segregation*

Pierre L. van den Berghe

Conquest Military conquest is the commonest origin of plural societies, (societies composed of distinct ethnic or racial groups). It is also the most frequent origin of inequality between ethnic and racial groups. The other principal origin of plural societies is peaceful immigration, whether voluntary, semi-voluntary (e.g. indenture), or involuntary (e.g. slavery and penal colonies). Conquest, of course, is also a form of immigration, namely one in which it is the dominant group which comes in and disperses to establish control over the natives. What is commonly meant by immigration, however, is a situation in which the dominant group is indigenous, and in which immigrants move in peacefully and disperse to assume a subordinate position. Conquest and peaceful immigration lead to very different situations of race and ethnic relations.

Plural societies originating in conquest are frequently dominated by racial or ethnic minorities who exert their control through superior military technology and organization rather than numbers. Being often ruled by minorities, such societies are typically highly despotic and characterized by sharp ethnic or racial cleavages and a large degree of legally entrenched inequality between ethnic groups.

Unlike in countries that owe their pluralism to peaceful immigration, conquest leads to relatively stable or slowly changing ethnic boundaries, largely because the conquered groups typically retain a territorial basis and remain concentrated in their traditional homeland. In contrast to immigrant groups who often disperse on arrival in their host countries, conquered groups, by staying territorialized, find it easier to retain their language, religion, and culture. Furthermore, the dominant group often does not even seek to assimilate the conquered. So long as the conquered remain submissive and pay taxes, they are commonly left relatively undisturbed in running their daily affairs at the local level. They may even retain their native elite, under a system of indirect rule.

Two principal types of conquest can be distinguished, depending on the level of technology of the conquered. Where the natives belong to small-scale, stateless, thinly settled, nomadic groups of hunters and gatherers or simple horticulturists, the outcome is often their displacement by the invaders. Sometimes there is a definite policy of genocide, but often epidemic diseases, frontier warfare, and loss of a territorial basis for subsistence combine to bring about the destruction of native cultures as functioning groups, and the relegation of the remnants of their population to native reserves. In these 'frontier' situations, which characterized countries like Canada, the United States and Australia, the conquerors essentially replaced the indigenes, both territorially and demographically. The aboriginal societies were not only fragile and defenceless; their small numbers and their resistance to subjection made them virtually useless to the conquerors as a labour force.

Whenever the conquerors encounter a settled peasant population belonging to a stratified, state-level, indigenous society, however, the situation is very different. Initial resistance may be stronger, but, once control is achieved, the conquerors find an easily exploitable labour force (which often continues to be under the direct supervision of the collaborators from the former ruling class of the conquered groups). The result is exploitation rather than displacement. Examples are most traditional empires of Europe, Asia, Africa, and precolonial America, as well as most Asian and African colonies of Europe.

Read:

Interethnic Relations, by E.K. Francis (Elsevier, 1976), a broad sociological treatment of ethnic and race relations, especially strong on Europe and North America.

Patterns of Dominance, by Philip Mason (Oxford University Press, 1970), much like the above, but more historical, and strongest on Asia and Africa.

See *Colonialism; Native peoples; Race; Slavery*

Pierre L. van den Berghe

Cox, Oliver C. (1901-74) He was born in Trinidad and died in the USA. He studied law at Northwestern University in the USA and then continued these studies for a higher degree in law at University of Chicago. While there, he contracted polio and the subsequent physical disabilities persuaded him that he would not be able to practise law. He chose to take a Master's degree in economics and then completed a PhD in Sociology in 1938. Thereafter he became Professor of Sociology at Lincoln University, Missouri and, later, at Wayne State University.

Quantitatively, his main area of interest and writing was on the nature of capitalism as a system. This is evident in his following major publications: *The Foundations of Capitalism* (New York: Philosophical Library, 1959) and *Capitalism as a*

System (New York: Monthly Review Press, 1964). The nature of capitalism and its evolution from the feudal system of Europe was the subject matter of one of his later articles, 'The problem of Social Transition' (in *American Journal of Sociology*, 1973, 79, pp. 1120–33). However, his name is known primarily through the renewed interest in the 1960s and 1970s in his earlier book *Caste, Class and Race* (New York: Doubleday, 1948; reprinted in 1959 and 1970 by Monthly Review Press). This became both the object of attack by radical 'black' sociologists in the United States and of admiration by marxist and leftist writers in Britain. The former regarded Cox as an assimilationist on the strength of some of the claims made in this text. The latter interpreted the text as the 'classic' marxist analysis of the origin of racism and of the relationship between class and 'race'. Both groups were referring to a text which was a product of an earlier time and set of concerns. Moreover, Cox's claims and predictions from that earlier time were contradicted by the events of the 1960s, leaving him, so others have observed, a lonely and disillusioned man.

Much of Cox's work was influenced by the writings of Marx and this is clearly evident in *Caste, Class and Race*. In this text, he defends two main contentions. First, he argued that 'race relations' cannot be reduced to caste relations and so the text develops an extensive critique of W. Lloyd Warner and John Dollard. Second, he argued that what he preferred to define as 'race prejudice' (he rejected the term racism) was not a natural phenomenon but was a direct consequence of the development of capitalism, from which he concluded that a solution to the 'race problem' could be found only in the transition from capitalism to a democratic and classless society. It was in developing this second argument that Cox attempted to set out a detailed theoretical and historical account of the relationship between class and 'race'.

When viewed historically, Cox's text, published in 1949, was significant because it attempted to reassert the significance of marxist categories of analysis in a context which was, to say the least, unfavourable to marxism. This should be recognized, even when one goes on to argue that Cox's use of some of the marxist categories was grounded in what would now be regarded as a very limited selection of Marx's work. Indeed, the way in which the concept of class is defined and employed has led others to argue that the work cannot easily be regarded as being within the marxist tradition. Cox's tenuous relationship with marxism is confirmed by the afore-mentioned article in the *American Journal of Sociology* of 1973 which is concerned with the transition from feudalism to capitalism and which makes no reference to the new classic marxist contributions of M. Dodd and P. Sweezy, let alone vol. 1 of Marx's *Capital*.

Read:

Caste, Class and Race by Oliver C. Cox (Monthly Review Press, 1970), which, despite later criticisms, remains a challenging contribution when viewed historically.

The Idea of Race by Michael Banton (Tavistock, 1977), where Cox's later work is located and criticized in the context of an analysis of the tradition of 'race relations' analysis.

'Class, race and ethnicity' by Robert Miles in *Ethnic and Racial Studies* (1980, vol. 3 no. 2, pp. 169–87), for a critical analysis of Cox's attempt to theorize a relationship between class and 'race'.

See *Dollard; Marxism and race relations; Race relations; Racism*

Robert Miles

Creole A term that is used quite freely in race and ethnic relations, which has a quite specific meaning. It was originally taken from the Portuguese *crioulo,* meaning a slave brought up in the owner's household, the word became *criolli* in Spanish and *creole* in French, and came to take a particular meaning in the state of Louisiana in the early 1800s. After the Louisiana Purchase of 1803, those of French and Spanish descent called themselves creoles as if to distinguish themselves ethnically from Anglo-Americans who began to move into Louisiana at the time. The creoles evolved their own distinctive styles of music and languages. The term later came to refer to the group of 'coloureds', that is the products of miscegenation (black and white mixture). They were a selfconscious ethnic group who perceived themselves as different and separate. Based in New Orleans, they spoke French and developed their own educational institutions, such as Xavier University.

In a West Indian context, creole referred to the descendants of Europeans who were both born and lived in the Caribbean; it was also used to distinguish a West Indian-born slave from an African one. Those born in the islands developed their own dialects, musics and culture and the word creole came to mean anything created anew in the Caribbean (it probably stemmed from the Latin *creara* for created originally). So particular dishes, dialects, art forms, etc. were known as creole and this denoted something very positive and original. Nowadays, the term creole describes homegrown qualities exclusive to ethnic groups, particularly in language and dialect.

Read:

Ten Generations by Frances J. Woods (Louisiana State University Press, 1972), the life story of an extended family of American creoles, who were something of an elite.

West Indian Societies by David Lowenthal (Oxford University Press, 1972), defines creole culture as based on a part history of slavery and a present legacy of colour, and covers the whole development of creole culture. Less impressive, but still useful in this context, is Eric Williams's *From Columbus to Castro: the history of the Caribbean, 1492–1969* (Deutsch, 1970).

Jamaica Talk by Frederic G. Cassidy (Macmillan, 1969), an interesting study of possibly the most important element of creole cultures: language.

See *Afro-Caribbeans; Kinship; Reggae*

Ellis Cashmore

Culture Defined by Sir Edward Tylor in 1871 as, when 'taken in its wide ethnographic sense' being 'that complex whole which includes knowledge, belief, art, morals, law, custom and any other capabilities and habits acquired by man as a member of society'. Since then, definitions have proliferated with little if any increase in precision. Sir Raymond Firth has written that 'If . . . society is taken to be an organized set of individuals with a given way of life, culture is that way of life. If society is taken to be an aggregate of social relations, then culture is the content of those relations. Society emphasizes the human component, the aggregate of people and the relations between them. Culture emphasizes the component of accumulated resources, immaterial as well as material . . .'

In the United States in particular, culture is regarded as possibly the most central concept of anthropology as a discipline, but it has not been built into the sort of theoretical structure which can cause it to be defined more sharply for use in the formulation of testable hypotheses. Whereas it may be convenient to refer to, say, 'Japanese culture' and its characteristics, and to recognize subcultures within such a unit, it is usually impossible to conceive of cultures as having clear boundaries. It is therefore impracticable to treat them as distinct and finite units that can be counted. Cultures tend to be systems of meaning and custom that are blurred at the edges. Nor are they usually stable. As individuals come to terms with changing circumstances (such as new technology) so they change their ways and shared meanings change with them.

It is important to bear in mind these limitations to the explanatory value of the culture concept when considering its use in the educational field. It is argued that the curricula for all subjects should be reviewed to ensure that schools make the maximum possible contribution to the preparation of children for life in a multiracial world, and in a society which includes groups distinguished by race, ethnicity and culture. At present there is a tendency to use the name 'multicultural education' as an official designation for programmes directed to this end, though the names multiracial and multi or polyethnic education are favoured by some people. All these names are open to the objection that there is no finite number of stable constituent units. The use of 'culture' in this connection is questionable since advanced technology is so readily identified with culture of the First World, the west. The culture of people living in India and Trinidad has many features in common with the culture of England: cars, radios, books and so on, but the things taken to represent the cultures of Indians and Trinidadians tend to be festivals, songs and recipes. This trivializes the cultures of the people who live in those societies as much as it would were English children told that their culture was exemplified by Guy Fawkes Day, Morris dancing and custard. It might be better to talk of education for cultural diversity were it not so difficult to know how much diversity is desired and how much is desired in comparison with the traditional educational aims of literacy and numeracy.

Read:

Elements of Social Organization by Raymond Firth (Watts, 1952), at page 27.

Culture: a Critical Review of Concepts and Definitions by A.L. Kroeber and Clyde Kluckhohn (Peabody Museum Papers, 1952), for a systematic review of definitions.

West Indian Children in our Schools (the 'Rampton Report'), an official report which tried to outline the nature of multi-cultural education. (Cmnd 8273, HMSO, London).

See *Boas; Ethnicity; Kinship*

Michael Banton

D

Darwin, Charles (1809–82) Charles Darwin was the grandson of Erasmus Darwin, a pioneering writer on what has come to be known as evolution. Charles accepted the unpaid post of naturalist on board *HMS Beagle* for its 1831–6 voyage of exploration in South America, contracting in Peru a debilitating disease which later obliged him to lead a secluded life. Apart from natural history, he wrote on geological, zoological, evolutionary, botanical and psychological subjects. Darwin is sometimes thought of as the discoverer of the theory of evolution, but this is seriously misleading. Since at least Linnaeus, many naturalists had been doubtful about the fixity of species and had speculated about a possible sequence of development, but they had no satisfactory explanation of how living forms could change. Darwin supplied the missing theory of change with the conception of natural selection introduced in his book, *On the Origin of Species by Natural Selection, or the Preservation of Favoured Races in the Struggle for Life*. It assumes the existence of variability within populations and explains how in particular environments adaptive characteristics would be favoured. In his 1871 book *The Descent of Man*, Darwin developed his theory of sexual selection, seen as a special case of the more general theory. Those individuals which are more attractive to members of the other sex are more likely to attract mates and leave offspring. Evolution can then be seen as a process favouring the characteristics of the individuals which produce the greatest number of offspring likely themselves to reach the stage of reproduction.

Darwin's research method was highly systematic. From the time when, in 1838, he grasped the idea of struggle within populations as an explanatory principle, he worked to gather evidence that bore upon the critical hypotheses.

He later wrote, 'how odd it is that anyone should not see that all observation must be for or against some view if it is to be of any service.' Again, 'False facts are highly injurious to the progress of science, for they often endure long; but false views, if supported by some evidence, do little harm, for every one takes a salutary pleasure in proving their falseness; and when this is done, one path towards error is closed and the road to truth is often at the same time opened.' He himself, having written out his theory in outline, then devoted some eight years to revising the classification of an apparently insignificant class of barnacles because this enabled him to test his hypotheses about the evolution of sexuality.

Darwin's influence upon the history of racial thought was profound. His demonstration of the mutability of species destroyed the doctrines of the racial typologists who assumed the permanence of types. He showed the debate between the monogenists and polygenists to be scientifically unproductive. He introduced a new conception of 'geographical races, or sub-species' as 'local forms completely fixed and isolated'. Because they were isolated they did not interbreed and so 'there is no possible test but individual opinion to determine which of them shall be considered as species and which as varieties'. Darwin made no attempt to classify human races, observing that the naturalist has no right to give names to objects which he cannot define. As is to be expected, there are weaknesses in Darwin's work: he thought the acquired characters might be inherited; he believed that inheritance was an equal blending of parental characters, etc. Such problems were resolved when the scientific study of genetics became possible. As Jacob Bronowski once wrote 'The single most important thing that Charles Darwin did was to force biologists to find a unit of inheritance.' Not until the statistical reasoning of population genetics had taken the place of the typologists' dream of pure races were the implications of Darwin's revolution for the understanding of race fully apparent.

Read:

Charles Darwin: Evolution by Natural Selection by Sir Gavin de Beer (Nelson, 1963; Doubleday, 1964), the most authoritative biography.

The Triumph of the Darwinian Method by Michael T. Ghiselin (University of California Press, 1969), a stimulating account of Darwin's method.

DARWINISM

'The nature of the Darwinian revolution' by Ernst Mayr in *Science* (vol. 176, 1972), assesses the impact of Darwin's thought.

See *Darwinism; Eugenics; Heritablity; Social Darwinism*

Michael Banton

Darwinism Currently taken to refer to at least four theories or hypotheses which can be considered separately. The first, and principal use, is to denote the theory of evolution according to which the diversity of living forms arose through modification by descent, most if not all forms having originated from common ancestors. The second use refers to the argument that evolution is the result of natural selection, supplemented in some species by the process of sexual selection. The third use is to designate the view that evolution occurs at a uniform and slow rate – as opposed to recent theories of 'punctuated equilibria' according to which there are occasional catastrophes (such as that which appears to have eliminated all the dinosaurs), separated by periods of relatively slow evolution. The fourth use is that which sees Darwinism as claiming that the processes which underlie the evolution of species also lead to the emergence of new species. The theory of evolution proper does not depend upon acceptance of Darwin's argument about selection as its cause, or upon any assumption that evolution is gradual, or that selection is sufficient to explain speciation. It is general theory which can be used to generate falsifiable hypotheses.

In practice, it is often difficult to separate these usages since the theory of evolution is less convincing if it cannot account for the origin of life, and particularly of the genetic code. Under the influence of population genetics Darwinism developed into a mathematical theory of differential reproduction. Natural selection has come to mean that some individuals leave more offspring than others without explaining which individual will leave more. The idea that it is the individuals best adapted to their environment which leave more offspring is assumed, but has no explicit place in the theory. So, in the words of C.H. Waddington, an eminent modern geneticist, 'The whole guts of evolution – which is, how do you come to have horses and tigers and things – is outside the mathematical theory.' If an explanation of the evolution of the horse is to be persuasive, it would help were there a series of horse fossils available from one region relating the age of the rock strata to the phases of their evolution, but for horses and many other species the fossil record is woefully deficient. No evidence can be found for the transitional forms predicted by the theory. One of the chief differences between reptiles and mammals is that the former have a single earbone and at least four bones in the lower jaw whereas mammals have two further earbones but only one jawbone. It is suggested that some of the reptiles' jawbones moved to permit the evolution of the mammalian ear, but how this could have happened remains a mystery. Moreover, while it is undergoing an evolutionary transition, an animal still has to feed itself, reproduce, and evade predators, so that even if a particular change may in the long run confer a great advantage it must not entail any serious disadvantage in the short run. This also increases the difficulty of accounting for the evolution of flight in birds.

Awareness of the limitations of Darwinism has in recent years stimulated attempts to find scientific support for the doctrine that the origin of human life is adequately explained in the first book of Genesis. The scientific study of evolution is a search for truth. Those who speak for creationism seek to use science to bolster a religious belief.

Read:

The Neck of the Giraffe by Francis Hitching (Pan Books, 1982), for a popular account of the difficulties of Darwinist theory.

Darwin by Wilma George (Fontana, 1982), provides a recent short account of Darwin's work, as does *Darwin* by Jonathan Howard (Oxford University Press, 1982).

See *Darwin; Eugenics; Heritability; Social Darwinism; Sociobiology*

Michael Banton

Disadvantage A euphemism for the result of discrimination and exploitation, the term 'disadvantage' conveniently hides the causality of status differences and is, thus, currently fashionable in western capitalist states, especially in the United States. Indeed disadvantage implicitly puts the burden of explanation for inferior status on supposed disabilities of the victims. Underprivilege is an equally convenient obfuscation of the sources of inequality.

DISADVANTAGE

The concept of 'disadvantage' has been central to a set of ameliorative strategies devised in the United States, supposedly to redress ethnic and racial differences, mostly in income, education, and access to employment and schools. Certain minorities are defined as disadvantaged or underprivileged, and, therefore, qualified for affirmative action. Existing differences are principally ascribed to racial or ethnic factors, to the nearly complete exclusion of class. Minorities are alleged to be in a 'disadvantaged' position partly because of ethnic or racial discrimination against them, and partly because of unfortunate failings of their own which they must be helped to overcome (e.g. lack of education, lack of a work ethic, hedonism, 'externality', or the latest psychologistic fad).

Social remedies for disadvantage consist mostly of making supposedly benign exceptions for minorities rather than in changing the class structures which perpetuate inequalities. Affirmative action, or positive discrimination takes the form of racial and ethnic quotas in university admissions and in hiring, remedial courses for minorities, racial busing for school 'integration', and the like. The common denominator of some fifteen years of these policies has been their lack of success, or even their boomerang effect (in the form of white backlash, increasing salience of racial consciousness, and devaluation of credentials of all minority group members).

Long before the United States, the government of India, both under British rule and since independence, adopted similar policies to relieve the disadvantage of the 'backward' castes. The results were quite similar: far from reducing the significance of caste status, a political incentive was created for people to organize along caste lines, and to claim 'backward' status for economic or political advantage. In Israel, too, the government has initiated policies of benign discrimination in favour of Oriental Jews, though not toward Arabs, whose position is far worse, and who suffer from much more blatant discrimination.

Read:

Affirmative Discrimination, by Nathan Glazer (Basic Books, 1975), a critique of the policy and of its impact in the United States, by an American sociologist.

Minority Education and Caste, by John Ogbu (Academic Press, 1978), a lucid analysis of the source of educational 'disadvantage' for minority groups in the United States, Britain, India, Nigeria, and elsewhere, by a Nigerian anthropologist.

See *Affirmative action; Discrimination; Minorities; Racism*

Pierre L. van den Berghe

Discrimination: categorical and statistical The distinction between these two forms of discrimination turns upon the motivation of the discriminator. Categorical discrimination is the unfavourable treatment of all persons socially assigned to a particular category. Statistical discrimination is the unfavourable treatment of persons arising from a belief that people in the category to which they are assigned are more likely to possess negative attributes. The category in question may be constructed by reference to race, religion, gender or any of the criteria used to divide members of a society. The legal definition of direct discrimination should encompass all instances of categorical discrimination in which the complainant has suffered less favourable treatment. The legal definition of indirect discrimination is sufficient to offer remedies against the practice of statistical discrimination, so there is a parallel between the two distinctions, but they are not the same. The categorical-statistical distinction derives from economic analyses which see the former kind as the expression of a form of prejudice whereas the latter is a kind of optimizing behaviour. The direct-indirect distinction requires an examination of the intention behind an action that is the subject of complaint. Direct discrimination occurs when a person is treated less favourably on the ground of the other person's supposed colour, race or ethnic or national origins. Indirect discrimination occurs when an unjustifiable condition is imposed which is such that only a small proportion of persons in the victim's racial group can comply with it.

Read:

'Categorical and statistical discrimination' by Michael Banton, *Ethnic and Racial Studies*, vol. 6, no. 2, 1983, for a fuller discussion.

Legal Control of Racial Discrimination by Laurence Lustgarten (Macmillan, 1980), for lawyer's review.

See *Institutional racism; Police and race relations; Prejudice*

Michael Banton

Dispersal In the 1960s, with the influx of immigrants into the inner city areas of Britain's conurbations, local authorities began to turn to central government for a social policy lead. Whereas previously the problems regarding the concentration of immigrants in these areas had been discussed almost entirely in the arena of education, other sectors of social welfare provision were beginning by the late 1960s to experience difficulties. These problems were compounded by the increasing fears of both politicians and officials that Britain was about to experience the sorts of problems already encountered in the United States with the ghettoization of its large cities. Accompanying this ghettoization was the imagery of social decay, crime, and racial violence. However, one of the major differences was that Britain, unlike the USA possessed a large amount of publicly owned housing stock, and with it the ability, if desired, socio-spatially to engineer large sections of the population.

It was apparent to local authorities that natural 'dispersal' away from the inner-city areas was not occurring, and the question of dispersal based on housing allocation – to move entire families – was considered. It was seen as a possible way of achieving both the theoretical goal of social integration, and the practical objective of alleviating the increasing social welfare burden placed upon the inner city.

Various pieces of research and reports had touched on the concept. The most significant being that of the Cullingworth Report of 1969, which devoted a whole section to the question (paragraphs 397–413) and which concluded: 'any policy of dispersal in the field of housing must be implemented with great sensitivity, with no element of compulsion or direction, and can proceed only at the pace of the needs and wishes of the people involved' (Cullingworth 1969, paragraph 409).

Although the possibility of voluntary ecological dispersal appeared to have gained at least tacit governmental support by 1969, central government decided to leave such initiative as a local option rather than part of a national policy.

In England, Birmingham City Council put its own policy of dispersal into operation in February 1969. Although it had previously discussed the concept at a General Purpose Committee meeting in May 1968, the council's decision followed ultimately from a threatened rent strike and petition by white residents opposed to the placing of a black family into a block of flats already accommodating one black family. Although the council rejected the petition, they agreed with the philosophy that dispersal was the best way to achieve integration, alleviate social welfare problems, and prevent possible ethnic conflict. The council, therefore, decided on a policy, the basis of which was to be the housing of black families in a set ratio to whites in council property: a maximum of only one in six properties could be allocated to blacks within a given block of flats, maisonettes or streets.

In 1975, the city council offered and allocated to an Irish woman a council house; it was subsequently realized by the council that the woman was married to a West Indian, and because the house was 'a white segregated' property due to the set-ratio policy, the offer was withdrawn. The case was taken to the Race Relations Board, and, although both the Birmingham Housing Committee and the Housing Department argued that set-ratio dispersal was in the spirit of fostering integration between whites and blacks even if it was not strictly to the letter of the 1968 Race Relations Act, the Board ruled that discrimination had occurred. Birmingham's dispersal policy was formally suspended in October 1975.

The key to a fair appraisal of the concept of dispersal is *choice*, whilst the opportunities for voluntary geographical dispersal away from the inner cities must equally be available to both black and white. By ignoring the wishes and benefits concentration may afford ethnic communities, any policy or discussion of involuntary dispersal (in my opinion the possibility of having a 'policy' of voluntary dispersal being something of a misnomer) must reveal an ethnocentric bias which at its best is problematically untenable and at its worst institutional racism.

Read:

'The practice of dispersal in Britain' by H. Flett, G. Henderson and B. Brown, *Journal of Social Policy* (1979).

'Dispersal and choice – towards a strategy for ethnic minorities' by N. Deakin, *Environmental Planning Journal* (1970).

See *Busing; Ghetto; Pruitt-Igoe*

Carl A. Bagley

Dollard, John (1900–) A United States psychologist who, having undergone psychoanalysis in Berlin, became the first writer to apply Freudian interpretations to black-white relations in North America. According to Freudian doctrine, social living and human culture require a degree of orderliness and discipline which conflict with the desires of the young human. Socialization entails frustration. The basic reaction to frustration is the aggressive response designed to reassert mastery, but a child finds it unprofitable to attack a parental figure who is responsible for his or her socialization. The child must either turn the aggression in on itself or store it up, waiting for a convenient opportunity to discharge it on a suitable scapegoat. The first key concept is therefore that of generalized or 'free-floating' aggression held in store; the second, that of social permission to release this aggression on a particular target group; the third, that scapegoats must be readily identifiable (as the Negro's skin colour served as a sign telling the prejudiced person whom to hate). According to this view racial prejudice was always irrational. In a later article, Dollard distinguished between direct and displaced aggression according to whether it was discharged against the agent of the frustration (direct) or a scapegoat (displaced); he stressed that in a situation of direct aggression some displaced aggression would also be released, adding an emotional element which might be responsible for the irrational behaviour often observable in situations of rational conflict. Dollard's main contribution is his book *Caste and Class in a Southern Town* (1937), which brings together the Freudian interpretation and a description of black-white relations in the Mississippi town of Indianola. In it, blacks and whites are presented as separate castes after the manner of W. Lloyd Warner, though without carrying through the sort of analysis Warner's students, Allison Davies, B.B. Gardner and M. Gardner achieved in their book about another Mississippi town published a little later under the title *Deep South*.

Read:

'Hostility and Fear in Social Life' by John Dollard, *Social Forces*, vol. 17 (1938), a short but comprehensive statement of Dollard's views about prejudice.

See *Discrimination; Myrdal; Prejudice; Scapegoat*

Michael Banton

Dual labour market The concept of a dual labour market originated from the observation that there were qualitative differences in the nature of the labour market in which blacks and whites were employed. It developed out of the attempt to conceptualize racial divisions within the urban labour market and was subsequently extended by Doeringer and Piore (1971) to incorporate other marginal groups. In its most elementary form, the theory proposes a basic division between employers operating in two spheres: (1) the primary market, providing high wages, internal structures with career opportunities, nonarbitrary management and secure employment; and (2) the secondary labour market, offering low wages, no career opportunities, arbitrary management and insecure employment. Since its original formulation, the theory has been subject to certain refinements; for instance, it is now generally recognized that the same employer can straddle both markets: one part of the organisation providing primary sector conditions, another part operating in the secondary sector.

It has also been contended that there are significant methodological problems with the dualist theory, not least in the failure of its proponents to demonstrate empirically a simple duality in the segmentation of the labour market. In all, recent attempts to operationalize the theory have suggested that the situation is more complex and the market structure more highly differentiated than the 'dualists' originally anticipated. In other words, attempts to conceptualize labour markets in dichotomous terms, especially at the local level, are misleading.

In general, it is argued that educational credentials assume a major role in determining at which point school leavers gain entry into the labour market. Recent research by Osterman (1980) on the youth labour market in the USA, for example, supported the hypothesis that low educational achievers are confined to the secondary market. Research carried out in the UK, however, suggests that formal qualifications do not necessarily play the determinative role in the allocation of occupational positions that much conventional wisdom would give them. In this context, visible signs such as skin colour are important criteria not only in determining the position of an applicant in the occupational hierarchy but also in determining whether access is obtained at all.

DUAL LABOUR MARKET

The continuing maldistribution of black and south Asian workers in the labour market which sees them disproportionately represented in the lower echelons – or secondary sector – of the labour market can only partly be attributed to their school performance. In short, the disadvantages experienced by colonial migrants in the labour market is consistently and systematically being reproduced amongst their offspring.

Read:

Getting Started: The Youth Labour Market by Paul Osterman (MIT Press, 1980), an American study concluding that educational underachievers occupy positions in a secondary labour market.

Internal Labor Markets and Manpower Analysis by P.B. Doeringer and M.J. Piore (D.C. Heath, 1971), analyses the concept of the dual labour market based on empirical research carried out in the USA.

The Working Class and the Labour Market, by Bob Blackburn and Michael Mann (Macmillan, 1979), a study of unskilled male workers in Peterborough, UK. It examines the utility of the 'dualist' argument and considers it, *en passant*, in relation to the occupational position of black and South Asian workers.

Racial Disadvantage in Britain, by David Smith (Penguin, 1977), based on a series of investigations carried out by the PEP, it remains the most comprehensive analysis of the experiences of colonial immigrants in relation to the housing and labour markets of the UK.

See *Afro-Caribbeans; Asians in the UK, Labour*

Barry Troyna

Emancipation In Roman Law, *emancipare* meant literally 'to transfer ownership', specifically the release of a child from paternal authority. By extension, emancipation came to mean the freeing of slaves, and, in an even broader sense, the lifting of legal restrictions on certain groups, as when we speak of the emancipation of Jews in eighteenth- and nineteenth-century Europe, of serfs in nineteenth-century Russia, or of women in twentieth-century Europe.

In the context of race relations, 'emancipation' usually refers to the collective manumission of slaves in specific countries or colonial territories, especially in the western hemisphere. France was the first to issue an emancipation proclamation of its slaves, in 1794, but the edict was rescinded by Napoleon in 1802, and actual emancipation only took place in 1848. Britain legally abolished slavery in its empire in 1833, with a 5–7-year transition period of 'apprenticeship'. Most Spanish American colonies emancipated their slaves within a few years of achieving independence from Spain in the 1820s. In the United States, the first emancipation proclamation was issued in 1862, but it only became effective in 1865. Brazil was the last major country of the Americas to abolish slavery in 1888, only a couple of years later than in the remaining Spanish colonies of Cuba and Puerto Rico.

The late eighteenth-century saw the rise of an abolitionist movement in Europe and America, especially in Britain, France, the United States, and Brazil. The movement achieved its first major success when Britain and the United States outlawed the transatlantic slave trade in 1807. However, it was not until the early 1860s that the trade was effectively abolished. Rates of manumission of individual slaves during the slavery period differed widely from territory to territory. Some countries that were late in abolishing slavery, like Brazil and Cuba, had much higher rates of manumission than countries where final abolition came earlier (e.g. the British colonies and the United States).

Whether slavery is considered extinct in the world at present is largely a matter of definition. A number of traditional forms of serfdom and clientage subsist in parts of Africa, Asia, and even Latin America, which are difficult to distinguish from domestic slavery. As for massive, chattel slavery, the Soviet and Nazi concentration camps would seem to qualify as modern revivals of slavery.

Read:

Slave and Citizen, by Frank Tannenbaum (Random House, 1946), a classic account of differences between the slave regimes in various parts of the western hemisphere.

Race and Class in Latin America, edited by Magnus Mörner (Columbia University Press, 1970), especially Part 1 on 'The abolition of slavery and its aftermath.'

See *Brazil; Race; Racism; Slavery*

Pierre L. van den Berghe

Environmentalism Environmentalist explanations of racial diversity were first developed in the eighteenth-century. The Bible presented all mankind as descended from Adam and Eve. How then could differences of physical appearance have arisen? The French naturalist Buffon maintained that originally there was one species of man which, after being dispersed, changed 'from the influence of climate, from the difference of food, and of the mode of living, from epidemical distempers, as also from the intermixture of individuals'. The attainment of civilization depended on a society's ability to develop a social organization appropriate to its environment. The environment of tropical West Africa was seen as a particularly adverse one so that one strand in the defence of the slave trade was the belief that it provided an opportunity for Africans to attain human fulfilment in a more favourable setting. The natural humanity of West Africans was denied neither by the slave traders nor by the contemporary books of geography. Some eighteenth-century writers assumed that the prevailing adaptation to environment had been achieved over a long period and that it was dangerous for people to migrate to a region with a different kind of environment. The implication of Voltaire's *Candide* was that it was best for people to remain and cultivate the gardens of their own country. Europeans who settled in North America were expected to degenerate, and biblical support was found for the view that God had determined the bounds of each nation's habitation (*Acts* 17: 26).

The high point of eighteenth-century environmentalism in its application to race relations was the 1787 *Essay on the Causes of the Variety of Complexion and Figure in the Human Species* by Samuel Stanhope Smith (later president of Princeton College). Smith insisted that the Bible showed all men to be of one species. There was a general association between skin colour and the degree of latitude marking out a people's habitat once allowance had been made for the 'elevation of the land, its vicinity to the sun, the nature of the soil, the state of cultivation, the course of winds, and many other circumstances.' Colour, he wrote, might well 'be considered as a universal freckle'. Races could not be clearly distinguished from each other and it was therefore impossible to enumerate them with any certainty. All that stood in the way of the advancement of Negroes and other peoples of non-European origin was their removal to a better environment. If Negroes 'were perfectly free, enjoyed property, and were admitted to a liberal participation of the society, rank and privileges of their masters, they would change their African peculiarities much faster.'

Environmentalist explanations of racial diversity were under sharp attack during the first half of the nineteenth-century from writers who stressed hereditarian causes of difference. Both kinds of explanation were brought together in Darwin's theory of natural selection. With the establishment of genetics as a field of scientific research, it became possible to examine the relative importance of environmental and hereditarian explanations of particular observations. It is quite reasonable, however, to describe as environmentalists those writers who stress the relative importance of social cultural, economic, nutritional and similar factors in the differential performance of individuals of different socio-economic status or different ethnic group membership when, for example, taking intelligence tests.

Read:

The Image of Africa by Philip D. Curtin (Macmillan, 1964), a historical study of environmentalist thought.

Mirage in the West by Durand Echevaria (Princeton University Press, 1957), another historical study.

White Over Black by Winthrop D. Jordan (University of North Carolina Press, 1968), a study of the type of thought in the USA; see also reading for *Heritability.*

See *Darwin; Hereditarianism; Heritability; Sociobiology*

Michael Banton

Equality There are a bewildering number of senses in which this concept can be used, but uniting them all is the assertion that, in all public matters, humans should be both treated identically and given exactly the same degree of access to scarce resources. This said, there are usually additional clauses providing for circumstances in which humans may not be treated equally. For example, those with sufficient identifiable qualities, such as intelligence, are more readily granted access to educational institutions or more senior occupational posts. Equally, a person with apparent physical attributes may be given access to professional sporting establishments and allowed to develop his or her so-called abilities.

This is to acknowledge that all people are not born equal yet should be given the chances to develop what capacities they have. In race and ethnic relations this takes on a particular importance: for instance, if blacks as a category of people are not regarded as having the same inherent abilities as whites, then it seems perfectly justifiable *not* to grant them equal access to facilities and not to treat them equally. Take education: if it is accepted that blacks do not have the same intellectual equipment as whites, then they can be denied access to certain types of education. Here we see the danger of the kind of argument put forward by Arthur Jensen and others. If a fundamental inequality is proposed, then equal treatment and access becomes a nonissue.

If, on the other hand, we accept that all people are *not* born equal, but also that categories of people *cannot* be separated out on the basis of such characteristics as skin colour, or phenotype, then there is no justification for administering a system of unequal access and treatment. Individuals may have, for a variety of reasons (including biological and social ones) different abilities, but there is no reason to suppose that we cluster those differences into groups and assert that 'races' are inherently unequal. It may well be that on measurable tests of intellectual ability, blacks do not perform as well as whites; yet this may well be due to the lack of opportunities available to them to develop these abilities in childhood. Hence, they do not develop them, fare badly in examinations and are denied access to higher education. This is one way in which inequality is transmitted from one generation to the next.

Read:

The Pursuit of Inequality by Philip Green (Martin Robertson, 1981), a detailed examination of the forms that inequality can take and how those forms are rationalized.

Race, IQ and Jensen by James R. Flynn (Routledge & Kegan Paul 1980), a complete appraisal and critique of the race and intellectual inequality theories.

See *Affirmative action; Intelligence and race; Racism*

Ellis Cashmore

Ethiopianism 'From the first day on which an African was captured then blessed by some swaggering Portuguese cleric and consigned to a terrible Atlantic crossing, there have been two distinct Africas,' writes David Jenkins in his book *Black Zion*. 'There is the geographical entity with its millions of social realities, and there is the Africa of the exiled Negro's mind, an Africa compounded of centuries of waning memories and vanquished hopes translated into myth.'

That Africa of the mind has periodically surfaced in many different forms and inspired all manner of social and religious movements. Ethiopianism refers to such movements; it is the expression of black peoples in the Diaspora, uprooted from their spiritual homeland and scattered throughout the world. So we find it in the United States, the West Indies and the UK, not to mention South America.

The strain to return to Africa has existed since the earliest slave days. Jenkins notes how slaves being transported to the Americas would throw themselves overboard still locked in irons in vain attempts to swim home. In the early 1830s, Samuel Sharpe, a Jamaican slave, organized a rebellion based on the belief in a messianic deliverance to Africa. Sharpe used a combination of Christian concepts, particularly the idea of 'second coming' and African beliefs, to generate enthusiasm for his uprising. Before him, slave preachers from America had travelled to the West Indies to establish what was called Native Baptism, again a fusion a Christianity of African beliefs.

Africa has surfaced in many forms amongst black Americans. At the turn of the nineteenth century, Paul Cuffee, a black sea captain living in Massachusetts, attempted a migration programme, but succeeded in returning only thirty-eight people to Sierra Leone. After Cuffee, the vision of a mass migration of blacks to Africa was sustained, albeit with some modifications, by various leaders, one of whom, Bishop Henry M. Turner succeeded in settling an estimated 500 people in Liberia.

One of the most vivid expressions of Ethiopianism came in the 1920s with the Universal Negro Improvement Association (UNIA) under the leadership of Marcus Mosiah Garvey whose slogan 'Africa for the Africans' captured the philosophy of the movement. Blacks in the USA and the West Indies were implored to abandon hopes of integration into white society and turn their sights towards Africa.

Garvey adopted the national colours of Ethiopia for the UNIA and constantly referred to the Ethiopian empire as a source of inheritance and ancestry in counterposition to the imperial dominance of western powers. 'We negroes believe in the God of Ethiopia,' insisted Garvey. 'He shall speak with the voice of thunder that shall shake the pillars of a corrupt and unjust world and once more restore Ethiopia to her former glory.' Like other similar movements, the UNIA identified the whole African continent as 'Ethiopia', the idea being that, in ancient times, there was just one vast nation called Ethiopia; the conquering Europeans found it expedient to split up the continent into separate countries because it facilitated domination – the 'divide and rule' principle.

The great modern movement of Ethiopianism is Ras Tafari, sometimes known as the Rastafarian movement. This emerged in the 1930s, taking the basic ideas of the UNIA but grafting them on to an apocalyptic vision of the future in which the whites' political control of the west would be loosened and all black peoples would be returned.

In Europe the movement called *négritude* became a sort of cultural counterpart to the more obviously political movements. This gave artistic expression to what were taken to be distinct African modes of thought. One of its leading proponents, Leopold Senghor, told his followers to attempt to rid their minds of 'white' thoughts, reject white values and immerse themselves in Ethiopia, which he used synonymously with Africa.

Read:

Black Zion by David Jenkins (Wildwood Press, 1975), a clear exposition of the various manifestations of Ethiopianism since the early slave days, showing how they are sometimes purely religious, often a blend of both.

Black Exodus by Edwin S. Redkey (Yale University Press, 1969) covers much the same ground as Jenkins, but gives more emphasis to the American movements, particularly southern slave rebellions, such as Nat Turner's.

Black Nationalism by E.U. Essien-Udom (University of Chicago Press, 1962), essentially a study of the Nation of Islam, but with interesting sections on its forerunners, such as the Moorish Science Temple of America and Father Divine's Peace Mission.

See *Black Power; Garvey; Nation of Islam; Négritude; Rastafarian movement*

Ellis Cashmore

Ethnicity The actual term derives from the Greek *ethnikos*, the adjective of *ethnos*. This refers to a people or nation. In its contemporary form, ethnic still retains this basic meaning in the sense that it describes a group possessing some degree of coherence and solidarity composed of people who are, at least latently, aware of having common origins and interests. So, an ethnic group is not a mere aggregate of people or a sector of a population, but a self-conscious collection of people united, or closely related, by shared experiences.

Those experiences are usually, but not always, ones of deprivation; for example, characterizing immigrants and their descendants. The original migrants might have left their homelands to seek improvements elsewhere or maybe they were forcibly taken from their lands, as were African slaves. Conversely, the deprived peoples might have been the natural inhabitants of lands that were invaded and then alienated from them. North American Indians and Australian Aborigines would be opposite examples of this. Whatever the circumstances, the people coming under the total or partial domination of either a hostile indigenous population or a conquering group of intruders go through experiences of deprivation. They may be materially deprived, culturally denuded, politically neutered; quite often all of these.

After they become aware of their common plight, their response may be to generate stability, support and comfort amongst others who undergo similar experiences. By emphasising the features of life, past and present, they share, they define boundaries inside which they can develop their own particular customs, beliefs and institutions – in short, their own cultures. The ethnic group, then, is a cultural phenomenon, even though it is based originally on a common perception and experience of unfavourable material circumstances.

Some have argued for the replacement of the word 'race' with 'ethnic group' though this argument seems to stem from a fundamental confusion. Ethnic groups do prosper in times of adversity and quite frequently there is a relationship between a group that is considered a distinct 'race' by the dominant population and the group that considers itself a unified people sharing a common experience. But whereas 'race' stands for the attributions of one group, ethnic group stands for the creative response of a people who feel somehow marginal to the mainstream of society. There is no necessary relationship between the two concepts, though, in actuality, there is often a strong overlap in the sense that a group labelled a race is often pushed out of the main spheres of society and made to endure deprivations; and these are precisely the conditions conducive to the growth of an ethnic group. These are the very people likely to band together to stress their unity or common identity as a way of surviving. Michael Banton has summed up the essential difference between an ethnic group and a 'race': 'the former reflects the positive tendencies of identification and inclusion where the latter reflects the negative tendencies of dissociation and exclusion.'

Ethnicity, then, defines the salient feature of a group that regards itself as in some sense (usually, many senses) distinct. Once the consciousness of being part of an ethnic group is created, it takes on a self-perpetuating quality and is passed from one generation to the next. Distinct languages, religious beliefs, political institutions become part of the ethnic baggage and children are reared to accept these.

The ethnicity may, of course, weaken as successive generations question the validity of the ethnic group. An example of this would be the responses of many children of South Asian migrants in the UK; the 'second generation' found the cultural demands (ranging from arranged marriages to dress restrictions, etc.) excessive and in sharp contrast to the culture they were associated with when away from their families. Whereas the original migrants found the maintenance of their culture highly necessary, their sons and daughters found it irrelevant. Yet the ethnic affiliation cannot be freely dropped as if a cultural option; frequently, it is deeply embedded in the consciousness through years of socialization within the ethnic group. The ethnic boundary is difficult to break out of.

On the other hand, ethnic awareness can be actively promoted to serve immediate purposes. The development of the Chicano movement attests to this. Disparate groups of Mexicans and people of Mexican descent were made aware of their own common plight, principally through the efforts of people like César Chávez (1927–) who galvanized agricultural workers into a strong ethnic-based trade union. In this case, ethnicity was used quite openly as a resource to promote the feeling of 'we' and 'them' (the white business-owners who exploited them) in the achievement of both short-term and long-term tangible goals. The generation of this 'we-ness' prompted confrontation in the form of strikes, sit-ins, boycotts and demonstrations. The Chicano ethnicity was not a mere spontaneous rearing of a new awareness, but a deliberate manipulation of people's perceptions of their own situations. In this sense, ethnicity can be used as an instrument in the effort to achieve clearly defined ends. The Italian-American Congressman Vito Marcantonio (1902–54) successfully drew on strong ethnic support to hold him in power in the 1934-40 period and his attempted reforms included ethnic progressive programmes.

In other situations, ethnicity may be, as Sandra Wallman put it, 'an utter irrelevance or a crippling liability'. Emphasizing or exaggerating cultural differences may not only distinguish a group from the rest of a population, but also incur the wrath of the wider society. Witness, for example, the experiences of Yosif Begun (1932–), one of countless

Russians sentenced to Siberian exile for the 'crime' of sustaining Jewish ethnicity through the teaching of Jewish language, history and culture. Western antisemitism still prevails, possibly sustained by the view that 'Jews keep themselves to themselves . . . they like to think of themselves as superior.' Despite the social mobility of Jews, their progress is still, to a degree, inhibited by such postures.

Situations such as these mean that the ethnic group is widely recognized by other nonethnics. The group has a significance quite apart from the members of the group. This does not make the group any more or less 'real' in an objective sense. The whole point about ethnicity is that it is as real as people want it to be. The group may have no significance at all outside the perceptions of the group members themselves; yet it is real to them and their subjective apprehension of the group motivates them to organize their lives around it.

For instance, it might be possible to expose many of the beliefs on which the Rastafarian movement is based as ill-founded. Rastas themselves feel united by a common ancestry as well as current material circumstances. The bonds that hold the 'brotherhood' together have their origins in a conception of an ancient Africa, united and glorious in a 'golden age'. The fact that many of the ideas held by Rastas may be erroneous does nothing to weaken the ethnic bonds, for Rastas themselves find them meaningful and structure their day-to-day lives around them. The strength of ethnicity lies at source in the subjective relevance it has for the group members.

There is a clear parallel between the Rastas' ethnic response and that of black Americans in the 1960s. Previous generations of blacks had attempted to imitate the lifestyles of middle-class whites, attempted – perhaps vainly – to move physically and intellectually away from the ghetto life and all its associations with the past. Pale skin and straight hair symbolized the attempt to remove the 'taint' of blackness and aspire to white standards. Young blacks in the 1960s reversed this. They plunged back into history in a search for their roots, and, to signify this, grew their hair into 'Afros' and changed their names to African equivalents, at the same time declaring 'black is beautiful'. For the blacks themselves, they were 'discovering' their past and, therefore, themselves. For others, they were creating ethnicity anew. True, they were basing that ethnicity on the conception of a common ancestry, but the way in which they reformulated it was a product of their imaginations. Thus the ethnicity was a subjective phenomenon that was lent credibility by the many thousands of members it attracted.

Ethnic growth, then, can emerge from a number of sources. It can be a defensive mechanism, as with, say Italians, who moved to America, faced antagonism and hardship and so turned in on themselves to recreate their own Italian culture in the new context. The basic characteristics of the culture were carried over and given fresh relevance. On the other hand, the Afro ethnicity of young blacks was a new construction.

Underlying these and other responses is the theme that ethnicity is basically reactive: it is elicited and shaped by the constraints and limits on opportunities imposed on the people who seek to be ethnic. Those people perceive that they are up-against something and organize themselves (survive) or advance themselves (achieve). But the ethnic group is always a reaction to conditions rather than a spontaneous stirring of people who suddenly feel the urge to express themselves through the medium of a group. As stressed before, ethnicity appears as a cultural phenomenon, but it is a response to material conditions.

The 'ethnic revival', as it is sometimes called, has prompted some writers, like Nathan Glazer and Daniel Moynihan, to theorize that ethnicity has already displaced social class as the major form of cleavage in modern society. Ethnicity, they conclude, is 'a more fundamental source of stratification'. While it seems untenable to dismiss class as the critical factor in all forms of social conflict, there is certainly sufficient material to predict that ethnicity and ethnic conflict will be, in the future, at least as significant as class conflict. Having stated this, it would be unwise to separate the two forms, except for analytical purposes, for there is often a very intimate connection between class position and ethnic response.

Ethnic groups are more often than not fractions of the working class, an underclass that is especially vulnerable to the kinds of exploitation that capitalism is based on. This is not to suggest that ethnic groups must stay anchored in this position. The actual fact of organizing ethnically is often instrumental in furthering the interests of the members and some groups, like Irish Catholics and Jews in the USA, overcome material deprivations and aspire to elites. Quite often the ethnic impulse spills over into political realms and strong political organizations are built up to represent the ethnic groups' interests. But nearly always the group starts life from a low-class position of marginality.

To sum up: (1) ethnicity is the term used to encapsulate the various types of responses of different groups; (2) the ethnic group is based on a commonness of subjective apprehensions, whether about origins, interests or future (or a combination of these); (3) material deprivation is the most fertile condition for the growth of ethnicity; (4) the ethnic group does not have to be a 'race' in the sense that it is seen by others as somehow inferior, though there is a very strong overlap and many groups that organize themselves ethnically are often regarded by others as a 'race'; (5) ethnicity may be used for any number of purposes, sometimes as an overt political instrument, at other times as a simple defensive strategy in the face of adversity; (7) ethnicity may become an increasingly important line of cleavage in society, though it is never entirely unconnected with class factors.

Read:

Ethnicity by Nathan Glazer and Daniel P. Moynihan (Harvard University Press, 1975), in its day an important statement cast in a liberal perspective.

Ethnicity at Work edited by Sandra Wallman (Macmillan, 1979), an interesting collection of papers, each examining some aspect of ethnicity as it surfaces in work contexts.

'Analytical and folk concepts of race and ethnicity' by Michael Banton in *Ethnic and Racial Studies* (vol. 2, no. 2, 1979), an appraisal of the utilities of both ideas.

See *Chicanos; Kinship; Migrant ideology; Politics and 'race'; Rastafarian movement*

Ellis Cashmore

Ethnocentrism See *Prejudice; Xenophobia*

Eugenics A social movement originated by Francis Galton (1822–1911), the author of *Hereditary Genius*. It is currently defined as an applied science directed towards the improvement of the genetic potentialities of the human species. Its history, particularly with respect to questions of racial relations, has been punctuated by controversy.

Galton argued that mental ability was inherited differentially by individuals, groups and races. He showed that this ability, like the physical trait of height, followed a normal curve of distribution within the population and that the relatives of outstandingly able individuals tended to be very able themselves. Galton drew on his own money to create a research fellowship and a eugenics laboratory at University College, London, which was directed by his friend Karl Pearson. Later he bequeathed funds to endow a chair of eugenics for Pearson. A Eugenics Education Society was founded in London in 1908 and similar societies followed in many other countries.

In Darwin's theory, a race is a line of individuals of common descent. A race which transmits more of its characteristics to future generations is fitter than other races and therefore is likely to predominate over them in the future. This gives rise to the same sort of controversy as other theories (such as Marx's) which claim to predict the course of future development. Those who adopt a 'naturalistic' stance contend that ethical decisions should be based on the knowledge of what is going to happen anyway. Antinaturalists insist that 'what is good' and 'what the future will bring' are questions requiring different kinds of answer. Their objections are expressed with humour in C.S. Lewis's 'Evolutional Hymn' (reprinted in *The Oxford Book of Light Verse*). Another position is that man is different from other forms of life in having the ability to direct the course of his future evolution. A government can enact legislation to prevent unfit persons (mental defectives, persons suffering from hereditary diseases, etc.) from having children; this is called negative eugenics. Equally, it can take action (through tax incentives, special allowances, etc.) to encourage persons considered to be of the best stock to have more children; this is called positive eugenics. The eugenics movement had a limited success when its campaign for the institutional segregation of the mentally backward led to the Mental Deficiency Act of 1913, but its political programme ran into massive opposition and petered out. Genetic counselling is currently available to persons who fear that any children they might have would suffer from hereditary defects. This is not normally provided under the name of eugenics but it can be seen as an example of a eugenic measure.

Read:

The Idea of Race in Science by Nancy Stepan (Methuen, 1982), pages 111–39 are especially important.

Eugenics and Politics in Britain, 1900–1914 by G.R. Searle (Woordhoff, Leyden, 1976), describes the estabishment of eugenics in its social context.

See *Darwinism, Heritability, Social Darwinism*

Michael Banton

Exploitation This has both a narrow and a more broad usage. The narrow usage is found within marxist writing to refer to the process by which a class of non-producers are able to live without working by extracting a surplus from a class of direct producers. This process of exploitation takes a number of different historical and structural forms. Within a feudal society, the serfs produced crops and other items both for themselves and for the various levels of the aristrocracy, either by directly working the lord's land (and handing over to him all the product), or by handing over a proportion of the product from their activity on their customary land. Despite variations in the specific form that the transfer of surplus took, what characterized the process was a legal/customary constraint upon the serfs to produce directly for the dominant class.

By way of contrast, for marxists the process of exploitation in a capitalist society is obscured by the very form that it takes. Within capitalism, the worker sells labour power for a wage to a capitalist. The capitalist uses the labour power, in combination with raw materials and machinery, etc., to produce commodities which are then sold. By virtue of the fact that the worker receives a given sum of money for every hour worked or item produced, it appears that he or she is fully rewarded for the time spent labouring for the capitalist. In fact, the value received by the worker in the form of wages is less than the value of the commodities that are produced as a result of the employment of his or her labour power. Profit originates in the difference between these two values (in the sphere of production) and not in the difference between the combined price of all the 'factors of production' and the price of the product as paid by the purchaser (in the sphere of exchange).

In both these instances, exploitation is being used to refer to the extraction of surplus value at the point of production. The process is, however, not simply an 'economic' one. Rather, it occurs within supporting political and ideological relations. Hence, in feudal societies, there were customary/legal definitions of the amount of time that the serf should spend labouring for the lord. And, in a capitalist society, the relationship between worker and capitalist is surrounded and linked by a wide range of legal provisions and ideological notions concerning a 'just wage' and 'acceptable' working conditions, etc. This integral political/ideological dimension to exploitation within marxist analysis provides the bridge to broader and, ultimately, non-marxist uses of the concept of exploitation.

To illustrate this point, we can take two examples, those of slave labour and contract, migrant labour. In the case of slave labour, the slave is owned as a thing by a master who receives the total product of the slave's labour, but in return for which the slave has to be provided with food, clothing and shelter. However, the ownership of a human being as a thing requires that the human being be divested partially, or completely, of humanity. Thus, one can identify a historical, *ideological* process by which those human beings who were enslaved were defined as less than human by virtue of their condition of 'heathenness' and, later, by their supposed 'race'. In the case of a contract, migrant worker, the entry into the society where capital employs his or her labour power in return for a wage is legally and ideologically structured in such a way that the conditions under which this exchange occurs are inferior to those applying to indigenous labour. Hence, the contract worker may have no permanent residence or voting rights.

These political and ideological processes are, in both cases, integral to the process by which a surplus product is obtained from the utilization of labour power. In other words, in marxist analysis, they are integral to the process of exploitation. However, it is common for the notion of exploitation to be used to refer directly to these ideological and political processes in themselves, and without reference to the appropriation of surplus value. This broader usage tends to arise from theoretical perspectives which regard wage labour as a natural or acceptable form of appropriation of labour power, against which other forms are then evaluated and analysed. Thus, in the case of slave labour, exploitation is used to refer to both the harshness of the treatment of the slave and the way in which the slave is dehumanized, as assessed relative to the 'freedom' of the wage labour. And in the case of contract, migrant labour, exploitation is located in the comparative legal/political disadvantages of the worker when compared with 'indigenous, free' labour.

We find parallels in the way in which writers analyse the position of New Commonwealth migrants and their children in Britain. This is judged to be the sole or primary product of racism and discrimination and therein, it is argued, lies their exploitation. In other words, racism and discrimination are forms of exploitation in and by themselves, as measured by the fact that 'white' people are not the object of such experiences and processes. In this usage, exploitation loses any direct connection with production relations and comes to refer to any process by which one group is treated less equally than some other. Thus, the many ways in which men treat women, 'whites' treat 'blacks', and parents treat children, can all fall within the rubric of exploitation. This move towards extreme generality, and the analytical problems that it causes, is evident in the way in which the notion of exploitation is increasingly qualified by a descriptive adjective as in racial exploitation, sexual exploitation and parental exploitation.

Read:

Capital, vol. 1, by Karl Marx (Penguin, 1976), where, in Parts 3, 4, and 5, he details his analysis of the nature of exploitation in a capitalist society through the concepts of absolute and relative surplus value.

Marx's Capital, by Ben Fine (Macmillan, 1975), which gives a brief account of surplus value and surplus appropriation in chapter 4.

Racial Oppression in America, by Robert Blauner (Harper & Row, 1972) as an example of an analysis which tends towards a broad utilisation of the notion of exploitation.

See *Capitalism; Labour; Marxism*

Robert Miles

F

Fascism Refers to a political movement which aspires to a particular form of authoritarian class rule within a capitalist society. It emerged in western Europe in the period after the First World War, although its ideology has much deeper roots in European political action and political thought. As a form of class rule, it is characterized by an acceptance of a form of capitalism as an economic structure and process, by the elimination of all independent working-class and other political organizations and by authoritarian forms of political rule and administration. The latter is evident in the rejection of bourgeois liberal conceptions of party organization and representation in favour of the establishment of a permanent political elite, and in the establishment of a corporate state. As an ideology, it is characterized by an extreme nationalism (which commonly but not characteristically becomes racism) and an 'irrationalism' which asserts that the interests of 'the nation' must always predominate over all other interests. Although fascist movements have existed in all European countries since the 1920s, only in Germany, Italy and Spain have they attained political power.

Fascist movements of the early twentieth century represented a revolt against bourgeois society and the liberal state as well as against the growing working-class political and trade union organizations. The early support for these movements came from sectors of the population excluded from both financial and political bourgeois privilege, and working-class organizations, notably petit-bourgeois, clerical and professional strata and the peasantry. Such strata were facing extreme political pressure from 'above' and 'below' in a context of the major social and economic dislocation in Europe after 1918, and so any explanation must take full account of both the nature of the strata that gave support to fascism and the structural conditions that permitted fascism to become a solution. Fascism represented a solution insofar as it constituted a new route to political power and promised through national reorganization a new and radically different political and economic future. This revived support from sections of both the petit-bourgeoisie and the working class, but the political and financial support of monopoly capital became the decisive factor in ensuring the attainment of political power. The route to political power was based upon only tactical support for electoral activity, combined with para-military organization and activity, not only for 'self-defence' but also for a coup d'état. Its vision for the future was a national state purged of all forms of internationalism (from finance capital to communism) and bourgeois privilege in which the ordinary man (and sometimes woman) would have his (and her) rightful place as a member of a national community. The explicit political subordination of women to the task of biological reproduction of the nation, with all its implications, has received particular attention in more recent analyses of fascism. It also aimed at dispensing with bourgeois parliamentarianism as a form of government, to be replaced by the rule of the fascist party which would embody all national interests.

The routes to power in Italy, Germany and Spain differ in important ways. However, in all three cases, the support of important sections of the ruling capitalist class became crucial, both in terms of political credibility and financial support. The emphasis on national regeneration and suppression of working-class political organization promised greater economic and political rewards to sections of the dominant class, faced with economic crisis and a strong and politically conscious working class, than did bourgeois parliamentarianism. It is in this sense that fascism, once in power, is to be understood as a form of class rule.

The relationship between fascism and racism is a particularly controversial issue. It was only in Germany that racism came to play a predominant part in political ideology and strategy and this has led some commentators to conclude that a firm distinction be drawn between fascism and nazism. It is certainly the case that the fascist movement in Germany explicitly reproduced a notion of German nationalism which was biologically based and excluded the Jews as an allegedly distinct and inferior 'race' which threatened biological extinction if allowed to remain. An explicit biological nationalism was not as important in Italy or Spain but it does not follow that the resulting treatment of the Jews makes German fascism a special case. Not only, in all three cases, was fascism an alternative form of class rule which guaranteed a modified capitalism, but, moreover, the historical coincidence of the generation of the ideas of 'nation' and 'race' as means of political mobilization in the nineteenth century means that nationalism contains within it the potential of becoming expressed by means of an explicit racism. This is not simply a matter of historical coincidence but also of the nature of nationalism per se, characterized as it is by the belief in the historical/natural existence of populations sharing a common heritage and culture which must receive expression and organization in a territorial state. The notion of natural, cultural distinctiveness can, in particular historical circumstances (given the predominance of the commonsense idea of 'race'), easily come to be expressed in terms of 'race'.

The defeat of the fascist powers in the Second World War has not led to the elimination of fascist movements in western Europe. Although the political ideology and strategy of fascism was discredited in defeat and in the discovery of the activities of nazism against the Jews and other sections of the German and other European populations, small fascist parties have been allowed to continue to exist and have, since the mid-1970s, shown signs of increasing support and activity throughout Europe. In some cases, particularly in Britain, this has been on the basis of the articulation of an explicit racism in reaction to the presence and settlement of migrant labour. But this should not be allowed to obscure the more general, common features of fascist movements, in particular their tactical support for bourgeois democracy combined with para-military, repressive activity of various kinds.

Read:

Fascism and Dictatorship by N. Poulantzas (New Left Books, 1974), which contains a challenging and influential re-interpretation of fascism from a marxist perspective.

'Racism, fascism and the politics of the National Front' by D. Edgar, in *Race & Class* (1977, vol. 19, no. 2 pp. 111–31), for an important discussion of the relationship between racism and fascism, with particular reference to Britain.

Fascism: A Reader's Guide, edited by W. Laqueur (Penguin, 1979), for a detailed academic analysis of fascism and an extensive bibliography.

See *National Front; Nationalism; Race; Racism*

Robert Miles

Gandhi, Mohandas Karamchand (1869–1948) Leader of the Indian nationalist movement which successfully repelled British colonial rule, Gandhi was born in Porbandar on the western coast of India and had an arranged marriage in the customary Hindu way at the age of thirteen. His wife Kasturbai was his lifelong supporter. At nineteen, he went to England to study law and graduated as a barrister before returning to India in 1891. Here his lack of self-confidence led him to accept a post in South Africa, where he felt professional demands were less stringent.

It was in South Africa that he first encountered racialism, a pivotal experience being when he was ejected from a Pretoria-bound train despite holding a first-class ticket – Indians were allowed only in third-class compartments. His ejection was based solely on his colour. After this, he committed himself to campaigning for the rights of Indians in South Africa through the vehicle of the Natal Indian Congress, formed in 1894.

To attain his objectives, Gandhi came to formulate his central method of nonviolent civil disobedience, or passive resistance, which later became known as *Satyagraha*, meaning 'truth force'; for example, whenever he or his followers were beaten or imprisoned, there would be no retaliation, only a refusal to comply with others' demands. In the years that followed, the method was adopted by movements the world over, particularly by Martin Luther King's Southern Christian Leadership Conference.

During his twenty-one year stay in South Africa, he edited an influential publication, *Indian Opinion*, which was distributed throughout South Africa. He became internationally renowned for his campaigns. His intermittent imprisonments served only to elevate his status. During the Anglo-

Boer War, 1899–1902, Gandhi organized an ambulance corps in support of the British government. At this stage, he believed in the virtues of British colonial rule. The reversal of this opinion was to feature centrally in his subsequent operations in south Asia. After the war, the civil disobedience continued, culminating in a massive protest march in 1913 which resulted in the granting of many of Gandhi's demands for Indians.

His growing reputation in South Africa was constantly relayed to India, thus producing an invitation by the Indian National Congress (INC) for him to return to India to help his own country win *swaraj*, that is self-rule. He took up the invitation in 1915, taking over the unofficial leadership by 1921. The INC was formed in 1885 mainly as a liberal middle-class movement dedicated to reviving interest in traditional Indian culture; it later developed a political edge when it campaigned for greater freedom from British political control. Gandhi was responsible for transforming the INC from a more or less elitist organization into a mass movement with the support of the Muslim League and other smaller movements. Instead of constitutional lobbying, the INC opted for mass direct action in the form of nonviolent civil disobedience.

Gandhi was able to unify and mobilize the movement to such measures because his leadership was premised on charisma; in Gandhi, Indians saw not only a leader, but a person endowed with supernatural powers. This he acknowledged: 'Men say I am a saint losing myself in politics. The fact is I am a politician trying my hardest to be a saint.' He came as a messiah, bringing images of sainthood with his severe dietary restrictions, his vows of celibacy, his insistence on wearing only homespun *khaddar* and his utopian vision of an independent, agrarian India freed of the modern science and technology, which, he argued, were instruments of western domination.

At the outbreak of the First World War, at Gandhi's insistence, India offered support to Britain in anticipation of a stronger elected element in government led by the Indian National Congress and the Muslim League. This was provided in the Montagu-Chelmsford Reforms of 1919, but was insufficient to stem the tide of postwar dissatisfaction. The British government, in its concern for the maintenance of order, passed the Rowlatt Acts which gave the government greater powers to punish Indian dissidents.

Gandhi implemented a massive campaign of civil disobedience and urged his followers to withdraw from all schools and government positions. Whenever violence erupted, Gandhi embarked on extended fasts as if to blackmail his followers into ceasing their violence. This invariably succeeded. One such incident was when nearly two thousand villagers burned alive twenty-one Indian policemen in their station in Chaura Chaura in the United Provinces in February 1922.

One of the nonviolent protests against the reforms of 1919 turned into an atrocity when General Dyer ordered British troops to fire on a crowd of unarmed Indians at Amritsar, the result being 379 people killed and 1,137 injured. General Dyer himself said, after the massacre: 'It was no longer a question of merely dispersing the crowd, but one of producing a sufficient moral effect. My intention was to inflict a lesson that would have an impact throughout all India.'

During the events leading to the Amritsar incident, Gandhi's attitude towards the British colonialists changed completely: he became convinced that 'the British government today represents satanism.' This change led him into alignment with some factions of the INC who were strongly anti-British, and served to win him the leadership of the organization.

There were three decades of turmoil in India before the country won its independence from the British in 1947. Although Gandhi's influence was in decline in the years immediately preceding independence, it was his charismatic leadership which gave the Nationalist movement its impetus on a mass basis, for which he became known as the *Mahatma*, 'the great soul'. In 1948, he was assassinated by a Hindu extremist.

Martin Luther King acknowledged Gandhi as his inspiration and used the INC as the model for his own movement. King, like Gandhi, demanded great, almost inhuman self-discipline of his followers in restraining themselves when subjected to violence. As Gandhi strove to acquire independence and equality for Indians, King strove for freedom and equality for black Americans.

Read:

M.K. Gandhi: An Autobiography (Penguin, 1982), the Mahatma's own account of his experiences and philosophy translated from the original Gujerati.

Gandhi by George Woodcock (Fontana, 1972), a short, readable introduction to the career of Gandhi.

The Selected Writings of Mahatma Gandhi edited by Ronald Duncan (Fontana, 1983), a useful guide to the political opinions and general philosophy of the man.

See *Chicanos; Civil rights movement; Equality; Power; Smuts*

Gita Jairaj

Garvey, Marcus (1887–1940) One of the enduringly influential black leaders of this century. His actual achievements do not compare with those of King, Washington or even Du Bois, but his general thrust to elevate black people by forcing them to recognize their African ancestry was to have a lasting impact right into the 1980s.

Born in Jamaica, Garvey travelled throughout the West Indies and Central America before starting his organization in the USA. His Universal Negro Improvement Association (UNIA) went strongly against the grain of other black American movements. As his biographer E. David Cronon puts it: 'Garvey sought to raise high the walls of racial nationalism at a time when most thoughtful men were seeking to tear down these barriers.' Whereas leaders such as W.E.B. Du Bois and his National Association for the Advancement of Colored People (NAACP) were campaigning for the greater integration of blacks and whites (principally through legislation), Garvey declared integration impossible and implored his followers to make a sharp break with whites. His simple aim was to restore all blacks to what he considered their rightful 'fatherland', Africa, 'If you cannot live alongside the white man, even though you are his fellow citizen; if he claims that you are not entitled to this chance or opportunity because the country is his by force of numbers, then find a country of your own and rise to the highest position within that country,' was Garvey's message and he summed it up in his slogan, 'Africa for the Africans.'

To show that this was no empty slogan, Garvey made efforts to realize his ambition by buying a steamship line, called 'Black Star' and even entered into what were ultimately abortive negotiations with the Liberian Government to make possible a mass migration. Garvey, at the peak of his popularity, claimed four million followers all willing to forsake America and migrate to Africa to start a new life as what Garvey called 'The New Negro'.

This concept of the New Negro was pivotal in Garvey's movement. Blacks were told to rid themselves of any notions of inferiority and cultivate a new sense of identity; they were urged to take pride and dignity in the fact that they were truly Africans. Their subordination was the result of whites' attempts to control them not only physically, but mentally too. One method used by whites was religious instruction: blacks were taught to believe in conventional Christianity and worship whites' images. But Garvey augmented his UNIA with a new, alternative religious movement called the African Orthodox Church. Its leader, George Alexander McGuire, instructed UNIA members to tear up pictures of white Christs and Madonnas and replace them with black versions. Garvey explained: 'Our God has no colour, yet it is human to see everything through one's own spectacles, and since white people have seen their God through white spectacles we have only now started to see our own God through our own spectacles.'

Often, Garvey would fuse his practical policies with biblical imagery, sometimes hinting at the inevitability of the exodus to Africa: 'We have gradually won our way back into the confidence of the God of Africa, and he shall speak with the voice of thunder that shall shake the pillars of a corrupt and unjust world and once more restore Ethiopia to her ancient glory.' Messages like this and continual reference to Ethiopian royalty helped generate the kind of interest that eventually turned into the Rastafarian movement, members of which even today regard Garvey as a genuine prophet.

At a time when black organizations, particularly in the States, were assiduously trying to implement gradual integrationist policies, Garvey's programme was an outrage. He was vigorously condemned by people like Du Bois and there were assassination attempts. Further notoriety came when Garvey entered negotiations with the white racist movement, the Ku Klux Klan; in a bizarre way, both harboured the same ideal: the removal of blacks.

Throughout the 1920s, Garvey's influence spread in the USA and in the West Indies and he cultivated a mass following. The steamship line failed and negotiations for a migration to Africa broke down, so his following eventually faded. A spell in Jamaican politics ended after a series of clashes with the law and Garvey left for England where he died in 1940, his dreams unfulfilled.

Yet his influence amongst blacks continued; as his wife was to express it, 'Garvey instilled in them *new concepts* of their rightful place on earth as God's creation.' Garvey had instigated what he called 'a second emancipation – an emancipation of the minds and thoughts.' He identified the evil not so much in whites who controlled blacks, but in the minds of blacks themselves: they accepted their own inferiority and so failed to recognize their own potential. Garvey provided a blueprint for banishing the sense of inferiority with his conception of the New Negro. Even in the 1980s, Garvey is revered by a great many blacks as one of the most important leaders not in terms of practical achievements, but in terms of transforming consciousness.

Read:

Philosophy and Opinions, 3 vols, by Marcus Garvey (Cass, 1967), a collection of speeches and essays edited by Garvey's wife Amy Jacques Garvey; the best account of the complex, sometimes contradictory, patterns of Garvey's thought.

Black Moses by E. David Cronon (University of Wisconsin Press, 1974), a well-researched biography of the man and his movement with attention given to the social contexts of the times.

Marcus Garvey edited by E. David Cronon (Prentice-Hall, 1973), a useful introduction to the main themes of Garvey's philosophy with comments from the editor.

See *Black Power; Ethiopianism; Ku Klux Klan; Nation of Islam; Rastafarian movement*

Ellis Cashmore

Genotype The underlying genetic constitution of an organism in respect of a particular trait or traits, as opposed to the phenotype or appearance of that organism. All people with brown eyes have the same phenotype in respect of eye colour, yet some of them may carry a recessive gene for blue eyes and therefore have a different genotype. For predicting inheritance, it is the genotype which is important.

Genes control enzymes and in that way control the nature of physical characteristics. They are located on chromosomes and since all chromosomes exist in pairs, so do genes. The two members of a gene pair may be either identical or different. A person who carries blue-eye genes on both chromosomes is said to be homozygous for that characteristic; someone with a blue-eye gene on one chromosome and a brown-eye gene on the other is heterozygous in that respect. If a man who is homozygous for brown eyes and a woman who is homozygous for brown eyes have children they will all be brown-eyed. If a man who is homozygous for blue eyes has children with a woman who is homozygous for brown eyes the outcome is more complicated. Every egg cell the mother produces will contain one brown-eye gene; every sperm cell the father produces will contain one blue-eye gene. No matter which sperm fertilizes which egg, the fertilized ovum will be heterozygous, containing one blue-eye and one brown-eye gene. Each child will be brown-eyed since the brown-eye gene forms more of the chemical (tyrosinase) which colours the eye; it is therefore said to be dominant, whereas the blue-eye gene is recessive; although it is part of the genotype it cannot be seen in the phenotype.

If the father and mother are both heterozygous with respect to blue and brown-eye genes, they will form sperm and egg cells with one blue and one brow-eye gene. When these cells interact, three combinations are possible for the ovum: two brown-eye genes; one gene of each; two blue-eye genes. Since the one of each combination is twice as likely as either of the others, and since the brown-eye gene is dominant, the probability is that of four children three will have brown eyes and one blue.

This example oversimplifies the inheritance of eye colour because, as everyone can see, there are eyes of other colours than blue and brown. Possibly other genes at other places in the chromosomes or other kinds of eye-colour genes are involved in the production of the relevant chemicals, but the example serves to clarify the differences between phenotype and genotype. It also illustrates Mendel's laws: firstly, that inheritance is particulate, resulting from the interrelation of distinctive genes rather than from the blending of hereditary elements to produce a mixed character; and, secondly, that characters are independently inherited, so that a child's inheritance of his father's eye colour does not indicate the likelihood of his inheritance of his father's hair or skin colour.

GHETTO

Read:

The Race Concept, by Jonathan Harwood and Michael Banton (David & Charles, 1975).

Genetics, Man and Society, edited by Mark Lipkin and Peter T. Rowley (Plenum Press, 1974), the proceedings of a symposium held at the American Association for the Advancement of Science.

See *Heritability; Phenotype*

Michael Banton

Ghetto The congregation of particular groups who share common ethnic and cultural characteristics in specific sectors of the city often takes the form of a segregated area and is described as a ghetto. The concept ghetto, however, is notoriously imprecise and in popular usage it has assumed pejorative connotations. Areas such as Hampstead in London, Solihull in Birmingham (England) and Bel-Air in Los Angeles are rarely considered as urban ghettos despite their homogeneous nature: after all their residents are overwhelmingly white and middle-class. In contrast, areas in those cities such as Brixton, Sparkbrook and Watts – which contain relatively large black populations – are frequently characterized as ghettos. Clearly then, the term ghetto refers not only to areas of ethnic and cultural homogeneity but symbolizes all that is negative about city life: high crime rates, pollution, noise, poor quality housing, bad sanitation, and so on.

On the whole, most commentators agree that, technically, a ghetto should comprise a high degree of homogeneity, all residents sharing similar backgrounds, beliefs, etc. They should also be living amidst poverty, in relation to the rest of the city's population. By these two criteria, then, New York's Harlem and the Watts district in Los Angeles can be defined legitimately as ghettos. In the UK, however, the term ghetto is wholly inappropriate even to areas such as Brixton, Notting Hill and Sparkbrook. Despite the concentration of colonial migrants and their children in these and other districts within the major urban centres of the UK, they are nowhere approaching all-black areas. On the contrary, whites continue to constitute the majority of residents in these areas with the presence of blacks and south Asians largely confined to a few streets. But, despite its technical wrongness, the term ghetto continues to be popularly applied to these areas. In short 'ghetto' is emotive and racist in its connotation.

The origins of the term ghetto can be traced back to Europe in the Middle Ages, when it described how Jews voluntarily established corporate areas within the city, largely for protective purposes. The voluntaristic nature or otherwise of the 'ghettoization' process, however, is a contentious issue. Some writers adopt a 'choice' model of interpretation in which they focus on the attitudes and behaviours of ghetto residents themselves. Those who put forward the 'constraint' theory tend, in contrast, to adopt a broader perspective which engages more directly with social and political processes. In other words, theirs is a more deterministic account of ghetto formation. Not surprisingly, these different interpretations of the process lead to contrasting appraisals of their function. Louis Wirth (1928), for instance, presented a romantic version of ghetto life in Chicago in the 1920s in which he stressed its voluntaristic nature, and hence, its positive community features. On the other hand, Robert Blauner sees ghettos as an 'expression of colonized status' and a means by which the white majority is able to prevent blacks dispersing and spreading discontent. He argues that black ghettos in the USA are controlled by white administrators, educators and policemen who live outside the ghetto but effectively administer its day-to-day affairs. In other words, they exert 'direct rule' over the black communities, a relationship which Blauner terms internal colonialism. Under this system, blacks in the ghetto are subject people, controlled from outside: the 'burn, baby, burn' episodes of the 1960s, therefore, represented an attempt by the ghetto dwellers 'to stake out a sphere of control by moving against (USA) society and destroying the symbols of its oppression' (1972).

In the UK, a similar debate surrounds the pattern of ethnic segregation in the cities: some writers stress the discriminatory practices of the housing market as the determinant of migrant residence; others insist that clustering is actively sought by the migrants and occurs quite independently of such discriminatory practices.

Read:

The Ghetto, by Louis Wirth (Chicago University Press, 1928), an account of ghetto life in Chicago in the 1920s by a student and colleague of Robert Park, co-developer of the 'urban ecology' theory.

Racial Oppression in America, by Robert Blauner (Harper & Row, 1972), presents the theory of internal colonialism amongst a number of other essays designed to reveal the inadequacy of existing theoretical analyses of American race relations.
Ethnic Segregation in Cities, edited by Ceri Peach, Vaughan Robinson and Susan Smith (Croom Helm, 1981), a collection of papers by geographers and sociologists on ethnic segregation in cities both in the UK and USA.

See *Dispersal; Inner city; Internal colonialism; Kerner Report*

Barry Troyna

Gobineau, Joseph Arthur de (1816–82) A Frenchman born into a bourgeois family with aristocratic pretensions, who claimed the title 'Count'. Educated in German as well as in French, Gobineau earned a living from journalism until 1849, after which he obtained a succession of diplomatic appointments up to 1877. It would seem that in the Paris salons Gobineau obtained an acquaintance with contemporary anthropological speculations, notably with those of Victor Courtet de l'Isle, author of *La Science politique fondée sur la science de l'homme*. These were important to his four-volume *Essay on the Inequality of Human Races*, the first two volumes of which appeared in 1853 and the last two in 1855. The question of racial inequality receives little attention in Gobineau's remaining writings (which included twenty-six other books).

Some sections of the *Essay* are unequivocal in asserting a philosophy of racial determinism, but there are ambiguities and inconsistencies, so that different commentators emphasize different themes of the work. If anything can be seen as the book's central problem, it is probably the assertion that 'the great human civilizations are but ten in number and all of them have been produced upon the initiative of the white race' (including, apparently, those of the Aztecs and the Incas, though their civilizations are never examined). What explains the rise and fall of civilizations? Alongside this problem, and at times overshadowing it, is the author's desire to lament the breakdown of the old social order and to insist that the process of degeneration has advanced so far as to be irreversible. To answer the historical question Gobineau contends that races differ in their relative worth; and that 'the question on which the argument here turns is that of the permanence of type'. Whereas the whites are superior in intellect they are inferior in the intensity of their sensations so that 'a light admixture from the black species develops intelligence in the white race, in that it turns it towards imagination . . .' Mixtures of blood seem to be necessary to the birth of civilizations but mixtures, once started, get out of control and the 'historical chemistry' is upset. Thus there is a subsidiary theme in the book which stresses the complementarity of races as well as their hierarchical ordering. Logically there is no reason why the inability of racial types to lose their fundamental physical and moral characteristics, plus the idea that 'ethnic workshops' can be built to diffuse a civilization, should not lead to the birth of an eleventh. The prophecy of decline ('what is truly sad is not death itself but the certainty of our meeting it as degraded beings') therefore has its origin not in Gobineau's borrowed anthropology but in his personal pessimism.

One message that the book conveyed is the impotence of politics: nothing that men do can now affect the inevitable outcome. Nor does it lend support to nationalism, since Gobineau's 'German' and 'Aryan' are not to be equated with *die Deutsche* but include the Frankish element among the French population. The country which has best preserved Germanic usages and is 'the last centre of Germanic influence' is England, though in some degree the leadership of Aryan-Germanism has passed to Scandinavia. Gobineau emphasizes status differences as well as racial ones ('I have no doubt that negro chiefs are superior' he writes, 'to the level usually reached by our peasants, or even by average specimens of our half-educated bourgeoisie'). If it had been taken seriously, therefore, the *Essay* would not have appeared of ideological value as a basis for German nationalism or for claiming European racial superiority. But because of its ambiguities and its pretensions as a comprehensive philosophy of history, its political potential was greater than that of other works in the typological school. The first volume was quickly translated into English because it appealed to white supremacists in the south of the United States. The Wagnerian movement in Germany cultivated Gobineau's ideas and in 1894 a Gobineau Society was formed to give them publicity. In Hitler's Third Reich, the *Essay*, suitably adjusted, became a popular school reader.

GOBINEAU, JOSEPH ARTHUR DE

Michael Biddiss states that in the political literature of Nazism there are many phrases and conceptions echoing Gobineau's work: 'above all, there is in the *mode* of thinking every similarity'.

Read:

Father of Racist Ideology: The Social and Political Thought of Count Gobineau by Michael D. Biddiss (Weidenfeld & Nicolson, 1970), for a biographical treatment.

Gobineau: Selected Political Writings by Michael D. Biddiss (Cape, 1970), is a particularly useful anthology.

See *Chamberlain; Haeckel; Race*

Michael Banton

Haeckel, Ernst (1834–1919) A famous German zoologist, academic entrepreneur, and popularizer of science, who built a vacuous philosophy of life called 'monism' on a Darwinian foundation. He coined a variety of new terms, some of which have survived; among them was the 'biogenetic law', that ontogeny recapitulates phylogeny. This doctrine had been discussed in biology since the 1820s and appears in Robert Chambers's anonymously published *Vestiges of Creation*. All embryos were supposed before birth to pass through the earlier stages of evolution so that European babies passed through Ethiopian and Mongolian stages in the womb.

Haeckel's significance for the study of racial thought lies firstly in his decisive influence upon the development of the Volkish movement, a special kind of romantic German nationalism. Haeckel and the Monists were an important source and a major inspiration for many of the diverse streams of thought that later came together under the banner of National Socialism. Secondly, he publicized a distorted version of Darwinism in which racial differences were fundamental. Haeckel wrote of 'woolly-haired' Negros, 'incapable of a higher mental development' and of Papuans and Hottentots as 'fast approaching their complete extinction'. One of his major theses was that 'in the struggle for life, the more highly developed, the more favoured and larger groups and forms, possess the positive inclination and the certain tendency to spread more at the expense of the lower, more backward, and smallest groups'. In this way, Haeckel and the Monists became the first to formulate a programme of racial imperialism and *lebensraum* for Germany. Haeckel himself supported the Pan-German League, one of that country's most militant, imperialistic, nationalistic and antisemitic organizations.

Haeckel had a direct and powerful influence upon many individuals important to the rise of racial anthropology and National Socialism. One of them was Ludwig Woltmann, a member of the Social Democratic Party who attempted to fuse the ideas of Haeckel and Marx, transforming the latter's concept of class struggle into a theory of world-wide racial conflict. Another was Adolf Hitler. According to Daniel Gasman, Hitler's views on history, politics, religion, Christianity, nature, eugenics, science, art and evolution, however eclectic, coincided with those of Haeckel and were more than occasionally expressed in very much the same language. At least two significant ideological contacts can be established between Hitler and the Monist League that propagated Haeckel's doctrines. Among many Nazi scientists and intellectuals there was a general acclaim for Haeckel as an intellectual ancestor and forerunner, but he was never lauded as a major prophet of the movement (as was Houston Stewart Chamberlain). Chamberlain's conception of race derived from the pre-Darwinian theory of racial typology which permitted enthusiasts to regard the Aryans as being of distinctive origin and permanently superior. Darwinism was included in the German curriculum in biology but the Nazis were suspicious of a doctrine which attributed an inferior anthropoid ancestry to all men and was incompatible with their belief that Aryans had been racially superior from the very beginning.

Read:

The Scientific Origins of National Socialism by Daniel Gasman (Macdonald, London, and Elsevier, New York, 1971).

See *Aryan; Chamberlain; Social Darwinism; Volk*

Michael Benton

Hegemony From the Greek *hegemon*, meaning leader or ruler, this term has become associated with a particular brand of twentieth-century marxism, especially that espoused by the Italian Antonio Gramsci (1891–1937). Hegemony describes the total domination of the middle class (bourgeoisie) not only in political and economic spheres, but also in the sphere of consciousness. Marx theorised that the dominant ideas of any age are the ideas of the ruling class and this is taken as a central point in Gramscian interpretations of capitalist societies. What is accepted as commonsense, the obviously correct way things are, is not a neutral perception of the world, but a particular way of grasping reality which fits in neatly with the existing social order. In other words, the bourgeoisie's leadership extends from the material world into people's minds.

For Marx, consciousness was not separable from material existence; this means that what goes on in our heads can never be divorced from how we live the rest of our lives; so practices such as how we feed and clothe ourselves, our place in the social order, how we work, are all influences on our consciousness. People have a certain view of reality and, for the most part, they believe in the legitimacy or 'rightness' of that reality. Under capitalism, the working class (proletariat) live in a social order which works against their true interest: they are systematically exploited. However, and this is crucial, they do not oppose that order because they believe in its legitimacy; so they accept their own subordination. They believe it is part of commonsense.

The actual mechanisms through which commonsense is disseminated and transmitted from one generation to the next (thus ensuring the perpetuation of capitalism) are complex, but the Algerian philosopher Louis Althusser (1918–) has offered an influential version using the concept of an Ideological State Apparatus (ISA). An ideology is a way of viewing reality; for Althusser (and other marxian theorists), ideologies distort or mask true reality and serve ruling-class interests (i.e. enable them to keep control). Through schooling, going to church, attending to the media, people piece together a picture of reality. By accepting this commonsense picture of reality, people make themselves available for exploitation by those who dominate (and therefore control agencies like education, the media, etc.). One of the critical features of this is that the people accepting the commonsense remain unaware of their exploitation. Hence there is a hegemonic control and the bourgeoisie maintains its leadership without having it seriously questioned.

The relevance of all this to race and ethnic relations became apparent in the early 1980s, particularly through the theoretical work of the University of Birmingham's Centre for Contemporary Cultural Studies (England). Racist ideologies are seen as components of commonsense: ideas about the inferiority of blacks and Asians have deep roots in history, but they are 'reworked' over and over again and serve to divide working-class people. 'Problems' connected with so-called racial groups are interpreted as 'pathological' because these groups are seen as somehow different. This kind of commonsense thinking operates at local levels (for example in riots and unemployment) and at international levels, as Errol Lawrence points out: 'The relative "under-development" and poverty of many "Third world" countries is of course not viewed as the outcome of centuries of imperialism and colonial domination, but rather is thought to be expressive of a *natural state of affairs,* in which blacks are seen as genetically and/or culturally inferior.'

Images of primitiveness, backwardness and stupidity are associated with blacks and Asians and these are unquestioningly accepted as part of commonsense. They are integrated elements of a wider ideology, however, and the ideology's strength rests on people's failure to unmask it and examine alternative ways of viewing reality. So racism, in this Gramscian interpretation, is not a peculiarity of extreme right-wing forms of society, but part of everyday commonsense knowledge in modern society. The continued subordination of blacks and Asians is as much the result of ideology as it is to do with the more easily identifiable form of inequalities in work, housing and education.

Read:

'Just plain common sense: the "roots" of racism' by Errol Lawrence in *The Empire Strikes Back*, edited by the Centre for Contemporary Cultural Studies (Hutchinson, 1982), a strongly argued case for understanding racist ideologies within a Gramscian framework; this article uses interesting historical material to show how imperialist regimes created racist images that have been transmitted from one generation to the next and have gained purchase in the context of the 'organic crisis' of capitalist societies.

The Prison Notebooks by Antonio Gramsci (Lawrence & Wishart, 1971), the bible of this strain of marxian thought, it contains the theoretical basis for the exploration of hegemony and ideology.

The New Racism by Martin Barker (Junction Books, 1981), contains plenty of interesting historical and contemporary material on the different shapes and effects of racism in different social contexts, particularly useful on demonstrating how racist ideologies can be smuggled almost undetected into modern political debates where the 'race' issue is ostensibly not a priority.

See *Ideology; Marxism and race relations; Media and race relations; Power; Racism*

Ellis Cashmore

Hereditarianism The argument that racial differences are hereditary arose in opposition to the belief that, since all mankind is descended from Adam and Eve, diversity must be a product of adaptation to environment. In 1520, Paracelsus maintained that peoples 'found in out-of-the-way islands' were not descended from the sons of Adam; early hereditarian theories followed this thesis by claiming that racial differences had existed from the beginning of humanity. At the start of the nineteenth century, the influential French anatomist George Cuvier classified *Homo sapiens* as divided into three subspecies, Caucasian, Mongolian and Ethiopian, each of which was further subdivided on geographical, linguistic and physical grounds. He represented the races as constituting a hierarchy and contended that differences in culture and mental quality were produced by differences in physique. This line of reasoning was developed into an international school of racial typology as expressed in Britain by Charles Hamilton Smith (1848) and Robert Knox (1850), in France by Arthur de Gobineau (1853), in the United States by Josiah Clark Nott and George Robbins Gliddon (1854) and in Germany by Karl Vogt (1863). This school has more often been referred to as that of 'scientific racism'. Its adherents maintained that racial types were permanent forms, at least for the period for which evidence was available, and might have been separately created. The stricter typologists, like Knox and Nott, believed that the various human types were adapted to particular zoological provinces. Just as marsupials were peculiar to Australia, so Australian Aborigines exemplified the kind of men who belonged in that province. Other animals would not long survive there. It was the height of foolishness for Europeans to attempt to colonize North America, Australia or tropical regions because they were not suited to these environments; if they attempted it their descendants would degenerate and die out. The typological theory of racial differences appeared some three decades before the main phase of European imperial expansion and its doctrines provided little, if any, support for imperialist campaigns.

Whereas environmentalist theories offered explanations for the diversity of racial forms and hereditarian theories for the stability of these forms within particular environments, both kinds of explanation were brought together in Darwin's theory of natural selection. With the establishment of genetics as a field of scientific research, it became possible to examine the relative importance of hereditarian and environmental explanations of particular observations. It is quite reasonable, however, to describe as hereditarians those writers who stress the importance of genetic inheritance relative to environmental influences in the differential performance of individuals of different socio-economic status or different ethnic group membership when, for example, taking intelligence tests.

Read:

The Leopard's Spots by William Stanton (University of Chicago Press, 1960), an historical study of hereditarian thought.

The Black Image in the White Mind by George M. Frederickson (Harper Torch Books, 1971), another historical account.

The Idea of Race by Michael Banton (Tavistock, 1977), a more general review; see also readings for heritability.

See *Environmentalism; Heritability; Race*

Michael Banton

Heritability A measure of genetic inheritance. More technically, a heritability estimate for a particular trait expresses the proportion of trait variation in a population which is attributable to genetic variation. Suppose, for example, that in a certain population individuals vary in stature. If the variation can be traced to genetic differences the heritability estimate for stature will be 1; if it can all be traced to differences in the environments of individuals the estimate will be 0.

Every organism is the product of both inheritance and environmental influence. A hereditary trait (like skin colour) may be modified by environment (e.g. sun tanning). Equally a trait sensitive to environmental modifications (like weight in man) may be genetically conditioned. Geneticists speak of genes being 'switched on and off' by environmental stimuli. The difficulties involved in studying the interactions between heredity and environment can be illustrated by the inheritance of genes for yellow or colourless legs among certain kinds of chicken. If they are fed on white corn they all have colourless legs. If they are fed on yellow corn, or on green feed, some have yellow legs. If those belonging genetically to the yellow-leg variety are fed, some on white and others on yellow corn, the former have colourless and the latter yellow legs, so that the difference can be attributed to an interaction between environmental factors (i.e. nutrition) and genetic ones. This is why heritability has to be estimated for particular populations and the estimates for different traits in the same population vary substantially.

There was an angry debate in the early 1970s about the heritability of intelligence as measured by IQ tests. Studies in the United States had consistently recorded an average of about 15 percentage points difference in the scores of black and white samples, while Asian-Americans regularly scored better than whites. It was not in question that environmental factors could account for individual IQ differences of 20–30 points, or that US blacks and whites differed in several IQ-relevant environmental respects. The dispute centered upon whether environmental differences could account for all the differences between groups. Hereditarians such as A.R. Jensen maintained that since heritability estimates for IQ can be as high as 0.8, the inter-group difference is likely to be in part genetic. However the available heritability estimates only expressed the relative importance of environmental factors for IQ differences within the white population, and no reliable estimates were available for the blacks. The hereditarian argument was blocked by the lack of evidence that environmental differences operated between the groups in the same way as within the white population. Moreover, if discrimination against blacks in the United States was itself an intellectual handicap this made inter-group comparison impossible because like was not being compared with like.

Read:

The Race Concept by Michael Banton and Jonathan Harwood (David & Charles, 1975), for an elementary exposition.

Race, Intelligence and Education by H.J. Eysenck (Temple Smith, 1971), a statement of hereditarian views.

The Science and Politics of I.Q. by Leon J. Kamin (Penguin, 1977), gives a critique of the evidence about intelligence; the opposition of views is analysed in 'The race-intelligence controversy' by

Jonathan Harwood in *Social Studies in Science* (vol. 6, 1976 and vol. 7, 1977).

See *Environmentalism; Hereditarianism; Intelligence and race*

Michael Banton

Holocaust The term used to describe the atrocities committed by German Nazis in the Second World War. In January 1942, German ministers met to discuss what was perceived as a growing 'Jewish problem'. The result of the meeting was known as *Die Endlosung* – the final solution. This involved the systematic extermination of up to 6 million Jews mostly in mass gas chambers. Hence the term 'holocaust', from 'holo' (whole) 'kauston' (burnt).

Surviving members of the Nazi regime were tried at Nuremberg and convicted of genocide (the deliberate destruction of a whole nation or 'race' or ethnic group of people). Genocide was described as a crime under international law in 1948.

Read:

Holocaust by Gerald Green (Corgi, 1978), a survivor's account on which a television series was based.

The Holocaust and the German Elite by Rainer C. Baum (Croom Helm, 1981), looks at the political machinations behind the divisions which lead to the holocaust.

The Holocaust Kingdom by Alexander Donat (Secker & Warburg, 1965).

See *Fascism; Zionism*

Ellis Cashmore

I

Ideology This concept is the object of continuing debate and argument, although all uses of it suggest that it refers to a complex of ideas. This reflects the origin of the term in the late eighteenth century when it was used to refer, in a technical sense, to the science of ideas. It took on another meaning around the same time, one of which is still predominant in commonsense discourse and in conservative political thought. This uses the term in a pejorative sense to refer to impractical or fanatical theory, to ideas which are abstract and which ignore 'the facts'. Neither of these two uses are of any direct relevance to the way in which the concept is employed analytically now.

Contemporary analytical usage reflects the different ways in which the concept was employed by Marx. In Marx's own writings, one finds two distinct usages. The first is his use of the concept to refer to false and illusory descriptions of reality, a meaning that is synonymous with the notion of false consciousness. This usage is found clearly expressed in *The German Ideology*, written by Marx and Engels in 1846. This notion of ideology is used by both marxists and critics of marxism in combination with a mechanical interpretation of the base/superstructure metaphor. This is evident in arguments which claim that ideology is the reflection and product of ruling-class interests and has the function of obscuring from the working class the 'real' nature of its domination and exploitation by capital.

The second use of ideology in Marx's writings is to refer to the complex of ideas which correspond to particular sets of material interests and experiences. This usage is found in Marx's later work, notably in the *Grundrisse* and *Capital*. However, this usage itself fragments into two different emphases. On the one hand, ideology is used to refer in a general sense to the content of the forms of consciousness which come into being and are reproduced in the course of the reproduction of material life. On the other, it is used to refer to the structural fact of consciousness: in this sense, ideology is used to refer to a particular level or dimension of a social formation. However, both usages are usually associated with a further distinction between ideology and science, which implicitly (if not explicitly) returns us to an elaboration on the theme of illusion. The introduction of the concept of science as a polarity is necessary in order to permit a critical evaluation of the nature and content of ideology in these two second senses.

The work of Althusser and Poulantzas has been the site of much of this recent debate, from which has emerged some important clarifications and developments. One of these is pertinent to an analysis of racism and nationalism as ideologies. It has been argued recently that although ideologies refer to accounts of the world which are, in totality, false, they must be analysed and understood in such a way as to allow for the fact that people who articulate them can nevertheless make sense of the world through them. This means that ideological generation and reproduction cannot be understood simply and solely via some notion of false perception or ruling-class domination. The latter may be empirically the same in particular instances but this is not the complete substance of ideology. Rather, it is more important to explain why and how ideologies 'work' in relation to the essential relations of the mode of production, thus allowing a certain autonomy to the formation and reproduction of ideology. Thus, ideologies are mistaken, not so much because of false perception or indoctrination, but because of the determinate forms in which production relations can be experienced and expressed phenomenally.

The other important clarification to emerge from recent debates is consequent upon renewed interest in the work of Gramsci, from which has emerged the concept of commonsense. This refers to the complex of ideas and perceptions, organized without coherence, which are a consequence of both historical tradition and direct experience and by which people negotiate their daily life. The term ideology can refer to this commonsense which is characterized not only by its 'matter of factness' but also by its internal disorganization. Ideology can therefore refer not only to a complex of ideas which are the product of 'systematic' thought but also to the internally contradictory and incoherent set of ideas through which daily lives are lived.

These general debates are refracted in the ways in which racism is analysed as ideology. One classic, marxist tradition has been to argue that racism is an ideology created by the ruling class in a capitalist society to justify the exploitation of colonial populations and to divide the working class. This clearly reproduces the notion of ideology as an illusory creation of the bourgeoisie. More recently, drawing upon the second general notion of ideology found in Marx, racism has begun to be analysed as an ideology (complex of 'facts' and explanations) which refract a particular experience and material position in the world capitalist economy. It has independent conditions of existence, although those conditions are not themselves fully independent on the material parameters of the social formation. From this perspective, what is significant is that the ideology of racism allows sections of all classes to intellectually interpret and understand the world in a way which is consistent with their experience. Although the illusory nature of the ideas are openly acknowledged (on the basis of analytical historical analysis of the idea of 'race', i.e. science), it has been argued that they nevertheless provide at one level a relatively coherent explanation of the world as perceived and experienced. In its extreme form, in this argument, racism becomes one further dimension of the ideological level of the social formation. Within this level of the social formation one can therefore identify an ideological struggle and conflict, between racists and antiracists, which is not assumed to be between purely proletarian and bourgeois forces.

Read:

On Ideology, by Centre for Contemporary Cultural Studies (Hutchinson, 1978), for a detailed account of recent developments within marxist analysis in the debate about the nature of ideology.

The Concept of Ideology, by J. Larrain (Hutchinson, 1979), for a more general historical account of the different usages of the concept of ideology, both marxist and non-marxist.

Marx's Method, by Derek Sayer (Harvester, 1979), for a recent analysis of the nature and place of ideology in Marx's historical materialism which explicitly rejects the notion of ideology as a conspiratorial creation.

IMMIGRATION LAWS: UK

See *Hegemony; Marxism; Nationalism; Racism*

Robert Miles

Immigration laws: UK The seventeenth and eighteenth centuries saw the UK and other western European powers occupy vast portions of Africa, Asia and the West Indies. This colonial expansion laid the economic basis for the development of western capitalism: the colonies provided a source of cheap labour, raw materials, and in some cases, markets.

In the years immediately following the end of the Second World War, the UK exploited this source of cheap labour to the full. The introduction of the 1948 Nationality Act by the Labour government facilitated access to this source and while some members of what is commonly referred to as 'the lunatic fringe' of the House of Commons protested at the unregulated influx of black (and later south Asian) migrants, their demands tended to fall on deaf ears; quite simply, such considerations were subordinated to the country's economic priorities. The UK was experiencing rapid economic growth and the import of cheap labour to fill the subordinate levels of the labour market was essential. Nor did central government intervene in the settlement of the migrants in the UK. They were seen and treated simply as factory fodder and no attempt was made to facilitate settlement by the provision of educational, housing and welfare advice and facilities

It was not until the economy began to take a turn for the worse in the mid-1950s and the demand for labour in major industries began to recede that the efficacy of the UK's *laissez-faire* approach to immigration came to be seriously questioned. Local authorities which had borne the brunt of migrant settlement complained that their limited resources were stretched to the full; and the outbreak of violence between blacks and whites in Notting Hill and Nottingham in 1958 indicated the resentment felt by some sectors of the white population towards the black migrants. Against this background of imminent social and economic stress, 'race' and immigration policies emerged as a serious subject for political debate.

At the risk of oversimplification, two courses of action were available to the government: first, the implementation of policies designed to ameliorate the social problems highlighted by the settlement of colonial migrants in certain parts of the UK. Alternatively, government could abandon its traditional 'open door', or noninterventionist immigration policy and impose controls on entry. On the face of it, this second approach was entirely unnecessary; as the leader of the opposition Labour party explained in the House of Commons in the early 1960s, migration was self-regulating: as the economy had entered a downward phase and the number of job vacancies gradually diminished, the number of immigrants from the Caribbean had fallen accordingly. Nor was there much prospect of long-term unemployment at that time so that claims that the migrants would spend long periods drawing social security benefits were completely untenable.

In the event, the Conservative government eschewed the more constructive and logical step of attacking social problems through policies to improve the lot of black and white residents. Instead, it embarked on a policy of surrender by acceding to the increasingly vociferous demands from within its own party ranks for the introduction of controls. The Commonwealth Immigrants Act 1962 formally marked the end of the UK's *laissez-faire* approach to immigration, established a precedent for the introduction of progressively more restrictive and, *de facto* racially discriminatory immigration legislation, and presaged the start of what the lunatic fringe in parliament had identified as the defining characteristic of the race relations debate: numbers.

Briefly, the Act qualified the right of free entry into the UK for migrants from the New Commonwealth; that is, black and brown migrants. Although skin colour was not openly declared the criterion for entry, the exclusion of citizens of the Irish Republic from the constraints of the Act signified its racially discriminatory nature.

By 1965, selective immigration control had become bipartisan policy; despite its vehement opposition to the 1962 legislation the Labour party had, by 1965, completed a *volte face* on this issue and for the sake of political expediency introduced an extension of the earlier Act. In short, 1965 marked the point of consensus in Westminster based on an identification of black and brown people as 'the problem' and 'turning off the tap' as the solution to that problem. 'Keeping numbers down is good for race relations' became the organizing principle of this bipartisan policy. As Labour

MP, Roy Hattersley, put it in 1965: 'Without integration, limitation is inexcusable; without limitation, integration is impossible.'

This principle has subsequently been put into practice by both major political parties in 1968, 1971 and, most recently, in 1981 with the new Nationality Act. The effect of these laws has been successively to emasculate the citizenship rights of black and brown people and to confer second-class status on them. In all, these selective controls have institutionalized the notion of differential rights and status between white and nonwhite populations in their relation to the UK. The 1971 Immigration Act, for example, effectively ended all primary immigration (that is, heads of households) from the New Commonwealth and placed colonial migrant workers in the UK on an equal footing with, say, 'guest workers', or, Gastarbeiter in West Germany. The 1981 Nationality Act went even further by curtailing, amongst other things, the citizenship rights of black and brown people brought up in the UK.

In 1978, Ann Dummett pointed out that although immigration laws formally constitute part of the country's external policies, they cannot be divorced entirely from its general policy on race relations; this is because they express, 'by means of their definition of wanted and unwanted newcomers, what kind of society each Government is aiming for'. The pertinence and veracity of this observation in the case of the UK is clear. As external immigration controls in the UK have become more restrictive, so the government's reliance on internal controls, such as passport checking and police surveillance of 'suspected' illegal immigrants has become correspondingly greater. The 1981 Nationality Act will ensure that this pattern of internal harassment is sustained. Not only will this serve to consolidate the racial basis of the UK's immigration laws, it will undermine even further the welfare and security of the country's black and brown communities.

Read:

'The role of government in Britain's racial crisis' by Michael and Ann Dummett in *Race in Britain: Continuity and Change* (Hutchinson University Library, 1982), edited by Charles Husband, pinpoints the role of party politics and government in the legitimation of racism in the UK, through racially discriminatory legislation and the surrounding debate.

Slamming the Door by Robert Moore and Tina Wallace (Martin Robertson, 1975), uses the case study of Asians expelled from Uganda in the early 1970s and discouraged by the UK government to enter that country, to document the inhuman consequences of UK immigration policies.

Passport Raids and Checks by Paul Gordon (Runnymede Trust, 1981), a clear exposition of the development, purpose and effect of the UK's internal immigration controls.

See *Anti-discrimination laws; Immigration laws (USA); Institutional Racism; Politics and race relations;*

Barry Troyna

Immigration laws: USA The history of US immigration policy falls into five distinct periods: 1609–1775 (colonial period); 1776–1881 (open door phase); 1882–1916 (regulation phase); 1917–1964 (restriction phase); 1965–present (liberalization phase).

In the seventeenth century, colonial immigration policy was shaped by the need for labour to work the virgin lands of the New World. Schemes were designed to attract people to the colonies from Europe and the British Isles. Transportation was laid on and subsidies for the purchase of land and tools for new settlers provided. Bounties were paid to those who could secure the services of indentured labourers and take them to America.

The availability of work and property was the major incentive for migrating, though the religious policy of most of the colonies was also a magnet. Apart from New England, all areas tolerated most varieties of Christianity. Some places became religious enclaves, such as Maryland for English Catholics, and Pennsylvania for Quakers. There were three important components established in this phase: (1) local government exercised jurisdiction over immigration and settlement; (2) local government and private entrepreneurs were responsible for recruiting immigrants from overseas; (3) economic developments stimulated an active search for new sources of labour, so that policy was directed toward encouraging the flow of immigrants.

The British government's refusal to recognize general naturalization acts bred conflict as it restricted settlement in the areas where labour was required. In fact, this was one of the grievances that led colonists to take up arms against the

British in 1775. The War of Independence brought with it a new concept of national identity and the new Americans began to see themselves as a unique 'frontier people'. This influenced the Constitution drafted in 1787 and made foreign people ineligible for high political positions until they fulfilled residential qualifications.

Congress passed federal laws in 1790 allowing for the granting of citizenship to any whites who resided and abided by the law for two years. This was a very relaxed policy and laid the basis for the massive growth of population in the nineteenth century. From 1820–60, there was some regulation of migrant traffic at major entry ports, particularly New York, and ships' masters were made to give details of their passengers, making it possible to identify and possibly deport the infirm and destitute who could make no meaningful contribution to the labour force. Criteria for entry were such things as medical health, trade or craft and religion, so there was little control over immigration. Federal officials kept no records of immigrants until 1820. The emphasis was very much on getting as much manpower as possible; so much so that there was some intense competition between states.

By the 1870s, over 280,000 immigrants a year were disembarking at American ports. Overwhelmed by the growing volume, Congress declared existing state laws regulating immigration unconstitutional and enacted a series of statutes to bring immigration under Federal control.

In the late nineteenth century, the Federal government erected the bureaucratic structure to operate the new immigration control. Restrictions gradually got tighter as speculation about the links between immigrants and social problems mounted. One notable flashpoint arose over the issue of Chinese workers: labour organizations felt threatened by the nonunionized, unskilled labourers who were willing to work for low wages. Pressure resulted in new legislation preventing Chinese workers from acquiring citizenship (thus making them more amenable to control).

The Chinese Exclusion Act of 1882 was a significant move in identifying a group thought to be unassimilable and threatening. Again, in the 1890s, a group was perceived as undesirable: these were 'new immigrants' from southern and eastern Europe who were filing into urban centres. More stringent rules were added in regard to health and competence; about 15 per cent of migrants were being rejected by the end of the century.

However, the 'alien wedge' continued to be driven in, particularly by the Japanese in California. In 1910, the Dillingham Report on the harmful effects of immigration argued, albeit implicitly, that the 'new immigrants' were racially inferior to those from northern and western Europe. So, people like Slavs and Sicilians became the source of panic as they were thought to be incapable of becoming 'Americanized'.

The 1917 Immigration Act was the first of a sequence of severely restrictive statutes based on the report. Restricted zones were located, literacy tests introduced and a ranked order of eligible immigrants drawn up. No limits on the western hemisphere were imposed and the lack of restrictions on neighbours ensured a steady, cheap supply of Central American labour. Southern and eastern European immigration was sharply curtailed and no labour was allowed from the so-called Asiatic Barred Zone (including India, Indo-China and other smaller Asian countries). This effectively signalled the beginning of the era of restriction. Quota systems were later introduced, allowing for annual quotas of immigrants from specific countries. The thrust of later acts was to select those groups considered best suited to American society.

There were inadequate methods of classifying national origins that undermined the quota system and the effort to thwart 'unassimilable' groups was not effective. However, by the 1930s, the system was fully operative and immigration began to drop, especially with the onset of the Great Depression; large portions of the quotas went unfilled. In fact, for the first time in its history, the number of people leaving the USA exceeded the number entering. The Second World War prompted the US government to make special provisions for groups suffering hardship as the result of war experiences.

Perhaps the most significant piece of immigration legislation in modern times is the McCarran-Walter Act of 1952: this tightened restrictions on migrants from the colonies of quota-receiving countries, so that black immigrants from the West Indies who had previously entered under the British quota were sharply cut down (this, in turn, stimulated many migrants to turn to the UK as an alternative and so precipitate a massive rise in West Indian migration to Britain). There were, however, liberalizing elements in the Act, such as the allowance of no less than 85 per cent of the total annual quota to northern and western European countries and the extension of quotas to Asian countries.

The Kennedy administration attacked the national origins quota system as having no 'basis in logic or reason' and its reform eventually resulted in the 1965 Hart-Celler Act (the provisions of which took effect in 1968). The quota system was abolished and the ceiling on annual immigration raised to 290,000, at the same time removing any preferential treatment for western countries (this was later revised in 1976 to give western immigrants with training, skills or family ties priority).

The reforms since the mid-twentieth century have served to dismantle some of the exclusionary measures installed when the Federal government assumed control over immigration without removing the crucial link between immigration flow and labour requirements which has become a feature of all industrial societies. The importance of this link is reinforced by the concern over illegal immigration, particularly from Mexico (over half a million arrests and deportations take place annually and between 1 and 8 million Mexicans are thought to reside illegally in the USA). In the UK, illegal immigration from south Asia arouses similar anxiety.

Read:

The Distant Magnet: European Emigration to the USA by Philip Taylor (Eyre & Spottiswood, 1971), analyses the movements from Europe and the 'pull' factors drawing people to America.

The Uprooted, 2nd edition, by Oscar Handlin (Little Brown, 1973), by a writer whose other main work, *Immigration as a Factor in American History* (Prentice-Hall, 1959), is taken as a classic text on the whole subject.

'The social organization of Canadian immigration law' by E. Cashmore in the *Canadian Journal of Sociology* (vol. 3, no. 41, 1978), an analysis of how Canadian policy operated the link between manpower requirements and immigration flow to show how immigration law is used as a set of strategies by economic elites; provides a theoretical model for understanding the operation of all immigration laws.

See *Anti-discrimination laws (USA); Immigration laws (UK);*

INNER CITY

Institutional racism; Migrant ideology; Politics and race relations
Ellis Cashmore

Inner city A term that is now well-established in British political discourse, where it is synonymous with a problem. Thus, the 'inner city' is considered to be a legitimate object of political debate and policy because it is defined as being characterized by certain negative features, such as a declining economic base, poor housing conditions, vandalism and high rates of crime. To these negative characteristics is now usually added that of the presence of New Commonwealth migrants and their children, although the interpretation of that presence differs. On the one hand, it is argued that this presence in such undesirable and hostile conditions is a component part of the disadvantage that such migrants and their children face. On the other, it is argued that this presence is the cause of at least some of these undesirable conditions, in particular, the high crime rate.

This political definition of a problem was firmly established in the course of the Labour government of 1974–9 but the origins lay, first, in the facts of residential settlement of the New Commonwealth migrants of the 1950s and 1960s and, second, in certain policy initiatives taken by the Labour Government of 1966–70. The pattern of residential settlement was a function of (1) the pattern of labour demand; (2) the effect of discrimination; (3) the limited financial resources of the migrants. The consequence of these three factors was a residential concentration of the migrants in urban areas characterized by a housing stock in transition and material decline. The particular policy initiatives included the Urban Programme (officially announced as a reponse to the 'immigrant problem') and the Community Development Project (which was explained as an initiative to find new ways of meetng the needs of all people living in areas of 'high social deprivation'). Both initiatives were explicitly defined in terms of dealing with the material and social problems of declining urban areas.

These initiatives were pursued by the Conservative government of 1970–4 which, in 1973, set up the Urban Deprivation Unit. Additionally, in the previous year, the Department of Environment had been authorized to set up studies of six urban areas with the aim of identifying a means of dealing with urban deprivation. These collectively became known as the Inner Area Studies. The notion of the inner city was logically and officially developed from this by the succeeding Labour government which published a White Paper, *Policy for the Inner Cities*, in 1977 in response to these studies. In this policy statement, the 'inner city' problem was defined as consisting of economic decline, physical decay, social disadvantage and the presence of ethnic minorities. Since 1977, the 'inner city' problem has become more narrowly defined in politics in terms of 'law and order' rather than in terms of economic/social deprivation.

There have been various criticisms made of this political conception of the 'inner city' which, collectively, led to the conclusion that the term has little analytical value. However, this has not in itself prevented the term from becoming widely used in academic as well as political discourse. There are two major, and linked, criticisms of the notion. The first is that, historically, there have always been areas of urban conurbations which have been characterized by physical decay and extreme social disadvantage. Thus, the new notion of 'inner city' is misleading insofar as it ignores this historical fact. Second, this inborn decay is a direct product of the nature of capitalist development, characterized as it is by a cyclical process of industrial development and by the consistent failure to adequately cover the full cost of the reproduction of labour power. The 'typicality' and integral nature of urban decay to the system of capitalist production is bypassed by the notion of there having emerged a new 'problem' of the inner city in the 1960s and 1970s.

But although there is nothing new in 'urban decay', what is novel is that the fact of decay has become politically recognized and defined in terms of the political construction of 'race relations' as a problem. It is in this sense that the notion of the 'inner city' refracts political events of the 1960s and 1970s.

Read:

Policy for the Inner Cities (HMSO, 1977), for the classic political definition of the 'inner city'.

'"The parallels are striking" . . . crisis in the inner city?' by C. Paris in *International Journal of Urban and Regional Research* (1977, vol. 2, no. 1, pp. 160–70) for a critique of the concept of 'inner city'.

Britain's Black Population by Runnymede Trust and Radical Statistics Race Group (Heinemann, 1980), for a summary of state initiatives in connection with the 'inner city' in chapter 2.

See *Anti-discrimination laws (UK and USA); Ghetto*

Robert Miles

Institutional Racism An expression introduced in 1967 by two black activists in the United States, Stokely Carmichael and Charles V. Hamilton. They differentiated individual and institutional racism and stated that the latter 'relies on the active and pervasive operation of anti-black attitudes and practices. A sense of superior group position prevails: whites are "better" than blacks therefore blacks should be subordinated to whites. This is a racist attitude and it permeates the society, on both the individual and the institutional level, covertly and overtly.' Such a formulation has great advantages for polemical purposes. It rolls into one ball cultural assumptions, motives, institutions, attitudes and beliefs about superiority. For purposes of social policy and remedial action these various components need to be distinguished and analysed separately. Since white society had been slow to respond to the results of such analyses it was very understandable that black activists should feel impatient with what to the victims of prejudice and discrimination is apt to feel like hair-splitting and an excuse for procrastination.

Read:

Black Power: The Politics of Liberation in America by Stokely Carmichael and Charles V. Hamilton (Penguin, 1967).

See *Black power; Racism*

Michael Banton

Integration A notion which has become part of the British politicians' philosophy whenever they are forced to comment on British 'race relations'. They consistently repeat that the ideal aim, following the migration and settlement of New Commonwealth citizens, is their integration into British society. This usage refracts a wider international political usage, particularly in the United States. It is used to refer to a process whereby a group with a distinctive culture (including religion) both adapts to and is accepted by a larger group without being forced to change its culture and associated practices in favour of those of the majority. This process of integration is commonly also defined as cultural pluralism, meaning the mutually accepted co-existence of different cultures within any given society. It is commonly contrasted with the notion of assimilation which refers to a process whereby a group changes its cultural beliefs and practices in favour of those of the group with which it comes into social contact.

The political aim of integration in Britain was clearly signalled in May 1966 when the then Home Secretary, Roy Jenkins, identified it as a policy goal defined as 'not a flattening process of assimilation but as equal opportunity accompanied by cultural diversity, in an atmosphere of cultural diversity'. However, this politically defined policy aim had already been clearly linked to the policy of preventing New Commonwealth migrants from coming to Britain by a fellow Labour Party MP, Roy Hattersley in 1965 when he claimed 'without integration limitation is inexcusable; without limitation integration is impossible'. From the mid-1960s to the late 1970s, both political parties have consistently supported the contradictory policies of integration and (racist) immigration control.

The policy of integration has been pursued in a variety of initiatives in Britain. For example, legislation in the 1960s made various forms of discrimination illegal and the Race Relations Board was set up with powers to enforce the Acts of 1965 and 1968. Additionally, the Community Relations Commission was established with the aim of encouraging 'harmonious community relations', partly by educative work and partly be acting as a channel for the expression of 'black' interests. These organizations were consolidated into one with the formation of the Commission for Racial Equality in 1976 which was given slightly strengthened powers. Thus, state intervention to ensure integration involved a limited attempt to eradicate social discrimination and limited action to encourage greater knowledge and understanding of 'black' interests and problems. The sincerity of these interventions was contradicted by the continuing legislation which aimed to reduce and, ultimately, prevent 'black' immigration.

The opposition to integration as a policy aim has been consistently voiced by Enoch Powell, fellow politicians on the right of the Conservative party, and by neo-fascists. Their claim is that cultural pluralism is an impossible goal because, so they maintain, it challenges the primacy of British culture. This view was given clear support by the Prime Minister of the Conservative government elected in 1979 when she claimed in January 1978 that 'people are really rather afraid that this country might be rather swamped by people with a different culture, and you know, the British character had done so much for democracy, for law and order and so much throughout the world that, if there is any fear that it might be swamped, people are going to react and be hostile to those coming in.' Although integration continues to be officially defined as a political objective, the notion of cultural equality is politically rejected by such a claim.

Although in the early phase of the New Commonwealth migration to Britain many migrants indicated a willingness to modify their cultural practices (eg. many Sikhs stopped wearing the turban, cut their hair and shaved), their continuing experience of racism and discrimination has convinced a significant proportion of them that 'integration' means in practice their subordination. The response of sections of migrants and their British-born children has been a militant assertion of an emerging new cultural identity which rejects many aspects of both the dominant culture and elements of their earlier cultural accommodation. For them 'integration' is synonymous with racism in the context of racist immigration controls and other practices of the state, and consequently they have concluded that integration into a society where racism is embodied in practices of the state is impossible and unacceptable.

Read:

Black Men, White Cities, by Ira Katznelson (Chicago, 1976), for a critical analysis of state initiatives in Britain to ensure integration.

Slamming the Door, by Robert Moore and Tina Wallace (Martin Robertson, 1975), for an account of the passage of the legislation which introduced racist immigration control in Britain and of the way in which the legislation is administered.

Introduction to Race Relations by E. Cashmore and B. Troyna (Routledge & Kegan Paul, 1983), contains a chapter 'Laws-Labour-Migration' which discusses the contradiction between integration policies and immigration control.

INTELLIGENCE AND RACE

See *Anti-Discrimination laws (UK and USA); Assimilation; Immigration laws (UK and USA); Politics and 'race'; Pluralism*

Robert Miles

Intelligence and race The issue of racial differences in intelligence has raged for well over a century, especially in relation to people of African descent. Blacks have long been regarded in the west as intellectually inferior to whites and Asians, and, starting in the nineteenth century, the racist doctrines of Arthur de Gobineau, of Houston Stewart Chamberlain (an intellectual mentor of Adolf Hitler), and others, have sought to give the stamp of scientific approval to theories of mental differences by race. With the First World War, when IQ tests began to be widely applied to army recruits, school pupils and other groups in the United States, interest in racial differences in intelligence was given another boost. Test results were used to 'prove' the inferiority not only of blacks, but also of eastern and southern European immigrants.

In more recent times, the work of Arthur Jensen and other psychometricians has kept the controversy alive, especially Jensen's 1969 article in the *Harvard Educational Review*, and his recent (1980) *Bias in Mental Testing*. For the last thirty years, however, the great weight of scientific opinion has been cast on the environmentalist side of the interpretation of group differences in IQ test performance. Jensen has been repeatedly attacked for asserting that black Americans were innately inferior in certain intellectual abilities, and that some 80 per cent of the variance in IQ performance is due to heredity.

Jensen's 'hereditarian' position has two principal components, which are, theoretically, separable. One consists of stating that the heritability of *individual* intelligence is high; and the other is to ascribe *group* differences in intelligence to genetic factors. The second statement in no way follows from the first. It is the consensus of most geneticists that human intelligence is determined by many genes, and that any assessment of such a complex set of abilities by an IQ test is suspect. Even if one accepts the validity of the test, to make statements of heritability concerning such a polygenic trait goes well beyond the scope of modern genetics. Finally, to transpose a guess on heritability of the individual phenotype to the level of group differences represents another giant leap beyond the data.

Indeed, any assessment of heritability is always time- and situation-specific: it only holds under a precise set of environmental conditions. The heritability of a given trait differs widely from group to group if environmental conditions vary (as they clearly do for white and black Americans). In short, Jensen's conclusions are not only based on unwarranted assumptions; they have absolutely no standing in human genetics.

There is much evidence that Jensen is wrong in attributing 'racial' differences in IQ scores to differences in native intelligence. Similarly disadvantaged groups, quite unrelated to Afro-Americans, have also shown an IQ score gap of about 10–15 points (the average white-black gap in the United States). This includes such disparate groups as European immigrant groups in the United States in the earlier decades of the twentieth century, and Oriental Jews in contemporary Israel. Conversely, some subgroups of Afro-Americans in the United States, notably people of recent West Indian extraction, do considerably better than old-stock continental Afro-Americans (who, like West Indians, come principally from West African populations).

Scarcely anyone denies that there is an important genetic component in phenotypic intelligence, but our rudimentary knowledge of human genetics does not permit even an informed guess as to degree of heritability. Perhaps the safest conclusion is that intelligence, like other behavioral phenotypes, is 100 per cent heredity and 100 per cent environment. Even if heritability of intelligence in one group could be ascertained, it would not be the same in another group, and within-group heritability would not be a valid base for explaining between-group differences.

It is, of course, possible that significant differences in frequencies of genes affecting intelligence exist between human groups, but no such differences have yet been found, nor is it plausible to infer any from existing data. The weight of evidence points to an environmental explanation of intergroup differences in IQ scores. In any case, mean differences between groups are much smaller than individual differences within groups. Individual differences in IQ performance are probably attributable to a mixture of genetic and environmental factors, in unknown proportions. Most problematic of all is the extent to which IQ tests are a meaningful measure of intelligence.

Read:

'How much can we boost I.Q. and scholastic achievement', by Arthur Jensen, in *Harvard Educational Review* (vol. 39, 1969, pp. 1–123), the most scholarly treatment of the hereditarian position.

Inequality, by Christopher Jencks (Basic Books, 1972), which argues for 45 per cent heritability of I.Q. test score phenotype, plus or minus 20 per cent.

The I.Q. Controversy, edited by N.J. Block and Gerald Dworkin (Pantheon, 1976), a collection of essays on I.Q. testing and its implications for social policy.

See *Darwinism; Environmentalism; Genotype; Hereditarianism; Phenotype; Racism*

Pierre L. van den Berghe

Internal colonialism A term first used by Robert Blauner to describe the situation of minorities in contemporary America. In classic colonialism, a country's native population is subjugated by a conquering colonizing group. In internal colonialism, by contrast, the colonized groups are minorities under white bureaucratic control; they have been conquered and forcibly taken to the USA, in the process having their culture depreciated or even destroyed. North American Indians and Mexicans were forced into subordinate statuses in much the same way as Asians, Africans and Latin Americans were conquered by Europeans. White Americans treated native populations (Indians and Mexicans) as colonizers treated the groups they colonized.

According to Blauner, blacks, although they were not conquered and enslaved on their own land, were nevertheless conquered and forced into subordinate status in America. This experience of lack of voluntary entry into the country marks blacks, Indians and Mexicans off from all other migrant groups. Europeans who enter the United States voluntarily (whatever their motives) form an immigrant minority.

The groups conquered and colonized undergo very unique experiences in the process of becoming a colonized minority: (1) they are forcibly made to exist in a society that is not their own; (2) they are subjugated to the extent that their social mobility is limited and their political involvement restricted; (3) their own culture is depreciated or even extinguished. As a result, the colonized group becomes trapped in a caste-like situation. This, in turn, affects that group's self-conception: it accepts the 'superior' ways of life of the colonizing group and tends to view itself as inferior.

Specific areas, likened to internal colonies, were the basis of segregation in all areas of urban life: politics, education, occupations and virtually every other area of social interaction. This spatial segmentation ensured that certain groups were herded together and were therefore easier to control by white bureaucracy.

By examining how the various minority groups first came into contact with white American society, Blauner contends, we can understand their differential treatment in the generations that followed. So: colonized minorities' positions are structurally quite different from those of immigrants. Whereas Irish, Italians, Poles and others have advanced socially (albeit in a restricted way), blacks, Indians and Mexicans have not. The latter groups remain disadvantaged with an almost lawlike persistence. Similarly, the institutions and beliefs of immigrants were never brutalized in the way colonized groups were. Underlying this is the fact that white racism is much more virulent when directed against colonized minorities than against immigrant groups.

Taxonomically, Blauner's thesis has many problems, not the least of which is: where do groups such as Puerto Ricans, Chinese and Filipinos fit? The experience of these groups leads to a more fundamental conceptual problem of defining forced and voluntary migration. As Blauner's argument rests on this distinction, it may be asked whether so-called voluntary movement to America might not be precipitated by a complex of circumstances that severely limit the emigrants' alternatives. It may well be the case that the migrants' conditions are so intolerable that a migration is imperative – if only in the interests of survival. Even more extreme would be cases in which political situations actually motivate the migration. Such instances weaken the notion of an involuntary movement.

Nevertheless, Blauner's model of internal colonialism has been an influential contribution to theories of race relations and has at least directed attention away from current circumstances and towards history as a starting point for investigation.

Read:

Racial Oppression in America, by Robert Blauner (Harper & Row, 1972), the text in which the author sets out his important thesis.

See *Colonialism; Ghetto; Migration; Pluralism; Power; Slavery*

Ellis Cashmore

Irish in the UK The geographical proximity of Ireland to Britain has ensured that there has been an Irish presence in Britain for many centuries. The increasing colonial domination of Ireland by England from the seventeenth century (some would date the beginning of this in an earlier period) has provided the economic and political context for this Irish presence over the past four hundred years. Within this period, the first record is of the wandering in England and Scotland of Irish paupers, but the numbers were not large. A more systematic (and welcome) presence arose from the development of a seasonal migration from Ireland to England and Scotland in the course of the later eighteenth century which provided a labour force for British farmers at harvest time. For much of the eighteenth century, this migration was relatively small-scale and it was only after 1790 that the numbers began to increase significantly. With the provision of a cheap steam-ship service in the early nineteenth century, the numbers rose to an estimated annual peak of 60,000 in 1841. Although the absolute numbers declined thereafter, the tradition of seasonal migration of Irish travellers continued into the middle of the twentieth century in some parts of Britain.

The stimulus for this migration lay not only in the changing forms and relations of production in Britain which both increased the seasonal demand for agricultural labour at harvest time and attracted existing rural labourers into industrial production. There was also the fact that changing relations of production in Ireland itself were making it extremely difficult for subsistence peasant producers to reproduce themselves. For many, obtaining a cash income became vital to maintaining a land-holding and one means of so doing was to migrate to Britain each summer. Hence, seasonal migration was well established by the 1830s and this contact led to a more permanent settlement, especially in the emerging industrial regions which were experiencing a growing demand for labour.

It is in this context that the effects of the potato famines of 1845–9 have to be assessed. The widespread starvation and destitution that was a product of the famine intensified a process of migration from Ireland to Britain which was already underway. However, the circumstances of the famine migration ensured that there was little prospect of return to Ireland and a large proportion settled in the growing industrial areas, especially around Glasgow, in Lancashire and Yorkshire, and in London. An equally large proportion either migrated directly to the USA, or remigrated there from Britain. The United States continued for the rest of the nineteenth century to provide the main attraction for the continuing stream of Irish migrants who were forced to seek a living elsewhere as the Irish economy stagnated, partly because of colonial domination. However, Britain, for reasons of geographical proximity and a continuing, although erratic, demand for various forms of industrial labour, remained the choice of some Irish migrants. In the latter part of the nineteenth century and early twentieth century, large numbers of Irish women migrated to enter domestic service, and, later, hospitals.

The Irish migrants of the nineteenth century, both seasonal and permanent, entered various forms of semi- and unskilled work. They became not only agricultural labourers but also industrial labourers, especially on railway, road, canal and dock construction. They also entered the declining cotton-weaving industry and provided manual labour in the growing coal and iron industries. The record shows that their housing and social conditions reflected this lowly position in the market for wage labour. In the areas of large-scale Irish settlement, they swelled the ranks of the growing army of wage labour and, on occasion, acted on the initiative of employers as strike-breakers. When combined with their Catholicism, this economic competition with other fractions of the working class provided a potent cause for riots, especially in the west of Scotland.

The Irish migrants and their descendants constitute the largest 'immigrant' population in Britain, although it is difficult to assemble precise figures because of the continuing free movement of labour in Britain from Ireland, even after the achievement of independence by the Republic of Ireland in 1923. Although an anti-Catholic agitation continued in the twentieth century in Scotland, there has been little political agitation against Irish migration and the Irish presence since the late nineteenth century. Perhaps, as a consequence, there has been only a limited academic interest in the migration and contemporary presence and so observations about the current Irish population would have to be based on casual observations and an assumed continuation of earlier historical trends.

Read:

The Irish in Britain by J.A. Jackson (Routledge & Kegan Paul, 1963), for the only substantial sociological account of the Irish presence in Britain.

The Irish in Scotland by J.E. Handley (John S. Burns, n.d.), for a detailed account of the Irish migration to Scotland and of the hostile campaign against their presence.

Exiles of Erin by L.H. Lees (Manchester University Press, 1979), for a recent and detailed account of the Irish in London.

See *Ethnicity; Migration; Minorities*

Robert Miles

J

Jim Crow The conclusion of the American Civil War brought about the 1863 Thirteenth Amendment to the constitution, the Emancipation Proclamation that provided for the freedom of all slaves. It also prompted the question of whether the whites' responsibilities towards blacks should end with the prohibition of physical bondage: should the federal government provide protection and economic resources for freed ex-slaves? In formulating answers to this, the federal government attempted to reconstruct the south on a new basis of equality.

So, when eight southern states tried via legal means, known as the 'Black Codes,' to deny blacks access to desirable, well-paying work, the Federal government introduced two additional amendments to provide: (1) equality of protection for all under the law; (2) equality of voting rights for all men (not women).

Reconstruction had barely begun when the military occupation of the south ended in 1875. The belief was fostered that blacks would prosper through their own initiative and application and without federal intervention. The Civil Rights Bill of 1875 was designed to grant equal access for all citizens to all public facilities. But only limited government aid was provided; economic security and political equality were matters of individual enterprise. Hostility towards blacks was rife, especially in the south and resentment surfaced whenever blacks did show enterprise. The Thirteenth Amendment ended slavery, but did nothing to erode the racist beliefs that underpinned slavery.

In 1883, the US Supreme Court ruled that the 1875 Bill did not apply to 'personal acts of social discrimination'. Effectively, this meant that state laws requiring segregated facilities for blacks and whites were constitutional. The feeling was that the federal government had done too much to help blacks in their transition to free men. So the US Supreme Court deprived the previous legislation of its cutting edge and restored the determination of civil rights to state rather than federal levels. What followed became known as the 'Jim Crow' era: Southern states enacted a series of statutes that provided for the segregation of blacks and whites in such spheres as education, transport, marriage and leisure.

The *Plessy* v. *Ferguson* case of 1896 was a legal milestone: the Supreme Court upheld the state of Louisiana's requirement that seating on trains be segregated. The doctrine emerging from this decision was that blacks and whites were 'separate but equal'. Mr Plessy was, he claimed, seven-eighths 'white', yet he was, for all intents and purposes,a 'negro' and therefore not allowed to travel in 'whites only' coaches. The doctrine of 'separate but equal' spread throughout the south and, by 1910, there was a virtual caste system in practice. It served to maintain blacks in their subordinate positions by denying them access to reasonable educations and jobs; sharecropping was their principal means of survival.

'Jim Crow' was a type of *de jure* segregation, a separation required by law. When the law was not available to support segregation, the forces of the Ku Klux Klan were invoked. Hence, lynchings were widespread and largely overlooked by legal authorities. Blacks were thus inhibited from challenging the segregation and were more or less forced into accepting their inferiority. Hence the name: 'Jim Crow' had been a common slave name and elicited visions of the typical black with a weak mentality, a congenital laziness and an aura of childlike happiness. In other words, blacks were provided with no facilities for improving their education, for showing skilful application nor for protesting aggressively against their conditions (at least, not without fear of violent reprisals); so they were virtually made to conform to the whites' popular 'Jim Crow' image of them.

The court decision that brought an end to the Jim Crow era came in 1954 with the *Brown* v. *Board of Education* case. Segregated schools were declared unconstitutional; the principle was then extended to buses, restaurants, parks, etc. Over the next decade the Jim Crow laws were gradually overturned, their total dissolution coming with the 1964 Civil Rights Act.

Read:

Race, Ethnicity, and Class in American Social Thought 1865–1919 by Glenn C. Altschuler (Harlan Davidson, 1982), a historical monograph detailing developments in this crucial period in American race relations.

See *Anti-discrimination laws (USA); Civil rights movement; Institutional racism; Myrdal; Segregation; Slavery*

Ellis Cashmore

K

Kenyatta, Jomo (c. 1889–1978) Born an orphan at Mitumi, Kenya, Kamau Johnstone (as he was christened) was given a rudimentary education at a Scots mission school and became a herd boy. He entered politics in 1922 when he joined the Kikuyu Central Association, of which he eventually became president.

Between 1931 and 1944, he visited Britain and studied for a year under the anthropologist Bronislaw Malinowski. During this time, he rose to the presidency of the Pan African Federation (with Kwame Nkrumah as secretary). During the war, he worked on the land and married an Englishwoman in 1942.

But it was after the war that Kenyatta rose to world prominence: he returned to Kenya and geared up his Kenya Africa Union for violent protests against British imperialism. The military wing of his movement became known as Mau Mau. He was arrested in 1952 and sentenced to seven years hard labour, though he was released in 1958, only to be exiled in a remote northern area.

Returning to Kenyan politics, he rose once more to a minister of the dominant KANU party; then, in 1963, he became its prime minister, retaining the post after Kenya's independence in December 1963. A year later, he was made the first president of the Republic of Kenya. Thus his career turned full circle: from a terrorist, or freedom fighter (depending on one's perspective), against the British to the first leader of a fully independent Kenya.

Read:

Jomo Kenyatta by Jeremy Murray-Brown (Allen & Unwin, 1979), a biographical account.

Facing Mount Kenya by Jomo Kenyatta, with introduction by

Bronislaw Malinowski (AMS Press, 1978), originally published in 1938 before his rise to power, this gives an insight into the early anti-imperialist thinking of the leader.

Kenya: A Political History by George Bennett (Oxford University Press, 1963), a more general discussion in which Kenyatta figures prominently.

See *Africa; Colonialism; Nkrumah; Power*

Ellis Cashmore

Kerner report On 11 August 1965 a confrontation between white police and young blacks in Watts, Los Angeles' largest black ghetto, marked the end of the period of nonviolent protest at black oppression in the USA and presaged the start of a series of 'race riots'. By the end of 1968, the catchword, 'burn, baby, burn' had been heard in virtually every major US city, coast to coast, north to south. In 1967 alone, over 150 'race riots' were recorded during the 'long hot summer', the most serious taking place in Newark and Detroit. By the end of 1968, police had reported 50,000 arrests and more than 8,000 casualties.

Black and white left-wing radicals characterized the 'riots' as revolutionary insurrection, comparable to the colonial rebellions in Africa and Asia. White reactionaries, while agreeing with this description, maintained that the episodes had been inspired by foreign agitators and black communists and urged the authorities to meet fire with fire. President Johnson, on the other hand, tended to agree with moderate black leaders that the relatively small caucus of young trouble-makers had acted against the will of the vast majority of black Americans.

In his address to the nation on 27 July 1967, Johnson announced his intention to set up a National Advisory Commission on Civil Disorders under the chairmanship of Otto Kerner. The aim: to tease out the causes of the riots, to examine the characteristics of the areas affected and people who participated, to appraise the media's presentation and treatment of the riots and its effects, and, most importantly, to pinpoint strategies which would avert the possibility of further disorders.

The more speculative accounts of the 'burn, baby, burn' disorders were largely repudiated by the wealth of statistical and documentary material presented by Kerner and his colleagues in their 1968 report. Not surprisingly perhaps, in view of the significance and authority with which the Commission was endowed, some of the Commissioners' results and research methodology have since been subject to careful scrutiny by social researchers and, in some instances, found to be flawed. Even so, the profile of 'the typical rioter' sketched out by the Commissioners has generally been accepted: a young, single black male who had been born and brought up in the state and who shared a comparable economic position to blacks who had not participated in the disorders. He tended to be slightly better educated than other ghetto residents, though he was positioned in the lower echelons of the labour market, rarely worked full-time and was frequently unemployed. Although he was slightly more likely than nonparticipants to have been brought up at home in the absence of an adult male, the statistical difference was insignificant and its impact marginal. The evidence adduced by the Commission, and subsequently verified by other research, suggested that the motives of the 'rioters' were primarily political: they were not responding to their own particular disadvantage nor indeed that of their local communities, but to the more general disadvantaged and oppressed position of the entire black community in the USA.

The most fundamental of the 'underlying forces' which had precipitated the disorders was, in the words of the Commissioners: 'the accelerating segregation of low-income, disadvantaged Negroes within the largest American cities'. As they put it in their conclusion to the report: 'Our nation is moving toward two societies, one black, one white – separate and unequal.' They identified three paths along which government policies could proceed: the first was the 'present policies choice' which, the Commissioners warned, carried the 'highest ultimate price' of an even greater likelihood of further civil disorders, perhaps surpassing even the scale of the 'burn, baby, burn' incidents. An 'enrichment' policy, or 'gilding the ghetto', constituted the second strategy. This recognized some of the positive aspects of ghetto life and was premised on the notion of separate but equal communities. Although a similar strategy had been advocated by many Black Power leaders, the Commissioners pointed out that 'gilding the ghetto' to enhance its status would require a considerable deployment of national funds.

The preferred course of ameliorative action combined 'gilding the ghetto' policies with 'programs designed to encourage integration of substantial numbers of Negroes into the society outside the ghetto'. In other words, the enrichment policy would be an interim measure: the goal was dispersal. This, they contended, would not only improve the educational and social standards of American blacks, but would also facilitate social integration and help secure social stability. Put simply, dispersal constituted the most effective means of crisis-management.

Despite its many limitations, the Kerner Commissioners made a deliberate attempt to present the disorders in a sociological perspective rather than one which dealt exclusively in a 'law and order' framework. Though the report tended to overlook the more insidious and ultimately more wide-reaching forms of institutional racism as an instrument of oppression in the USA, it highlighted the central role which white racism (and the modes of action that this impels) played in the outbreak of the disorders. In this sense, alone, it presented a far more sophisticated appraisal than its UK counterpart, the Scarman Report, though, like that document, it evoked a sporadic and highly selective response from central government.

Read:

Report of the National Advisory Commission on Civil Disorders (Kerner Report), with an introduction by Tom Wicker (Bantam Books, 1968).

Violence as Protest by Robert Fogelson (Doubleday, 1971), an analysis of the conditions underlying the 'burn, baby, burn' episodes which concludes that these episodes were protests against genuine grievances in the black ghettos.

'Parameters of British and North American racism' by Louis Kushnick (*Race and Class*, vol. 23, nos. 2/3, 1982), argues that despite its liberal pretensions, the Kerner Commission advocated coercion and co-option. Its recommendations for more effective police control, for instance, were most enthusiastically and expeditiously implemented.

See *Black Power; Dispersal; Ghetto; Riots: UK, 1981; Riots: USA, 1965–7; Scarman Report*

Barry Troyna

KINSHIP

Kinship To be distinguished from affinity (a relationship traced through marriage) and descent. It is also important to differentiate kinship as a personal network, as a means of recruiting corporate groups, and as a sentiment of identification. Sir Raymond Firth wrote: 'The way in which a person acquires membership of a kinship group is termed descent. The way in which he acquires rank and privileges is termed succession, and the way in which he acquires material property after the death of its former owner is termed inheritance.' Descent may be traced (i) from a male ancestor through males (patrilineal); (ii) from a female ancestor through females (matrilineal); (iii) through both simultaneously but for different purposes (double unilineal); or (iv) through a mixture of lines (variously called omnilineal, cognatic or bilateral). Two persons are kin when one is descended from the other (lineal kin, as with grandparent and grandchild) or when they are both descended from a common ancestor (collateral kin, as with a man and his brother or uncle). Any table of kinship requires a reference point, that of ego, from whom relationships are reckoned. When kinship is a basis for claiming rights it is also necessary to establish a boundary to the range of degrees of relationship (as the medieval German kinship group included kin only up to sixth cousins). It will be apparent that only some of ego's kin will be of the same unilineal kinship group as ego, so that kinship reckoning comprehends more persons in the present generation than unilineal descent reckoning, whereas descent lines can list large numbers of ancestors who would be outside the range of recognized kin. The rights of kinship can be created, as by adoption, and they depend upon the social recognition of relationships, not upon genetic relationships (or consanguinity).

Most men and women grow up in families and therefore experience relationships of kinship as principles organizing the social world. They are therefore apt to organize their perceptions of the natural world according to similar principles, seeing family resemblances and relationships in animals, plants, etc. They also utilize the sentiments of identification generated within the kinship network as norms for judging social relations. For example, fraternity is considered an important value on the assumption that brothers support and care for one another, ignoring the frequency with which, in some social systems, brothers struggle with one another for primacy. Sentiments of kinship are extended in many ethnic movements to comprehend a much wider network (for example, the use of 'brother' and 'sister' in the recent Afro-American revitalization movement). Relationships of descent are also replicated in the organization of ethnicity. Just as someone can be a MacDonald over against a Campbell, a Highlander in opposition to a Lowlander, a Scot and not an Englishman, but a Briton or a European when overseas, so an immigrant may be able to utilize a series of ethnic identities of different magnitudes according to the social situation in which he finds himself. One identity nests inside another in an order of segmentation.

Read:

Introduction to Social Anthropology 2nd edition by Lucy Mair (Clarendon Press, 1972), a textbook on the subject of anthropology which is clear; the other literature is extensive and, in some cases, very technical.

Human Types by Raymond Firth (New English Library, 1958), the source of the above quotation.

The Ethnic Revival by Anthony D. Smith (Cambridge University Press, 1981), for the parallel with ethnic consciousness.

See *Boas; Culture; Ethnicity*

Michael Banton

Ku Klux Klan At the end of the American War of Independence in 1865, slavery was abolished and about 4 million blacks were granted new social and legal rights, rights that southern whites had previously regarded as exclusively their own. In the same year, six men formed a secret organization taking its name from the Greek word for band or circle, *Kuklos*, and adapting the Scottish concept of clan to make Ku Klux Klan. At various stages in its development thereafter, the KKK opposed blacks, Jews, Catholics, Mormons and communists, whilst retaining one constant imperative: to uphold white supremacy. The Klan was and, indeed, still is one of the most vigorous white racist organizations in the USA and, to a much lesser extent, UK. Throughout its history, the Klan has fought to maintain the supposed purity of the white Anglo-Saxon Protestant – the WASP.

As with other fascist organizations, the KKK philosophy

was based on a vision in which the white race (its term) reigned supreme. For two hundred years of its history, America had housed a majority of Protestants of English descent, Anglo-Saxons. According to Klan philosophy, it was obvious that God constantly looked over, protected and designated whites as the supreme, ruling group. It was demonstrated by their material well-being compared to the other two main groups: (1) North American Indians were subhuman savages fit only for mass extermination; (2) blacks were also less than human and were to be used as a form of property to relieve whites of harder forms of labour.

The Klan believed that there was a divine plan in which the WASP was to dominate; this plan had been violated by the freeing of slaves and the growing presence of Catholics. William Randel quotes from a KKK manifesto: 'Our main and fundamental objective is the MAINTENANCE OF THE SUPREMACY OF THE WHITE RACE in this republic. History and Physiology teach us that we belong to a race which nature has endowed with an evident superiority over all other races, and that the Maker, in thus elevating us above the common standard of human creation, has to give us over inferior races a dominion from which new law can permanently derogate.'

The Klan chose an assortment of methods to achieve its aim. At the respectable extreme it ventured into national politics, both independently and through the Democratic party. At the other extreme, it simply annihilated whole groups of people. Just after its formation, the Klansmen used to clothe themselves in white robes and hoods and terrorize blacks: there were regular lynchings, castrations and destruction of blacks' properties. But, even as recently as 1978, in Greensboro, the Klan ambushed a meeting and killed five people; though perhaps the Klan's most famous atrocity of recent times was in 1963 when a church in Birmingham, Alabama, was bombed, killing four black girls.

The KKK has gained momentum since the 1920s when it acquired an organizational structure, principally through the influence of William Mason. Ostensibly, it took the form of a secret society, much like Freemasonry, with a hierarchy of lodges and a network of communications. The head of this 'invisible empire', as the Klan called itself, was the Imperial Wizard, and under his command were Grand Dragons, Grand Titans, Lictors and so on.

In the 1920s, racism was rife in the United States, and there was growing hostility to the new immigrants from Europe. Charles Alexander wrote of the southern branches in this period: 'The Klan was only doing what the regional majority wanted – preserving the American way of life as White Southerners defined it.' Randel estimates that, at this time, about 5 million people were in some way affiliated to the Klan. In some respects, it was regarded as a positive moral force and this image was fostered by philanthropic enterprises and churchlike rituals. Support was gained through charity appeals.

Its membership in the 1980s is impossible even to estimate if only because the Klan carefully preserves its status as a secret organization. It has international linkups with other fascist groups and has branches in the UK, where it established a base in the mid-1960s. Its presence in England was signalled by a spate of burning crosses either nailed to or laid at the foot of doors of selected persons, usually black or Asian.

Bill Wilkinson, an Imperial Wizard, illegally entered the UK in 1978 with the expressed intention of generating support, but it seems his impact was nugatory. The British scene at that stage was full of neo-fascist groups ranging from the 'respectable' National Front, through the virulent League of St George to the paramilitary Column 88. However, the Klan has maintained its principal strength in the USA and remains one of the most potent racist underground organizations.

Read:

The Ku Klux Klan by William P. Randel (Hamish Hamilton, 1965), a detailed account of the growth of the organization in America though this doesn't cover many aspects of the modern Klan or its activities in the UK.

The Ku Klux Klan in the Southwest by Charles C. Alexander (University of Kentucky Press, 1965), a specific case study of one segment of the KKK in the USA.

The New Fascists by Paul Wilkinson (Grant-McIntyre, 1981), although this doesn't deal specifically with the Klan it is an up-to-date overview of the 'fascist revival' with an interesting theoretical discussion of the 'golden age' of the 1930s.

See *British Movement; Fascism; National Front; Racism*

Ellis Cashmore

L

Labour Labour is at the centre of all forms of social life: without labour, social life would not be possible. Labour is the means by which the material conditions of life itself (food, shelter and, in many areas of the world, clothing) are prepared. For marxists, this must be the starting point of all social analysis. They maintain that the power to labour by human beings clearly distinguishes *homo sapiens* as a species from all other living creatures by virtue of the fact that it has the capacity to be consciously purposive and creative. That is, a human being is capable of consciously varying the nature and character of any product in accordance with a prior image of that produce. This applies to the produce of both mental and manual labour.

The way in which human labour power is brought into contact with tools, land and machines varies historically. The manner of its combination is a determinate characteristic of a mode of production and class structure. Within a capitalist mode of production, labour power is combined with capital by means of the wage, and those who supply labour power in such an exchange are defined as the working class. It is only by means of selling labour power that the working class can obtain the means by which to live and reproduce. Historically, this has given rise to a rather different and broader meaning to the notion of labour.

The resistance to the capitalist mode of production has, historically, first taken the form of organization at the workplace in an attempt to regulate the terms under which labour power is bought and sold. This organization took the form of trade unions. Second, resistance took the form of the development of an ideology and organizations which aimed to transcend the society which was dependent upon wage labour. These two forms of response on the part of wage labour to the capitalist mode of production have come to be known collectively and generally as the labour movement. Consequently, it is common to find references to the 'interests of labour', where labour serves as a general synonym for the working class and its interests.

The concepts of labour and labour power have tended to be absent from much of the British analysis of 'race relations' which has tended to operate with the categories of 'white' and 'black', so suggesting that skin colour marks the primary line of division. More recent critical approaches to this tradition of research, some explicitly located within a marxist framework, have set out a case for analysing the economic, political and ideological consequences of migration to Britain in terms which explicitly recognize the specific character of the way in which labour power is appropriated in a capitalist society.

Read:

Wage Labour and Capital by Karl Marx, in *Selected Works* (Lawrence & Wishart, 1968), by K. Marx and F. Engels, for a clear account of what is meant by labour power and the distinction made with labour.

Capital and Wage Labour, edited by Theo Nichols (Fontana, 1980), for an outline of the various contributions to the analysis of the complex interrelationship between capital and wage labour.

Labour and Racism, by Annie Phizacklea and Robert Miles (Routledge & Kegan Paul, 1980), for an example of an analysis which sets out to break with the traditions of 'race relations' research by beginning analysis with the form in which labour power is combined with other productive forces.

See *Capitalism; Exploitation; Migration*

Robert Miles

M

Marley, Bob See *Reggae*

Marxism and race relations The relationship between marxism and the analysis of 'race relations' is complex and ambiguous. This is primarily because many marxist writers have in varying ways rejected 'race relations' as a legitimate area or subject of analysis while others have claimed to have set out a specifically marxist analysis of 'race relations'. Additionally, some marxist writers have attempted a critical re-evaluation of particular problem areas, while others have set out a critique of what they regard as Eurocentric marxism and its inability to adequately analyse racism.

The classic marxist analysis of 'race relations' is that set out by O.C. Cox in *Caste, Class and Race* which contains two central assertions. The first is that what he defined as 'racial prejudice' was a specific creation of capitalism. The second is that he elevated what he called 'racial' and 'ethnic' systems to the same analytical status as class. This work is regularly and approvingly cited by writers who identify themselves with or indicate sympathy towards marxist analysis. It has also become the regular object of criticism by sociologists who regard its assertions as typical instances of the weaknesses of marxism. The most common object of criticism is Cox's claim of a deterministic link between capitalism and 'race prejudice'. This is characteristically taken as evidence of a vulgar materialism, in which the economic 'base' of society determines the 'superstructure', in this case the ideology of racism, and on the basis of rejecting this, sociologists are then able to reject all other claims made by marxist writers.

The 'base/superstructure' problematic has traditionally been the site of debate between marxists and sociologists.

More recently, it has been the site of debate within marxism itself, and the work of those marxists who have distanced themselves from such determinism (e.g. Althusser) has been an inspiration for a re-evaluation of the relationship between racism and capitalism. In various ways and to varying degrees, these marxists (e.g. Eugene Genovese) argue that racism has a relative autonomy in relation to production relations and so has origins and effects which are not immediately grounded in capitalism. Those marxists who identify themselves with such a position (e.g. Gideon Ben-Tovim and John Gabriel) are usually specifically concerned with an analysis of the effects of racism in contemporary western European and North American capitalist societies and may even consider themselves to be contributing to a specifically marxist analysis of 'race relations' in the manner of Cox.

There are three further strands within marxism which distance themselves from the latter perspective, one implicitly and the other two explicitly. The first is that long tradition of concern with the analysis of the interrelationship between capitalism and colonialism/imperialism. This has roots in the work of Marx and, equally, in Lenin's work, specifically *Imperialism, the Highest Stage of Capitalism*. As befits analysis concerned with nothing less than the historical development of the capitalist world economy, there are numerous competing claims and perspectives within this area of work. The contributions of writers such as Samir Amin, Andre Gundar Frank, Immanuel Wallerstein, Michael Barratt Brown, Paul Baran and Bill Warren are all central to this area. Although the writers do not necessarily express this view explicitly, their work all testifies to the importance of understanding the contemporary interrelationship between western European and Third World societies and peoples against the background of the necessarily uneven development of capitalism. This is not only a matter of analysing the capitalism/colonialism complex (e.g. the role of the slave trade in the development of capitalism) but also the uneven development of capitalism *within* western Europe. It is on the basis of such an analysis that marxists would argue that one can only understand the unequal terms upon which the freed slaves in the southern states of America eventually moved north in the early twentieth century, upon which West Indians came to Britain in the 1950s and upon which

Turks were recruited as 'guestworkers' in German factories in the 1960s.

The second is of more recent origin and takes the form of an explicit critique of the objects of 'race relations' studies, whether they be marxist or sociological. A central concern of this critique is the analytical status attributed to the notions of 'race' and 'race relations'. It is argued that both of these notions are historical, social constructions and cannot be used to describe or explain, but rather themselves require explanation. To do otherwise involves reification and the legitimation of commonsense. The alternative analysis focuses on the political economy of labour migration, within whose parameters the study of the significance and impact of racism can be undertaken. This alternative focus claims direct links to both the advance around the notion of relative autonomy of ideology and the work of those concerned with the development of capitalism as a world economy.

The third strand is identified by a concern to criticize what is sometimes called Eurocentric marxism. Much of the impetus for this position arises from the anti-colonial movements for liberation and a number of the key tests are direct or indirect products of those political struggles. The writings of André Cabral, and Eldridge Cleaver are commonly cited in this connection, but the most significant are those of Frantz Fanon. One of the central points made by such writers is that European marxist analyses and revolutionary strategies reflect their historical and geographical origins and so cannot apply directly to quite different contexts. Amongst those they have in mind, one can cite national liberation struggles in Africa and Southeast Asia, the 'colonial' position of 'blacks' in American society and migrants from the Caribbean and Indian subcontinent who have settled in Britain. In all these circumstances, racism is identified as the primary determinant of the economic and political circumstances of these different groups of people *and* as an ideology which unites the ruling and working classes within the 'oppressor nation'. Their conclusion is that the struggle against racism must have its own autonomous, organizational form and political strategy. One may cite as representative examples of this position the writings of S. Carmichael and C. Hamilton, A. Sivanandan and the Centre for Contemporary Cultural Studies Race Group. What links all these writers is their overriding concern to identify the presence and determinant effects of racism within contemporary, capitalist societies.

Read:

Marxism and the Concept of Racism', by J. Gabriel and G. Ben-Tovim, in *Ethnic and Racial Studies* (vol. 7, no. 2, 1978, pp. 118–54), for an example of the marxist critique of economic determinism as applied to racism.

Racism and Migrant Labour by R. Miles (Routledge & Kegan Paul, 1982), for a marxist critique of the notion of 'race' and 'race relations' as analytical concepts.

A Different Hunger by A. Sivanandan (Pluto Press, 1982), for a 'black nationalist' analysis of racism in Britain.

See *Capitalism; Colonialism; Cox; Exploitation; Ideology; Migration*

Robert Miles

Media and race relations For many people, the mass media of television, radio and the press are an important source of beliefs and values from which they build up a picture of their social worlds. On certain issues where local information is unavailable this dependence on the media assumes even greater proportions: as the only direct source of information and comments, its accuracy and credibility are virtually unassailable.

In this context, the media's presentation and treatment of race-related material is critical not only in reflecting but also in contributing to the nature of relationships between people of different ethnic and cultural groups. In the UK, for instance, the concentration of the black and south Asian communities in specific areas of the major urban centres ensures that a large proportion of the white, indigenous population has little direct contact with these communities. In this respect, they have to rely on the media for information about the size and nature of these communities and for details about their relationship to the wider society. Of course, media audiences do not receive media-conveyed information and images, *tabula rasa*; nevertheless, the media's potential to influence perceptions and conceptions on this and a range of other social and political issues remains enormous.

Now, despite journalists' claims to the contrary, what is presented in the newspapers and in radio and television news bulletins has been carefully selected from a vast range of potentially newsworthy items; in other words, 'news' is not a random reaction to random events, but a socially constructed phenomenon; and the process of newsgathering is directed by a set of uncodified, though widely shared, criteria, often called news values. The immediacy and drama of an event, its extraordinary or unusual features and the presence of an established personality constitute the most important of these criteria: the greater the number of these dimensions in an item – such as the assassination of a leading world figure, a natural disaster, or the outbreak of a 'riot' – then the more likely it is to appear as a news story. The close correspondence in the types of issues and events covered in the various news media exemplify how widespread are the journalistic assumptions about what constitutes 'news'.

From this perspective, it is understandable why report after report into the media's coverage of race relations has revealed the largely negative orientation of this reporting: the emphasis on crime, manifestations of racial conflict, and the presentation of black people as a problem routinely constitute the *leitmotif* of the coverage. A study of race reporting in the UK national press during the 1960s, for example, revealed an overwhelming emphasis on the question of numbers of 'coloured' immigrants entering the UK. The researchers, Paul Hartmann and Charles Husband (*Race and the Media*), concluded that the press continued to project an image of the UK as a white society in which 'the coloured population is seen as some kind of aberration, a problem, or just an oddity, rather than as "belonging" to the society'.

By the late 1970s, this pattern had remained substantially the same. Although there was less concern with immigration and numbers, black people continued to appear in the national and local press as the symbol or embodiment of a problem. This version of the 'reality of race relations' in the UK was common to all national newspapers.

But, while these deeply embedded journalistic values and assumptions about 'good news' habitually impel reporters to such issues, some members of the profession – cognizant of the potentially deleterious impact which insensitive, sometimes inaccurate, race-related stories may have on actual relations – have developed strategies and guidelines designed to improve the nature and content of this reporting. In the UK, professional organizations such as the National Union of Journalists (NUJ) have issued guidelines to their members discouraging sensationalism and gratuitous references to ethnic origins in their news reports. Other organizations, such as the Campaign Against Racism in the Media (CARM), take the view that an effective onslaught on racist tendencies and practices by media workers must include activists from within and beyond the profession. Different again is the suggestion that black media workers should establish their own organization to counteract racism in the mainstream media and to facilitate the growth of an independent black media. In 1980, the Black Media Workers' Association was formed in the UK to perform these and related functions.

But what effect do media images have on their audiences? One school of thought maintains that there is a direct and causal relationship between exposure to certain media images, such as sex and violence, and subsequent involvement in such behaviours. The claim that the media created a 'copycat effect' through its transmission of news about the USA disturbances in the 1960s and those in the UK in 1981 was premised on this assumption. In fact, the relationship is far more complex than these commonsense interpretations of media effects would have us believe; an argument which was forcibly advanced in the Kerner Report on the US disturbances, but which was sadly lacking in its UK counterpart, the Scarman Report.

The research evidence suggests that the media are likely to reinforce rather than change attitudes and in the specific case of race-reporting, there is no direct relationship between the consumption of mass media and the degree of racial antipathy expressed by people. This does not absolve the media from responsibility for the perpetuation of racial stereotypes and hostilities, however. The essentially limited and ethnocentric picture of the world which the mass media continue to project not only fails to challenge these stereotypes but also actively perpetuates negative perceptions of black people. The result, according to one study carried out in the UK, was that media-derived conceptions of blacks were 'more conducive to the development of hostility towards them than acceptance'.

The ameliorative action taken by organizations such as the

NUJ and CARM, the gradual infusion of blacks into the profession and the belated emergence of an independent black media and community-oriented programmes represent at least some active opposition to racism in the media. Nevertheless, while journalists continue to remain committed to the notion of news values as seemingly immutable tools of the trade, the impact of these initiatives on the media's coverage of race-related material is likely to be marginal.

Read:

It Ain't Half Racist, Mum, edited by Phil Cohen and Carl Gardner (Comedia Publishing Group, 1982), a series of articles and interviews which critically examine racism in the media, its impact on audiences and the initiatives currently being taken in the UK to oppose these practices.

Public Awareness and the Media: A Study of Reporting on Race, by Barry Troyna (Commission for Racial Equality, 1981), an empirical study of how local and national newspapers in the UK covered race-related issues (including the National Front) during the late 1970s and its impact on public understandings of these matters.

Television and the Riots, by Howard Tumber (British Film Institute, 1982), a critical appraisal of the notion that TV coverage of the 1981 disturbances precipitated a 'copycat effect'. Includes interviews with media workers, police, community workers and some residents in Toxteth, Liverpool.

See *Kerner Report; Powell; Riots: UK, 1981; Scarman Report*

Barry Troyna

Melting pot, the See *Assimilation*

Migrant ideology Refers to the complex of beliefs and intentions held by a migrant about his/her migration. These provide both a strategy for, and a measure against which to assess the outcome of, the migration. Typically, although not exclusively, migrants whose migration is motivated by the search for some form of wage labour intend their migration to be temporary and intend to return to their region and country of origin. The aim of their migration is to earn a cash sum with which to improve the material and status position of themselves and/or their family and they, therefore, maintain contact with their family while absent, often to the extent of remitting money, particularly where the cost of the migration has been met collectively by the family. Where such notions form part of the content of the migrant ideology, they therefore set tasks for the migrant to achieve. When these are not achieved, the ideology itself will be modified or the failure has to be rationalized in some way that is consistent with the ideology. The beliefs and intentions of migrants whose migration has been prompted by political factors can be quite different. In instances where the migration has been enforced very suddenly, the migrants may not have clear aims and intentions, other than to remove him/herself from political threat. The term is more commonly used by research inspired by anthropological perspectives, but also has a place in analysis by marxist writers who focus upon labour migration.

Read:

West Indian Migration: The Montserrat Case by S.B. Philpott (Athlone Press, 1973), an analysis of migration from one Caribbean island to Britain which pays particular attention to the significance of migrant ideology.

Between Two Cultures edited by J.L. Watson (Blackwell, 1977), for an analysis of a number of different migrations to Britain, several of which are concerned with the migrants' aims and intentions.

See *Immigration laws (UK and USA); Migration; Myth of return; Pentecostalism*

Robert Miles

Migration The concept of migration should be assessed in relation to that of 'immigration'. Much political and academic analysis operates with a concept of 'immigration', which, in turn, tends to stand for 'coloured immigration'. The notion of immigration strictly means to enter a foreign country as an intending permanent resident and is therefore inappropriate as an aid to the analysis of events in Britain and, indeed, throughout much of the rest of the world, in the recent and medium-term past. In the case of Britain since 1945, it is inappropriate because: (1) most of the people that entered Britain did not do so with the intention of permanent settlement; (2) they entered Britain as Commonwealth and hence, at the time, British citizens, with the consequence that it is misleading to consider them to have entered a foreign country. Viewed in this context, we can argue that the everyday use of 'immigration' is testimony to the success of politicians and the media in spreading the notion of New Commonwealth entrants to Britain as being foreigners at a time when they were British citizens. Since 1962, various legal measures have been taken to bring reality into line with this ideological fiction. Academic analysis which gives any prominence to this notion is therefore guilty of legitimating this fiction.

As an alternative, the notion of migration is a preferable analytical concept because it makes no assumptions about 'foreigner' or the intentions of those to which it refers. Migration means, in its most general sense, the movement from one place to another. Hence, as applied to human beings, it refers to geographical mobility followed by a period of settlement. This is, as yet, too general for particular historical analysis, but at least it does not begin by ruling out, by definition, otherwise significant comparative analyses. In order to make historical and comparative analysis possible, the concept of migration requires further elaboration. Migration has been a feature of all historical periods of human history but the extent and nature of migration has taken different forms in particular contexts. With certain important exceptions (including that of populations that lived a nomadic pastoral or raiding existence, or which were forced to move as a result of war), large-scale migrations of people did not take place until the breakdown of feudal relations began, and thereafter we can make a basic distinction between labour migration and the migration of political refugees.

The latter refers to the geographical movement of people as a result of political pressure. This is characteristically long-distance migration because the intention of those migrating is to move away from the political influence of those expressing hostility. There are many examples, ranging from the migration of various new Protestant sects from Europe to the Americas after the Reformation to the massive westward migration of Jews in the latter half of the nineteenth century as a result of persecution and pogroms. To these historical examples, one can add the case of the Kenyan and Ugandan Asians who were forced to leave East Africa in 1968 and 1973 respectively, and additionally that of the Vietnamese fleeing from the consequences of revolution in the latter half of the 1970s. The central defining and comparative dimension of these migrations is that they are, to varying degrees, forced migrations and that those who migrate rarely entertain any realistic notion or intention of returning to the place whence they have fled. The primary motivation to migration is political and ideological.

The former category of migration is motivated primarily by economic factors. Once feudal relations of production had broken down and a demand, and market for, labour power began to develop, the population of societies undergoing the transition to capitalism no longer experienced such uniform and strong pressures to live out a life in the small areas where one had been born. Slowly, over time and with the development of capitalism, migrations occurred which ensured that labour power was made available at new sites of production. These migrations tended to be, up to the end of the eighteenth century (with certain exceptions), short-distance and freely chosen (but against the background of economic pressure). They were, therefore, migrations internal to the emerging nation-states of the time and were the first phase of the transition from a rural, agricultural society to an urban industrialised society in Western Europe. The important exceptions included the enforced and brutal migration of Africans to the Caribbean and the Americas from the sixteenth century onwards (a trade which reached its peak in the eighteenth century) in order to provide a supply of labour power in emerging centres of colonial production. But Africans were not the only source of 'unfree' labour: significant numbers of Europeans were forced or kidnapped into identured servitude in the Caribbean and Americas, including people who turned out to be on the losing side in the English Civil War in the seventeenth century and in the Jacobite revolts of the eighteenth century in Britain.

The labour migrations of the nineteenth century were on an altogether different scale, both in terms of numbers and the geographical distance of the migration. They were prompted by the simultaneous speeding up of the breakdown in feudal relations in Europe and the development of capitalist relations of production in Europe and North America. Much of this movement took on the character of external migration in the sense that it involved individually chosen movement across national boundaries with the migrants eventually becoming permanent settlers. The migration of labour from Ireland to Britain and, later, to North America was just one part of this international migration of labour in the nineteenth century, a migration that continued both the historical transformation of the peasantry into a proletariat and the development of capitalist relations of production on a world scale. A further example is that of the large-scale migration of those released in the nineteenth century from slavery in the southern states of the USA to the north in the early part of the twentieth century. This migration was also stimulated by a new demand for wage-labour by a new phase of capitalist expansion.

The migrations into western Europe that occurred between the 1950s and the early 1970s were also labour migrations. The economic recovery following the end of the Second World War eventually resulted in labour shortages in crucial sectors in the leading European capitalist economies. These were solved by labour migration from either the Mediterranean periphery or Europe or from colonial or ex-colonial territories, but in a different form to the labour migration of the nineteenth century. With the exception of Britain, labour migration was directly organized by the state on behalf of capital: individuals were recruited in their country of birth to work on a short-term contract basis in the dominant European economies. Nevertheless, this continued the process of the proletarianization of sections of the world's remaining peasantry, although for many proletarian status has been temporary rather than permanent.

By placing the process of migration at the centre of analysis, one begins with a basis for comparative analysis which links population movements into the dynamic of capitalist development. Much of the sociological analysis of 'race relations' in Britain has failed in this respect, preferring to offer some preliminary comments on 'push/pull' factors in determining 'immigration' to Brtain before proceeding to consider the part played by racism and discrimination in determining 'immigration' to Britain before proceeding to The result has been that British sociological research has become insular and parochial by virtue of lacking any real, comparative basis, leaving the field open to both geographers and marxists to undertake comparative analysis of migrations within and into western Europe. However, a number of anthropological studies have focused upon the process of migration and this has encouraged a more comparative perspective on migration.

Read:

West Indian Migration to England, by Ceri Peach (OUP, 1968), an example of the sociological approach to migration from the Caribbean to Britain since 1945.

Exporting Workers, by Suzanne Paine (CUP, 1974), a detailed case study by an economist of labour migration into West Germany from Turkey.

Racism and Migrant Labour, by Robert Miles (Routledge & Kegan Paul, 1982), an extensive critique of the sociology of 'race relations' and an outline of an alternative framework for the analysis of racism which begins with production relations and their interconnection with labour migration.

See *Afro-Caribbeans; Asians in the UK; Capitalism; Irish in the UK; Marxism; Migrant ideology; Myth of return*

Robert Miles

Millenarian movements Sometimes known as millennial movements, these are groups of people who develop a consciousness of the world based on an imminent cataclysmic change in which the social order is to be transformed by some supernatural agency. In its own terms, the millenarian movement is almost always doomed to failure because the expected transformation never materializes and, as the vision of a transformed social order disintegrates, the coherence of the movement comes under pressure.

Millenarian movements are often found amongst ethnic minorities, particularly the severely oppressed. Lacking hope of tangible improvement in their material lives, they turn to other measures and the millenarian vision offers at least that – a vision. The inspiration of many such movements is found in the Bible; indeed, the concept of the millennium refers to the period of a thousand years in which Christ is said to reign on earth. The Book of Revelation has particular importance in its reference to 'a new heaven and a new earth' (21:1).

In colonial situations where the colonized people have been introduced to Christianity through, for example, missionary teaching, there is the possibility that a literal, rather than figurative, interpretation of the salvation process may take root. Historically, we find groups developing millenarian visions in areas exploited by Christian Europeans (though not exclusively), such as in New Guinea where natives believed the valued material goods of the west, the 'cargo', would be delivered to them by miraculous means, arriving with the spirits of the dead and ushering in the millennium; the movements collectively came to be called 'cargo cults'.

The most celebrated ethnically based movement of recent times is the Rastafarian movement, originating in Jamaica in the 1930s and spreading to many other countries in the 1970s. Its followers believed that there would be a transformation in which the white-dominated world they called Babylon (to depict its evil nature) would be destroyed and black people would be transported to Africa. The change would be organized by Haile Selassie in whom Rastafarian followers saw a supernatural power.

Both these movements lived up to the five criteria of a millenarian movement as specified by Norman Cohn: (1) that it will be a collective response; (2) that salvation will be activated in this world (as opposed to the 'afterlife'); (3) that the transformation will occur imminently; (4) that it will be total, overturning the entire social order; (5) that the change will be miraculously achieved with the help of a supernatural agency. Many movements incorporate some of the elements without being full-fledged millenarian responses; the Nation of Islam (Black Muslims), for example, would come very close, as would many black revivalist movements. Millenarian movements flourish amongst the impoverished groups and sometimes precede more political and practically based organizations geared to achieving social change rather than merely waiting for it to happen.

Read:

The Pursuit of the Millennium by Norman Cohn (Secker & Warburg, 1957), acknowledged as the most comprehensive and systematic study of millenarian movements in a sociological and historical perspective.

Magic and the Millennium by Bryan Wilson (Paladin, 1975), a magnificient scholarly attempt to analyse millenarian movements within a specific framework; this took ten years of careful study of hundreds of different movements and the end-product is essential reading for anyone interested in millenarian phenomena.

Disaster and the Millennium by Michael Barkun (Yale University

Press, 1974), a highly original interpretation of millenarian movements based on the view that outbreaks of the movement are usually preceded by sustained periods of deprivation caused by some natural or social disaster.

See *Nation of Islam; People's temple; Rastafarian movement*

Ellis Cashmore

Minorities In the field of race and ethnic relations, the term 'minority' has been confusing because of the double component of its meaning, the numerical and the political. In the United States, where the term has become entrenched in official terminology, a minority group is defined primarily in terms of disadvantage, underprivilege or some such euphemism for a combination of political oppression, economic exploitation and social discrimination. In recent American usage, the noun 'minority' can refer both to a racial or ethnic group, or to an individual member thereof. Since the groups that are so defined (principally Afro-Americans, Amerindians, Hispanics, and groups of Asian origin) are all numerical minorities of the total US population, this usage is relatively unproblematic in North America, although it may reflect class interests. (The only possible confusion is with the political usage of minority to refer to party representation in government, as 'the minority leader of Senate'.)

As a term to be used in the comparative study of race and ethnic relations, minority is a liability, since many numerical minorities have been politically dominant and economically privileged. Nearly all tropical colonies of European powers, for example, have been ruled by minorities, often very small ones of under 10 per cent, or even 1 per cent of the total population. Obviously, to speak of the indigenous populations of India, Algeria, Nigeria or South Africa as minorities in relation to their colonial masters does not make much sense.

Even in a political context such as that of the United States, where the ethnically and racially disadvantaged are numerical minorities, the term minority is an analytical liability. Its popularity, however, may well be due to the fact that it serves political interests precisely *because* it obfuscates reality.

First, in a representative system, where small numbers are

disadvantageous in themselves, it is not clear where the status of minority begins and ends. In the United States, for example, many voices have argued for the inclusion of groups such as Jews and Japanese Americans on grounds of past discrimination as well as small numbers, while others have sought to exclude them on the basis of above-average success on educational or economic indices. If minority status confers preferential access to resources (as under affirmative action policies in the United States), then, of course, the terminological confusion of minority can be manipulated for political and economic gain.

Secondly, the definition of minority in racial and ethnic terms, and the association of that term with political and economic exclusion from the majority mainstream represents an obfuscation of class realities. Specifically, it ascribes the status of dominant group (WASP, White Anglo Saxon Protestants, in fashionable US parlance) to a group much larger and much more diffuse than the actual ruling class of American society. It also, of course, divides the working class along ethnic and racial lines, and militates against class-based organization by rewarding ethnic and racial affiliation. Perhaps most insidiously, it disguises the fact that the United States is, like all societies, ruled by a small elite, not by a large amorphous group such as WASPs; that is, the term minority salvages the majoritarian myth of bourgeois democracy.

Read:

Protection of Ethnic Minorities, edited by Robert G. Wirsing (Pergamon Press, 1981), a good summary of the treatment of ethnic minorities in capitalist, socialist, and third world countries.

See *Affirmative action; Disadvantage; Internal colonialism*

Pierre L. van den Berghe

Mosley, Oswald (1896–1980) The argument has often been advanced that while the UK is not entirely immune to the appeal of fascist doctrines, the commitment of its people to moderation and democracy and, as a corollary, their resistance to all forms of extremism, have effectively inhibited the potential of fascist groups to secure electoral power. In recent years, the credibility of this argument has been underlined by the experiences of the National Front. On the face of it, an economic recession, rising unemployment, widespread hostility towards colonial migrants and their children, disillusionment with the 'old gang' of politicians generally, and their treatment of the immigration issue in particular, all suggested that the electorate might be especially receptive to a party such as the National Front which proposed radical solutions to these perceived problems. The fact of the matter is that despite the National Front's decision to offer 303 candidates in the 1979 general election – the largest-scale challenge of any insurgent political party in the UK since 1918 – it has consistently failed to mobilize support on any electorally significant level. The same fate beset the most auspicious of the NF's predecessors in the UK – the British Union of Fascists (BUF) – which functioned under the leadership of Oswald Mosley in the interwar years.

On his death in December 1980, newspaper obituaries on Mosley were largely eulogistic: they focused on his oratory skills, his charismatic personality and referred to contemporary assessments of him as the outstanding politician of his generation, capable of becoming either a Conservative or Labour prime minister (he had left the Conservatives in 1922 and joined the Labour party two years later). His failure to realize this potential was, according to these obituaries, partly due to his 'misplaced' political beliefs but largely to his decision to leave the established political arena and to form the New Party, the precursor to the BUF, in 1931. Only parenthetically, if at all, did these obituaries refer to Mosley's commitment to antisemitism, his belief in the notion of 'racial purity' and, in the twilight of his political career, his determination to introduce a policy of repatriation for colonial migrants in the UK. In short, they refused to highlight the racist and antisemitic impulse of many of his political beliefs.

In his autobiography, *My Life* (1968), Mosley repudiated claims that he was antisemitic, arguing instead that he and the BUF 'attack Jews for what they do and not for what they are . . .'; but, while Mosley did not endorse the brand of racial fascism of his contemporary, Arnold Leese, his speeches clearly indicate the presence of an emotive racism and his conception of Jews in a conspiratorial framework.

Mosley formed the BUF in 1932 at a time when fascist doctrines were making a significant impact in other parts of Europe, notably Italy and Germany, and as the unemployment levels were rising dramatically in the UK. Accompanied by a growing contingent of BUF members, or Blackshirts as they were called, Mosley began almost immediately on a routine of public engagements which often culminated in violence and disorder. Some of these meetings and rallies were held in public halls such as Belle Vue in Manchester or the Royal Albert Hall in London; others were deliberately and provocatively arranged in predominantly Jewish areas, such as the East End of London. The rationale was clear: although the chances of attracting mass conversion in these areas was small, the mere presence of the BUF would create tension and increase public awareness of its existence. It was a strategy which forty years later would be adopted by the National Front.

But until 1934 the BUF remained on the political fringes. In that year, however, it attracted the support of the Press Baron, Lord Rothermere, who used his various newspapers to promote the cause of British fascism. Largely because of Rothermere's affiliation, Mosley attracted the largest audience yet to a BUF demonstration held in Olympia, London, in June 1934. But the meeting was to mark the watershed not only in the development of the BUF but also for Mosley's political ambitions. The degeneration of the Olympia meeting into a battle between the Blackshirts and the antifascists, precipitated largely by the political violence employed by the BUF, persuaded Rothermere to disaffiliate his newspapers from the fascist cause. From then on, it was all downhill for Mosley: the withdrawal of support, the emergence of a more explicit antisemitic thrust in the BUF's political programme, the escalation of violence between the Blackshirts and antifascists, the 'Battle of Cable Street' in East London and the subsequent enactment of the Public Order Act (1936) which severely limited the BUF's activities, all effectively pushed Mosley into the political wilderness. By the onset of the Second World War, Mosley was thoroughly discredited and, along with other leading members of the movement, was interned by the government throughout the war, under Defence Regulation 18b, because of his antiwar propaganda and antisemitic views.

In 1948, he formed the Union Movement which, contrary to his BUF programme, advocated the notion of a politically united Europe. Eleven years later, at the 1959 general election, he made his final attempt to re-enter parliament when he stood as the Union Movement candidate in the North Kensington constituency. This contained the district of Notting Hill which, the previous summer, had been the scene of violent disturbances between black and white residents. He offered the electorate a policy of repatriation believing, as he wrote in his autobiography, 'that someone should give this electorate the opportunity to express legally and peacefully by their votes what they felt about the issues involved'. In the event, Mosley received less than 3,000 votes (8.1 per cent of the total vote) and forfeited his electoral deposit for the first time in his career: the result was 'one of the chief surprises of my life' as he later put it.

Read:

Oswald Mosley, by Robert Skidelsky (Macmillan, 1975), a comprehensive biography of Mosley which, nevertheless, has been criticized for presenting the politician in too favourable a light and for underplaying the part of antisemitism in the BUF's programme.

British Fascism, edited by Kenneth Lunn and Richard Thurlow (Croom Helm, 1980), focuses on fascism in the interwar years with five essays on Mosley and the BUF, including Skidelsky's response to criticisms on his biography.

The Fascist Movement in Britain, by Robert Benewick (Allen Lane, 1972), considers various aspects of the BUF including its organization, political programme, strategy and membership.

See *Aryan; Fascism; National Front; Politics and 'race'; Skinheads*

Barry Troyna

Muhammad, Elijah See *Nation of Islam*

Multiracial Education In the UK and elsewhere, multiracial education constitutes the new orthodoxy in the 'progressive' education movement, and lies in the long tradition of social democratic education. In the same way as, for instance, compensatory education initiatives of the 1960s were designed to repair the meritocratic credibility of schools by providing 'equality of opportunity' to pupils of working-class origin, so multiracial education, by using similar rhetoric, aims to ensure that ethnic minority group pupils are not short-changed in their schooling. Both rest on the notion that schooling provides the main instrument of social and occupational mobility.

As a diffuse and complex conception of educational

reform, multiracial education assumes a variety of different trajectories. However, as Brian Bullivant found from his comparative analysis of multiracial education policies and practices in six countries in the late 1970s, certain assumptions and modes of action have generally become 'part of the rhetoric and conventional wisdom of multiracial education' (1981). Of these, the most popular have been typified elsewhere as the 'benevolent multiculturalism' approach. This derives from the view that self-image is the key to achievement and because the education system has conventionally rested on assimilationist grounds and deliberately suppressed the importance of ethnic and cultural differences in the classroom, ethnic minority pupils have consequently developed negative group and self-images. This has led directly to their lack of confidence and motivation to succeed in public examinations, and in the absence of formal educational qualifications, they have been consigned either to the subordinate levels of the labour market or to the unemployment queues. Some commentators have extended the logic of this proposition further: the high levels of black youth unemployment, either directly or indirectly, contribute to the supposed alienation of these youths from society in general and therefore assumed an important role in the outbreak of violent disorders in the UK in 1981. It is for this reason, then, that there has been a flurry of educational activity along multiracial lines since the 1981 disorders: the aim has been to eliminate the 'root cause' of these problems, namely, the educational 'underachievement' of black pupils, by providing them with a classroom experience which is more relevant to their ethnic and cultural backgrounds. This, it is proposed, will restore their self-image, provide them with the motivation and confidence to succeed in school, particularly in public examinations, and once they are armed with equivalent qualifications to their white peers, black youths will achieve equality of opportunity in their search for a job. In short, multiracial education is endowed with enormous emancipatory powers and is predicated on the assumption that the determinants of structural equality lay fairly and squarely within the terrain of education.

Now, despite the enthusiastic reception offered by policy-makers, administrators and teachers to this new orthodoxy, multiracial education has not been without its critics. Some have argued that multiracial education initiatives designed to improve the academic performance of minority group pupils are no longer necessary if the research findings of Geoffrey Driver (1980) and Michael Rutter (1982) are to be taken seriously. Both researchers found that, contrary to popular opinion, black pupils were performing relatively well in public examinations. Then there are commentators, of quite different political persuasions, who have argued that by elevating the importance of ethnic and cultural differences in the classroom, multiracial education sanctions those differences; in other words, it is a divisive philosophy and practice which is essentially racist both in intent and effect. Different again is the view that these initiatives are misconceived and that their imperative for action – to restore black pupils' self- and group image – is erroneous. Maureen Stone (1981), for instance, insists that black pupils do not have negative images either of themselves or of their ethnic group and that efforts geared towards this goal will increase rather than alleviate educational inequalities because they constitute a departure from academically oriented goals. Finally, there are some who have scrutinized the main assumptions underpinning multiracial education initiatives and assessed empirically their efficacy. This has involved an interrogation of the claim that multiracial education can provide equality of opportunity by improving the academic performance of black pupils. The thrust of this critique has been to show that discriminatory practices in the labour market ensure that the life chances of black school-leavers are worse than those of their white counterparts, irrespective of academic qualifications. They have drawn attention, in other words, to the unassailable fact that skin colour has an independent and powerful impact on black youths' chances of social and occupational advancement. From this perspective, multiracial education is placed in an entirely different social and political context and is ascribed with far less ambitious properties. If the aim is to enhance the possibility of equality of opportunity, educational initiatives must assume a more direct and explicit antiracist trajectory. Local Education Authorities must guide their teaching and nonteaching staff in efforts to combat racialism in and around their schools, and antiracist philosophies and practices must permeate the pedagogic, organizational and curricular procedures of the school. In short, the antiracist struggle in school must be fought simultaneously on many fronts. Tinkering with educational methods and techniques will do little to remove the most serious obstacle currently facing black and brown youth: racism.

Read:

The Pluralist Dilemma in Education, by Brian Bullivant (Allen & Unwin, 1981), a comparative analysis of multiracial education initiatives in six countries and a critical appraisal of their underlyng assumptions.

'Multiracial education: just another brick in the wall?' by Barry Troyna in *New Community* (vol. 19, no. 3, 1983), disputes the emancipatory powers conventionally ascribed to multiracial education by looking at the relationship between schooling and the labour market.

'In defence of anti-racist teaching' by Andy Green in *Multiracial Education* (vol. 10, no. 2, 1982), considers many of the critiques of multiracial education and proposes the retention of the term for the purposes of more explicit antiracist approaches.

See *Rampton/Swann Committee; Supplementary schools; Underachievement*

Barry Troyna

Myrdal, Gunnar (1898–) Swedish economist and sociologist, and Nobel laureate (Economics, 1974). Among his prolific works are *Asian Drama, Beyond the Welfare State, Challenge to Affluence,* and *Rich Lands and Poor*. His main contribution to the field of race relations was his monumental study on black Americans, commissioned by the Carnegie Corporation of New York, in 1937, conducted through a large staff of collaborators between 1937 and 1942, and published in 1944 as a 1,300-page, two-volume, 45-chapter book, *An American Dilemma*. This massive research effort put its imprint on at least a quarter-century of scholarship on Afro-Americans, and the list of Myrdal's collaborators was virtually a *Who's Who* in the field: Charles S. Johnson, Guy B. Johnson, Melville Herskovits, Otto Klineberg, E. Franklin Frazier, St Clair Drake, Arnold Rose, Allison Davis, to name but a few.

An influential feature of *An American Dilemma* was its Appendix 2, A Methodological Note on Facts and Valuations in Social Science. This classic statement of the role of the social scientist's values in his research was widely acclaimed and emulated.

The central thesis of the book is that the United States has long lived with a painful dilemma caused by the discrepancy between its democratic and libertarian ideals of freedom and equality for all, and its shabby treatment of Afro-Americans first as disfranchised chattel slaves, then as segregated outcastes. Myrdal predicted that this dilemma would, however slowly and painstakingly, be resolved by bringing the treatment of blacks in line with the lofty ideals of the American Republic.

An American Dilemma was also influential in its analysis of white–black relations in terms of caste and class. The first statement in print of the caste and class school was authored by the American sociologist and anthropologist Lloyd Warner in his introduction to a 1941 book by some of Myrdal's collaborators, but the concept was widely adopted thereafter. Warner, Myrdal and others saw whites and blacks as representing two almost impermeable castes, characterized by ascriptive, life-long membership, hierarchy and endogamy. Each racial caste was internally divided into permeable classes, but class status was not directly transferable from one caste to another because the castes themselves were in a hierarchy.

Myrdal was not without his critics, however. In 1948, Oliver C. Cox published his massive attack on Myrdal and his associates, *Caste, Class and Race*. From a marxist perspective, Cox regards American racism as a capitalist device to divide the working class, and to produce false consciousness. He attacks Myrdal's idealist formulation of a dilemma, and analyses the situation in terms of the class interests of the ruling capitalists. He also rejects the description of Afro-Americans as a caste, stressing the non-consensual nature of the American system, compared to what he saw as the consensual nature of the classical Hindu caste system.

Read:

An American Dilemma, by Gunnar Myrdal (Harper & Row, 1944), the towering study of black Americans in the early 1940s.

Caste, Class and Race, by Oliver C. Cox (Doubleday, 1948), the scathing marxist critique of Myrdal.

The Negro in America, by Arnold Rose (Harper, 1948), a condensation of *An American Dilemma*.

MYTH OF RETURN

See *Caste; Civil rights movement; Cox; Race; Racism*

Pierre L. van den Berghe

Myth of return A notion that refers to a particular aspect of migrant ideology which relates to the failure of the migrant to realize initially defined objectives of the migration. Where the migrant sets out with a specific intention of return after what is conceived as a short period of wage earning, unforeseen factors can prevent the realization of this aim. Typically, the migrant underestimates the sums of money that can be saved and/or is faced with unanticipated political and ideological barriers to the realization of his/her aims. As an example of the latter, one can cite the imposition of racist immigration controls in the case of New Commonwealth migration to Britain, an action which imposed an unforeseen constraint upon the migrants. There are many other potential factors which can prevent the migrant returning to the region/country of origin as intended, to the point that return itself is continually postponed to the indefinite future. In so doing, the migrant becomes in reality a settler, but characteristically a settler whose migrant ideology retains the idea of return.

Although the migrant may have become a settler, as measured by the continued physical presence in the country to which he/she has migrated, the idea of return can have important effects on behaviour. It can serve as a rationalization for the experience of racism and discrimination or it can serve as a motivation for continued attempts at long-term saving. It will certainly serve to retain a material and cultural link with the country of origin which can, in turn, be a means of resistance to racism and discrimination.

Read:

Between Two Cultures, edited by James L. Watson (Blackwell, 1977), for a number of social anthropological accounts of various migrations to Britain, in which the concept of myth of return is used.

See *Asians in the UK; Migration; Migrant ideology*

Robert Miles

N

Nation of Islam The largest and most important black sectarian movement in the USA, the Nation of Islam argues for a strict segregation of blacks and whites and the establishment of an American state exclusively for blacks. Like members of the Rastafarian movement, the 'Black Muslims' (as members were popularly known), identify white society as a source of evil because of its continued exploitation of black peoples and its denial of their autonomy. 'White devils' is how the Black Muslims describe those who oppose their ideals.

The movement has no single origin, but is a descendant of many lines, traceable to the various black sects that emerged in Chicago and New York City in the first twenty years of this century. One such movement was the Moorish Science Temple of America founded in 1913 by Timothy Drew (1886–1929), who later changed his name to Drew Ali. The sect was based loosely on Islamic principles and adapted a version of the Muslim holy book, the Koran.

Drew bade his followers to look for their origins in the ancient Moors and constructed a complex, if improbable, historical theory to explain that blacks were the true Muslims and had their religion stripped from them by the whites. The black man had been so thoroughly exploited by whites that he was left without a God, without power and, importantly, without a land. Followers of the Temple became so absorbed with the theory that they openly attacked whites on the streets.

In 1929, Drew was murdered, but his followers, believing him to be a prophet ordained by Allah, remained convinced of a reincarnation. But the sect lost any coherence after Drew's death and fragmented into a number of other Moorish movements which retained the fundamental belief that blacks were Asiatics who invaded North Africa. In this theory, blacks were not a 'race', but a 'nation'.

Some unity was restored in the 1930s by W.D. Fard, who claimed to be the reincarnation of Drew and, later by Elijah Muhammad. Under these leaders the Nation of Islam began to attract a large following of blacks, all of whom were emplored to reconstruct, if only in their minds, a lost culture of black people in America.

During the 1960s and early 1970s, the sect profited from the deprivations suffered by urban blacks. Unemployment nearly tripled between 1968 and 1975; for young blacks, in particular, unemployment ranged from 35 to 50 per cent. Under such conditions and with little hope for the future, blacks were attracted to this movement which argued for total social and geographical separatism, insisting, like Marcus Garvey had in the 1920s, that integration was futile and that black people would only develop fully if they were given scope to expand away from whites. The political goal of the 'Black Muslims' was the granting of one whole American state for blacks alone.

The sect's credibility was enhanced by the adherence of Malcolm X, the black radical, and Muhammad Ali, who, more than anyone, popularized the sect on a global scale. (Ali, in fact, began a trend amongst black sportsmen in the States and a great many after him, like Dwight Muhammad Qawi, Kareem Abdul-Jabbar and Matthew Saad Muhammad, were converted.)

Elijah Muhammad outlined a programme that included the creation of separate hospitals, schools, industries, shops, etc. Practical self-help schemes were intended to support Black Muslim independence and promote what the leader called 'freedom from contempt', his idea being that white-dominated society effectively excluded blacks (and, for that matter, other nonwhites) from corporate and financial power bases, so blacks had nothing to lose by forming their own community.

Elijah's death in 1975 was followed by a relaxation of the strictures on membership: his son, Wallace, took over the leadership and admitted white adherents. The name was changed to the World Community of Islam in the West. This was accompanied by a change in ideology with Wallace campaigning for reformist measures rather than sticking to the claim for a separate state.

In more recent times, the sect has shed the rather disreputable image it gained in its association with Malcolm X (who split from the sect in 1964 and died in 1965) and the rumoured link-ups with various assassination attempts. For many blacks in the USA and, to a lesser extent in the UK, the Islamic movement has constituted a fresh and vital force and has functioned as a kind of resistance, albeit a symbolic resistance, to white society.

Read:

Black Nationalism: A Search for Identity in America by E.U. Essien-Udom, (University of Chicago Press, 1962), based on a two-year study in Chicago and New York City of the Nation of Islam and a number of other black movements which were broadly sympathetic with its aim – such as the National Movement for the Establishment of the 49th State.

The Black Muslims in America by C. Eric Lincoln (Beacon Press, 1961), an in-depth analysis of one branch of the movement, but with scene-setting background information.

Black Awakening in Capitalist America by Robert L. Allen (Anchor Press, 1970), places the Black Muslims in the broader perspective of black activism during the 1960s and 1970s.

See *Black Power; Ethiopianism; Garvey; Négritude; Rastafarian movement*

Ellis Cashmore

National Front Since 1945 there has been a number of fascist groups in the UK intent on 'tilling the soil of racial prejudice'. The size in membership of these groups varied enormously: some, such as the League of Empire Loyalists, which had been founded in 1954 by an ex-member of Mosley's British Union of Fascists, A.K. Chesterton, attracted around 3,000 supporters at its peak in 1957. Others, like the Greater Britain Movement, formed in 1964 by John Tyndall, probably never attracted more than 150 members. There were differences, too, in the life-span of these organizations and their mode of political action. All, however, vehemently opposed the dissolution of the British Empire and the settlement of black and brown colonial immigrants in the UK. In short, they accepted the basic fascist principle of white supremacy and geared themselves to the future restoration of the white race as unassailable leaders of the world.

NATIONAL FRONT

Until 1967, these various and disparate groups were of minimal political significance in the UK; but it was this continuing failure to secure a toehold in British politics which precipitated the decision of the leading fascist ideologies to unify their organizations into a coherent and electorally acceptable party: in 1967, the National Front (NF) was born.

Like the National Socialist Party in Germany in the 1920s and 1930s, the NF has adopted a 'two-track strategy' to attract publicity and, hence, to increase support and membership. On the one hand, it has contested local elections and parliamentary by- and general elections, though with little success. None of its candidates has ever won a seat, although two members of the breakaway National Party were elected to the council in Blackburn in 1976. Indeed, in only one parliamentary by-election, in West Bromwich in 1973, has an NF candidate secured a sufficient proportion of the votes cast to retain his electoral deposit. The nugatory performance of the NF in the 1979 general election made nonsense of its claim to be the 'fastest growing party in Britain'. All its 303 candidates lost their deposit and the party, in general, obtained only 1.3 per cent of the vote in the seats contested.

The other main thrust of its political activities has been its decision to hold demonstrations and meetings organized either around explicitly racist themes or within areas containing relatively large black, brown or Jewish communities. Quite rightly, these have consistently provoked opposition both from the local communities and from antiracist organizations such as the Anti-Nazi League and have often degenerated into volatile occasions. In 1974, for instance, an anti-NF protestor, Kevin Gately, was killed at the NF's demonstration in Red Lion Square. A little less than five years later, in April 1979, a London teacher, Blair Peach was killed as antifascists tried to prevent the NF's pre- general election meeting in the Southall district of London. Similarly spectacular, though not fatal, incidents have been provoked by the NF in Lewisham in London, Ladywood in Birmingham and the Manningham district of Bradford, amongst others. The NF insists that because it is a legally constituted electoral party which adheres to the procedures and rules of parliamentary democracy, it should be entitled to the rights and privileges enshrined in that political system; in other words, to exercise the right of free expression of opinion, to hold assemblies and demonstrations, and so on. From this perspective, anti-NF demonstrators are perceived as the main threat to parliamentary democracy because they seek to deny the party access to those rights and privileges.

But more careful scrutiny of the literature disseminated by the NF reveals that its commitment to parliamentary democracy is superficial – engendered by the imperatives of political expediency; simply its leaders have never entirely eschewed the notion of authoritarian rule. 'Good government can sometimes take a democratic and sometimes an authoritarian form', wrote John Tyndall, chairman of the NF between 1972–1980 and formerly founder member of the explicitly Nazi, Greater Britain Movement. The public face of the NF has consistently concealed the main constituents of its ideological armoury: the idea of racial nationalism, the obsessional belief in a Jewish worldwide conspiracy and a commitment to the doctrine of biological determinism all feature prominently in the lesser-known speeches and writings of its leading party members. In this sense, the 'racial fascism' of Arnold Leese and his pre-Second World War organization, the Imperial Fascist League, continues to provide the ideological inspiration for the NF.

Throughout its history, the NF's significance has been more symbolic than real. Its performance in the 1979 general election revealed that earlier fears about its electoral potential were largely misplaced. The results had led to the surfacing of bitter internal recriminations and provoked a series of breakaway movements which left the party in disarray and membership and morale at a low ebb. During the mid-late 1970s, however, it had assumed the role of a boundary marker, permitting an ideological shift to the right in mainstream political discussion and policy-making on race-related issues. For instance, Mrs Thatcher's decision to reinstate immigration into the centre of the political arena in 1978 was precipitated largely by fears that the absence of the issue from the party's political manifesto would encourage actual and potential voters to support the NF in the general election. As she put it, the refusal to discuss this issue within the 'big political parties . . . is one thing that is driving some people to the National Front'. Despite the party's subsequent demise, the legacy of its influence on the UK body politic remains.

NATIONALISM

Read:

The National Front by Martin Walker (Fontana, 1977), a detailed and exhaustive account of the origins of the National Front and of the political backgrounds and involvements of its leading personalities.

The National Front in English Politics by Stan Taylor (Macmillan, 1982), looks critically at various aspects of the party including its ideological background, its apparent electoral advances in the 1970s and the effectiveness of anti-NF groups such as the anti-Nazi League.

Fascists: A Social Psychological View of the National Front by Michael Billig (Academic Press, 1978), scrutinizes the consistencies between the NF and earlier fascist organizations and personalities. It also includes interviews with members of an NF branch in the West Midlands.

See *Aryan; British Movement; Fascism; Mosley; Politics and 'race'; Racialism*

Barry Troyna

Nationalism A term which refers to an ideology which was formulated after the French Revolution. It became a major determinant of political action in the course of the nineteenth century throughout western Europe and, in the twentieth century, throughout the world. Many writers want to draw a firm distinction between this conception of nationalism as an ideology and the notion of national sentiment which refers to a sense of collective solidarity within identified geographical and cultural boundaries. Thus, this distinction can account for the fact that a particular population may express some notion of national identity in the absence of a coherent and organized political movement to bring into being or reproduce territorial boundaries within which a state formation has political power.

As an ideology, nationalism contains three main ideas. First, it argues that an identified population should be able to formulate institutions and laws with which to determine its own future. Second, it maintains that each such population has a unique set of characteristics which identify it as a 'nation'. Third, and consequently, it claims that the world is divided naturally into a number of such distinct 'nations'. This combination of ideas and claims constitute the basis for political strategies and movements which, since the nineteenth century, have had a major influence on the way in which the world is organized politically. The formation and reproduction of national boundaries is, therefore, not a natural or inevitable process, but one which is the consequence of human actión in particular historical circumstances. Indeed, that process need not be directly prompted by the ideology of nationalism, as the example of England, France, Spain and Holland illustrate.

The origin of the ideology is the object of a continuing debate, although there is considerable agreement with the claim that it is connected with what some writers call industrialization and what others define as capitalist development. What unites these different theoretical traditions is the employment of the notion of uneven development. What is claimed is that from the late eighteenth century, the process of industrialization/capitalist development occurred in particular geographical areas, with the result that certain groups in adjoining areas desired to emulate the advances made elsewhere in order to share in the consequential material and political advantages. The ideology of nationalism was a means of politically mobilizing populations to construct a particular political framework for economic/capitalist development, i.e. to 'catch up' with the development of those who have developed first.

This process can be observed to have continued in the twentieth century particularly in connection with the consequences of decolonization. A rather different process occurred in connection with the redrawing of political boundaries after the two 'world wars' in Europe, although, again, nationalism was a prominent factor. Such a wide diversity of instances where nationalism has been a political force, particularly in the twentieth century, supports the contention that nationalism can be combined with political movements of the 'left' and 'right', a fact that can cause particular difficulties for marxist writers. One can illustrate this point by referring to the way in which nationalism has been a component elsewhere in the rise of fascism in Europe and in liberation movements in Africa and Southeast Asia. Moreover, the latter examples constituted political inspiration for black people in the USA in the 1960s where political resistance to institutionalized racism came to be expressed in terms of nationalism. For marxists, these examples have posed a problem insofar as they claim that classes constitute the major force for revolutionary change. The relative failure of marxists to be able to account for the political significance of nationalism in the twentieth century has been paralleled by the increasingly common claims by sociologists and political scientists that nationalism constitutes the major political force of the twentieth century.

The fact that nationalism emerged as a coherent and explicit ideology at the same time that racism was formulated as a 'scientific' doctrine is of significance. Both ideologies assert that the world's population is naturally divided into distinct groups, although the nature of the group and the foundation for supposed natural division differs. Nevertheless, the fact that racism asserts some form of deterministic relation between attributed or real biological features and cultural characteristics means that nationalism, although ostensibly focusing on cultural/historical differences, can nevertheless merge into or develop out of the former. This is particularly evident in British politics since the 1960s when expressions of British nationalism have increasingly come to contain a form of racism, although without explicit use of the idea of 'race' in the case of the main political parties. However, in the case of the neo-fascist parties, nationalism is expressed explicitly through a notion of 'race', in line with central strands of fascist ideology.

Read:

Nationalism in the Twentieth Century, by A.D. Smith (Martin Robertson, 1979), for an example of a sociological explanation of the nature of and explanation for nationalism since 1900.

The Break-up of Britain, by T. Nairn (Verso, 1981), for an influential marxist analysis of nationalism which breaks with both previous marxist analyses and sociological explanations.

Black Power: The Politics of Liberation, by Stokely Carmichael and Charles Hamilton (Penguin, 1969), for the best example of a political text written by black activists in the USA which utilizes the notion of nationalism.

See *Fascism; Ideology; National Front; Racism*

Robert Miles

Native peoples Prior to the expansion of Europe, many regions of the earth were occupied by peoples who lacked the art of writing, and who pursued technologically simple ways of life. Because Columbus thought he had discovered a new route to the Indies, the Europeans described the peoples of the Americas as Indians. The native people of Australia were called Aborigines. In Africa and Oceania the expression 'native' was commonly used. The Europeans described themselves as civilized but, ironically, the weaker the native peoples, the greater was the brutality shown towards them. In the United States and Australia, the native peoples were at times hunted by armed whites who regarded this as a form of sport. In Brazil and Australia diseases were deliberately spread amongst the native peoples and poisoned food left out for them.

In New Zealand, prior to the European invasions, there were about 200,000 Maoris. Before the end of the nineteenth century they seemed to be dying out, so many of them having succumbed to European diseases or having been shot by other Maoris using imported muskets. Then Maori cultural pride and the Maori birth rate began to revive. A similar three-stage sequence of defeat, despair and regeneration can be discerned among the Native Americans of the United States whose lands were appropriated more savagely than in the European colonies to the north and south. In North America European occupation was legitimated by international treaties, the 'Indian tribes' being regarded in law as nations on an equal status to that of the invaders. Different European powers were eager to make such treaties because they were in competition with one another. The political claims of Native Americans today are that the whites should observe the promises they made in these treaties. Australia is the one country where occupation had no basis in treaties and, two hundred years after the invasion, a pressure group has been formed to argue that it is not too late to draw up a treaty which would give legal recognition to native rights.

Governmental policies towards native peoples vary in many ways, but one unusual example is worth mention. It concerns that Swedish Sami Union (Sami is the name used for themselves by the people who are more generally known as Lapps). Conscious of their problems in dealing with a bureaucratic social order, the Union had for some time wanted better access to legal expertise. In 1962 the Swedish government appointed a legal councillor to work full-time in the service of the Union. The appointment was funded partly by the Sami themselves. As an ombudsman for the

Sami, the lawyer was able to invoke treaty rights that proved of great previously unsuspected value to the reindeer-herding Sami.

Read:

White Settlers and Native Peoples by A. Grenfell Price (Melbourne, Cambridge University Press, 1950), for a general review.

Ethnicity and Mobilization in Sami Politics by Tom G. Svenson (Stockholm Studies in Social Anthropology, 1976), contains an account of the Swedish action.

See *Colonialism; Ethnicity; Slavery*

Michael Banton

Négritude A movement begun in the 1930s by the Martinique born poet Aimé Césaire and other French-speaking black artists who wanted to rediscover ancient African values and modes of thought so that blacks could feel pride and dignity in their heritage. In its broadest sense, négritude was 'the awareness and development of African values,' according to Leopold Senghor, who helped develop the original ideas into a coherent political movement.

Though principally an artistic and literary critique of western society and its systematic suppression of blacks' potentiality by dissociating them from what were regarded as their true roots, négritude took on a more programmatic dimension with Senghor, who became president of Senegal. The impulse was, according to L.V. Thomas, 'the rediscovery of one's past, one's culture, one's ancestors and one's language.' Inspired by the African ethnographer and historian Leo Frobenius, Senghor delved into African culture to which he attributed the characteristic of being 'Ethiopian', as a way of coming to grips with the different conception of reality he presumed existed in ancient African societies.

Leo Kuper writes: 'Initially, *négritude* developed as a reaction to white racism, as dialectical opposition to cultural values imposed by whites.' But the Africa oriented to was not, as G.R. Coulthard puts it, 'of African civilizations or African cultural values, but of Africa itself as a vague geographical region, and the imaginary and emotional fatherland of all the Negroes in the world.'

Négritude never advocated a return to Africa in a physical sense, as did Marcus Garvey's UNIA or the Rastafarian movement, but sought only to make Africa's presence urgently felt by the millions of 'exiled', scattered blacks who had been 'brainwashed' into western ways of thinking. It was an attempt to create an African consciousness for blacks wherever they were; a return to Africa though realizing its presence in the *mind* of blacks. As the Haitian poet Jean Price-Mars put it: 'We belong to Africa by our blood.'

Like other Ethiopianist movements, négritude condemned conventional Christianity as a tool of colonialism designed to keep blacks in a state of subjection and perpetuate their physical and mental enslavement; it was seen, as Coulthard points out, in 'hypocritical connivance with colonialism and imperialism.' Colonialism had culturally denuded blacks to the bone, but as the négritude poet Leon Damas wrote:

> We have stripped off our European clothes . . .
> Our pride in being Negroes
> The glory of being black

This sums up the négritude effort: to upgrade black people not so much through overt political means, but through instilling them with a sense of history and culture compounded of the distinctive qualities deriving from Africa; a new pride and dignity in being black and being African.

Read:

Race and Colour in Caribbean Literature by G.R. Coulthard (Oxford University Press, 1962), an assessment and appreciation of négritude set in its historical context.

'Senghor and négritude' by L.V. Thomas, in *Présence Africaine* (vol. 26, no. 54, 1965), details the poet-president of Senegal's appreciable contribution to the movement and his attempts to convert it into practical policies.

Négritude: Essays and Studies edited by Albert Berrian and Richard Long (Hampton Institute Press, 1967), a most instructive series of papers exploring different aspects of the movement.

See *Africa; Black Power; Ethiopianism; Garvey; Rastafarian movement*

Ellis Cashmore

Nkrumah, Kwame (1909–72) With Kenyatta, regarded as one of the two great African nationalist leaders of the immediate postwar period. Kwame Nkrumah was widely known as the 'Gandhi of Africa'.

He was born in Ankroful, but educated at Lincoln

University, Pennsylvania, and the London School of Economics. In 1949, he returned to Africa to form the Nationalist Convention People's party with the slogan 'self-government, now'. A year later, he was imprisoned for twelve months for his role in organizing strikes amongst black workers.

On his release, he was elected as first municipal member for Accra and became what was known as the Leader of Business in the Assembly. In 1957, he became the first prime minister of the independent Commonwealth State of Ghana. Ghana became a republic in 1960. Nkrumah, like Kenyatta, symbolized the mounting Pan-African spirit: he challenged white domination at every opportunity without resorting to the open warfare tactics advocated by his Kenyan contemporary. On the other hand, his leadership was threatened by internal opposition to his drastic economic reforms and he often used dubious tactics to suppress his opposition (such as imprisoning critics without trial). Such opposition grew seriously, and in 1966, Nkrumah's regime was thrown by a military coup, whilst he was visiting China. He then went to Guinea where he was appointed head of State.

Read:

The Autobiography of Kwame Nkrumah (Panaf, 1973; first published in 1957), the leader's own account of his life.

Africa Must Unite by Kwame Nkrumah (Panaf, 1963), possibly his most important political tract.

Neo-Colonialism: The Last Stage of Imperialism by Kwame Nkrumah (Heinemann Educational Books, 1968), the theoretical background to Nkrumah's struggle against British rule.

See *Africa; Gandhi; Kenyatta; Power*

Ellis Cashmore

P

Paternalism The essence of paternalism is that it seeks to legitimate despotism by applying to relations of economic, social, and political inequality the model of familistic relations, especially between father and child. There is, of course, an element of despotism in parent-child relations, but the despotism is both tempered and legitimated by 'love'. In the colder phrasing of sociobiology, kinship makes for a commonality of genetic interests between relatives. Parents can indeed be expected to exert authority for the benefit of their children, if not all the time, at least much of the time, since their children's interests overlap with their own.

In the absence of such a commonality of genetic interests, unequal relations of power are characterized by a highly asymmetrical distribution of costs and benefits, that is, by exploitation. It is, therefore, in the interest of the dominant party to seek to disguise the coercive and exploitative nature of the relationship by claiming that domination is in the best interests of the oppressed. This is done by asserting that the dominated are in a state analogous to childhood, that is, are dependent, immature, irresponsible, and unable to run their own affairs, and that the rulers 'love' their subjects, and act *in loco parentis*, to the best interests of the oppressed.

Paternalism is probably the most widespread legitimating ideology of pre-industrial societies, and has been independently reinvented time and again in a wide range of social situations. It characterized, among others, patron-client relationships in many pre-industrial societies; god-parent–god-child ties in class-stratified Latin American countries; the white man's burden and civilizing mission ideology of European colonialism in Africa; master–slave relations in the chattel slavery regimes of the western hemisphere, and teacher–student relationships in universities.

The acceptance of the legitimizing ideology by the subordinates is generally a function of the degree of perceived benevolence in the relationship, and of the age difference between the parties. Thus, the model is more acceptable between teacher and students than between masters and slaves. As a type of race and ethnic relations, paternalism has characterized many societies, although acceptance of that ideology by the oppressed has always been problematic. Perhaps the two situations in which paternalism was most explicitly formulated as a legitimation of despotism are European colonialism, particularly in Africa, and plantation slavery in the Americas.

There has been much debate on the extent to which colonial subjects and slaves accepted their masters' view of them and internalized a sense of their own inferiority (the so-called Sambo mentality). There is much evidence that servility and subservience were only opportunistic survival mechanisms, although one cannot entirely discount that some slaves and colonials did indeed develop a dependency complex. This was probably more the case under slavery than under colonialism, because the slave plantation did, in fact, represent a somewhat closer approximation to a large family (though far from a happy one) than the typical colony.

Indeed, extensive mating (often forced, and nearly always extra-marital) between male owners or overseers and female slaves was characteristic of all slave regimes. For the dominant males, mating with slaves was a way of combining business and pleasure, hence the popularity of the practice, both in North and in South America. (The Latins tended to be less hypocritical and more open in their acceptance of miscegenation than the Dutch and English, but there is no evidence that the actual incidence of the practice differed between slave regimes.) These liaisons across racial lines did, of course, create numerous ties of sexual intimacy and of kinship between masters and slaves, and did make many plantations big families of sorts, albeit of a perverse type. The undeniable fact, however, is that sexual and kin ties across racial lines necessarily affected the master–slave relationship, and consolidated the paternalistic model of legitimation by giving it *some* factual basis.

Read:

Roll, Jordan, Roll by Eugene Genovese (Pantheon, 1974), an account by a marxist historian of the US plantation system from the slaves' point of view.

The Masters and the Slaves, by Gilberto Freyre (Knopf, 1964), the classic account of Brazilian slavery by a psychoanalytically oriented Brazilian sociologist.

Race and Racism, by Pierre L. van den Berghe (Wiley, 1978), an analysis of race relations in Mexico, Brazil, South Africa, and the United States, stressing the contrast between 'paternalistic' and 'competitive' race relations.

See *Africa; Apartheid; Brazil; Colonialism; Racism; Slavery*

Pierre L. van den Berghe

Pentecostalism A term used to describe a collection of religious sects that have proliferated particularly amongst blacks in the West Indies, USA and UK. Doctrinally, the assemblies revolve around the Day of the Pentecost spoken of in the Bible's Acts, 2: 1-2: 'And when the day of the Pentecost was now come, they were all together in one place. And suddenly there came from heaven a sound as of the rushing of a mighty wind, and it filled all the house where they were sitting.

Pentecostal members, or 'saints', were to await this day of judgment when they would reach their salvation; in the meantime, they were to withdraw as far as possible from the 'outside world' and restrict contact with outsiders. They believed themselves to be the 'chosen people', the saved who would be rescued on the day of the Pentecost when all others would be damned.

The precise origins of Pentecostalism are obscure, but it seems there were antecedents in both America and the West Indies, where there flourished a movement called native baptism. This was based on Christianity but was fused with elements taken from African belief systems. Slavery played a significant part in shaping native baptism, as Malcolm Calley points out: 'Possibly the most important role of slavery in the West Indies was to hinder the diffusion of a detailed knowledge of Christianity to the slaves thus stimulating them to invent their own interpretations and their own sects.'

Lay native baptist preachers were exposed to Christian

teaching in America and their mixture of biblical concepts and African ritualism was enthusiastically met by American and, later (in the 1780s), Jamaican slaves. Native baptism survived the attempts of plantation owners to suppress it and sprouted a variety of different forms which later transmuted into Pentecostalism.

The sects maintained a presence in the West Indies and USA after emancipation and grew in the UK in the 1950s and 1960s – coinciding with the arrival of tens of thousands of West Indian migrants. The response of the first wave of immigrants to white racialism was characterized by the writer Dilip Hiro as 'evasion': they turned inward, developing postures designed to minimize their visibility. Black clubs, shops and, of course, churches developed. Calley locates the beginnings of Pentecostalism in the UK in 1954 when services were held in private homes. By 1967, Clifford Hill revealed that a single branch of the movement, the New Testament Church of God, alone commanded a following of 10,861 congregations, employed fifteen full-time ministers and owned its own buildings, including a theological college for the training of its own ministry.

The growth of Pentecostalism is even more surprising when we consider the strictures placed on its members: forbidden were the consumption of tobacco and alcohol, the wearing of jewellery, or cosmetics, the use of bad language and sexual laxity. Avoidance of contact with the 'contaminated' outside world was recommended. Observance of these rules and adherence to Pentecostalist practices ensured the believer a special relationship with God, a relationship that was expressed through ecstatic experience in which the individuals became 'filled' with the spirit of God and threw convulsions, twitching and being able to speak in tongues (glossolalia): 'And they were all filled with the Holy Spirit, and began to speak with other tongues, as the spirit gave them utterance' (Acts, 2:4).

Pentecostalism indicates how many ethnic groups, particularly blacks in the USA and UK, rather than articulate any outright protest against their treatment by society, develop alternative lifestyles, creating their own autonomous religions, passively withdrawing and seeking salvation not in this world but in an afterlife.

Read:

God's People by Malcolm Calley (Oxford University Press, 1965), a detailed study of Pentecostalism's growth in the UK, but with useful chapters on the ancestry of the sects.

'Pentecostalist growth – the result of racialism?' by Clifford Hill in *Race Today* (vol. 3, 1972), the question in the title is answered affirmatively, the author arguing that Pentecostalism is a response to the ways in which blacks were treated in the first phases of their settlement in the British cities.

Black British, White British by Dilip Hiro (Monthly Review Press, 1973), refers to Pentecostalism, though the book is a more general statement on the black presence in Britain.

See *Migrant ideology; Millenarian movements; Myth of return; Rastafarian movement; Slavery*

Ellis Cashmore

People's Temple On 18 November 1978, 900 members of a religious sect led by the Reverend Jim Jones committed mass suicide at their commune in the jungle of Guyana. They were followers of Jones' People's Temple, a predominantly black movement taken to Guyana, mostly from California, for the purpose of creating an 'earthly paradise' in the hideaway called Jonestown.

It was Jones's apparent intention to establish a perfect community based on pure socialist principles without racism or sexism, where 'free love' would proliferate. Jones had espoused these principles during his years in Indiana and, later, California where he built up his following, particularly amongst black Americans, claiming he possessed miraculous healing powers. He warned his followers of the rise of the Ku Klux Klan, the rebirth of Nazism, and told them of his vision of an unavoidable genocidal apocalypse.

In 1970, he negotiated with the self-styled 'socialist' government of Guyana under the dubious leadership of Forbes Burnham, to shift his base to that country. This was to be site of his utopia. In its early days, Jonestown attracted great interest from black radicals in the USA who were intrigued by Jones's experiment. Later, however, it became increasingly obvious that Jones himself, contrary to his alleged socialist principles, was demanding absolute and total obedience from his followers and was enforcing his rules with harsh punishments; those who fled were threatened with death.

As the rumours that people were being held against their wills filtered back to the States, suspicion was aroused amongst journalists and politicians. After receiving one group of visitors, Jones sensed the danger they might have brought and ordered them to be killed. Three newsmen, a US Congressman and a Jonestown defector were executed. This precipitated the end of the Jones idealism and the leader bade his followers to poison themselves by drinking a specially prepared mixture of potassium cyanide and potassium chloride. Babies were given the poison by means of syringes. 'It's over, sister,' a man's voice was heard saying on a tape made during the mass self-sacrifice. 'Let's make it a beautiful day.' Nine hundred took their potions, lay down and writhed to death.

'We didn't commit suicide,' Jones recorded. 'We committed an act of revolutionary suicide protesting the conditions of an inhuman world.' Jones's followers performed the ultimate act of obedience; they unquestioningly followed his instruction to destroy themselves. (There were rumours that Jones warned that survivors would be tortured by the Guyanese army.) His leadership was based on charisma; clearly, the members of his sect considered him endowed with some sort of supernatural power and so were perfectly prepared to die for him and his ideals. His vision of the genocide inspired by racist groups was, in a way, similar to that entertained by Charles Manson with his prophecy of helter-skelter, the ultimate black v. white confrontation. In the modern world, the mass suicide of the People's Temple is unique.

Read:

Black and White by Shiva Naipaul (Hamish Hamilton, 1980), a descriptive account of a writer's visit to Guyana in the aftermath of the Jonestown suicides.

See *Black Power; Millenarian movements; Power*

Ellis Cashmore

Phenotype The visible or measurable appearance of an organism in respect of trait or traits. The phenotype is what one sees, the appearance or behaviour of an organism, in contrast to the genotype or underlying genetic constitution.

For example, all people with brown eyes have the same phenotype in respect of eye colour; equally, the behaviour of a particular strain of rats when confronted with a series of puzzles in a maze is a behavioural phenotype. The outward appearance of humans in respect of skin colour, hair form, bone structure, etc. is best identified as phenotypical variation; this is a relatively culture-free way of designating differences as opposed to the word race, the meaning of which varies from one historical period and one culture to another.

Read:

Personality and Heredity by Brian W.P. Wells (Longman, 1980), an introduction to the study of psychogenics.

The Race Concept by Michael Banton and Jonathan Harwood (David & Charles, 1975), discusses the concept.

See *Genotype; Intelligence; Racism*

Michael Banton

Pluralism This refers to a pattern of social relations in which groups that are distinct from each other in a great many respects share aspects of a common culture and set of institutions. Each group retains its own ethnic origins by perpetuating specific cultures (or 'subcultures') in the form of churches, businesses, clubs and media. It also encloses itself with its own set of primary group relations such as friendship networks, families and intra-group marriages. Yet, all those groups participate collectively in some spheres and, collectively, make up a 'plural society'.

J.S. Furnivall used societies in Burma and Indonesia as illustrations of plural societies: here people of very different ethnic backgrounds did not meet each other except in the marketplace, where they had to dispose of goods and services to other groups. The marketplace was the glue that held the different groups together like different pieces of stone in a mosaic. The mosaic is a useful metaphor for pluralism: one flat entity made up of many separate and distinct elements.

There are two basic types of pluralism: cultural and structural. Cultural occurs when groups have their own religions, beliefs, customs, attitudes and general lifestyles, but have others in common. Structural pluralism is when groups have their own social structures and institutions, while sharing others. For example, several groups may support a single government, and recognize the same law and use the same money; yet they might go to their own churches, speak a second language amongst themselves, have their own specialist educations and occupations and marry only within their own group.

Pluralism, as an analytical tool, purports to explain how many different groups with different backgrounds and, perhaps, different interests can live together without their diversity becoming a basis for conflict. This is especially so if power is distributed fairly evenly amongst the groups. Where one of the groups has control of power, conflict is likely to erupt. Historically, pluralism seems to apply to pre-industrial or industrializing countries like East African or Caribbean societies where there are more or less equal segments rather than hierarchial classes as in industrial societies.

The plural society is based on cultural and social heterogeneity (i.e. it is composed of diverse elements), but one that does not necessarily create deep divisions and produce serious conflict. Groups maintain their own distinct features and corporate identities, thus adding to the richness of society, without being excluded or relegated to lowly positions.

Pluralism has been used as an ideal in some circumstances, something to aim at; a society in which all groups can express their differences and cultivate their uniqueness without engaging in wholesale or even petty conflicts. The ideal encourages self-awareness and development in some spheres and unification and co-operation in others. This has been particularly popular in North American countries which house a variety of ethnic groups, but can foster only a limited unity despite attempts to balance out interests. But, well-intended as the goal maybe, it is constantly interrupted by racism which denies different groups access to certain types of resources (like well-paying jobs and good housing).

The term pluralism is also used in political science in a slightly different sense: it describes a situation in which there are several different interest groups segmentalized horizontally with no single group exerting complete dominance. The similarities with ethnic pluralism are apparent: division on the basis of difference without severe inequality of power; horizontal not vertical differentiation.

Read:

Netherlands India by J.S. Furnivall (Cambridge University Press, 1967, first published in 1947), this is a very early account of plural societies and provides the theoretical model for the later work by M.G. Smith, *The Plural Society in the British West Indies* (University of California Press, 1965).

Race Relations in Sociological Theory, 2nd edition, by John Rex (Routledge & Kegan Paul, 1982), deals with all the major theoretical contributions to race relations, including those of Furnivall and Smith.

'Pluralism: a political perspective' by Michael Walzer in the Harvard *Encyclopedia of American Ethnic Groups* (Harvard University Press, 1980), an assessment of the pluralist development of the USA.

See *Culture; Ethnicity; Native peoples; Power*

Ellis Cashmore

Police and race relations The National Advisory Commission which reported on the black riots in the United States in 1967 found that almost invariably the incident which started the riot had been the routine arrest of a black person. They considered that the police were not merely a spark which ignited a blaze. To many blacks the police symbolized white power, white racism and white repression; this did faithfully represent the attitudes of many policemen. The riots in British cities in 1981 reflected this pattern, though the injuries to participants and damage to property were much less. Lord Scarman found that '(1) The disorders were communal disturbances arising from a complex political, social and economic situation . . . (2) There was a strong racial element in the disorders, but they were not a race riot . . .' and, finally '(7) The riots were essentially an outburst of anger and resentment by young black people against the police.' He also noted that 'One of the most serious developments in recent years has been the way in which the older generation of black people in Brixton has come to share the belief of the younger generation that the police routinely harass and ill-treat black youngsters.'

In considering the question of harassment it is useful to draw upon the distinction between categorical and statistical discrimination. Some policemen are motivated to harass black youngsters by their personal prejudices: they are against blacks. Other policemen are motivated to harass black youngsters by the belief that they are more likely than other groups to be engaged in unlawful activities: they are against criminals. Any higher incidence of minority criminality is soon noticed by policemen and easily promotes sterotyping. If a large proportion of, say, car thefts, is committed by black youths, it is rational for police to investigate whenever they see a smart car driven by a young black since there is a greater likelihood of discovering an offender in this way than by random checks. It is rational in the same sense as it is rational for a manufacturer to discharge a noxious effluent into a nearby river when there is no law against environmental pollution. In securing his own ends more economically, the individual derives a private benefit while creating a public cost. Unless the policeman has some reason additional to minority status for stopping the minority driver he will contribute, firstly, to unwillingness to co-operate with the police among that minority and, secondly, to an amplification of the initial identification. Because minority drivers are stopped more frequently more offences will be discovered among them relative to their proportion of the total population even if there is no difference in the frequency with which they commit the offence in question. The initial belief will have turned into a self-fulfilling prophecy.

An analysis of the London figures for 1975 found that, after correcting for the age distributions of the populations in question, Asians were no more likely to be arrested than whites, but blacks were more than twice as likely to be arrested for indictable crimes. There is scarcely any friction between police and Asians; their relationship is affected by a different problem. A Home Office study in 1981 discovered that the incidence of racial attacks on Asians was fifty times greater, and that on blacks over thirty-six times greater, than attacks upon white people. The Home Secretary acknowledged that such attacks were more common than had been realized and that they seemed to be on the increase. The attacks were not orchestrated by extremist organizations, a conclusion that makes the evidence the more frightening. The police are dependent upon public co-operation to solve crimes of this kind; only limited co-operation had been forthcoming and the police had given the investigation of such attacks only low priority.

The British have been so anxious to keep issues of policing outside the arena of party politics that they have been unwilling to recognize that the allocation of resources for law enforcement is of real and increasing concern to citizens; it is a political matter even when it is not party political. The 1981 riots have helped to bring police methods into the area of public debate as never before in the country's history. Any policy for police-minority relations has therefore to form part of a larger policy for maintaining the peace within the nation. At present increased attention is being paid to the recruitment of minority police officers and of officers temperamentally suited to work in multiracial settings. Training programmes concerned with such settings are being developed but research studies in the United States and Britain have hitherto been unable to demonstrate that such programmes have improved either police attitudes or performance. In the long term, what matters is that minority interests should be adequately represented in bodies to which police chiefs are accountable; that offences by minority members are not pursued with disproportionate vigour; and that minority demands for services from the police evoke an equitable response.

Read:

Uprising! The Police, the People and the Riots in Britain's Cities by Martin Kettle and Lucy Hodges (Pan Books, 1982), for an account of the riots of 1981 and the background.

The Brixton Disorders, 10–12 April 1981, by Lord Scarman (Penguin Books, 1982), for the report of an official investigation.

The British Police, edited by Simon Holdaway (Arnold, 1979), brings together essays by sociologists.

See *Kerner Report; Racism; Riots (UK and USA); Scarman Report*

Michael Banton

Politics and 'race' The idea of 'race' has been taken up and employed as an object of political action in a variety of ways in different countries. Put another way, one can trace different forms in which political processes have become racialized. In the vast majority of these instances, the idea of 'race' has been employed in order to justify or legitimate discriminatory action of some sort. At the extreme, as in the instance of Germany in the 1930s and 1940s, the idea of 'race' was employed by the Nazi party to justify a solution to identified economic and political problems which involved mass murder of the Jews. In South Africa, from the early nineteenth century to the 1950s, the idea of 'race' was employed to justify the physical segregation and extreme exploitation of African labour.

Both these examples represent twentieth-century instances of a relationship that characterizes European colonial domination and expansion in the late eighteenth and nineteenth centuries, and the exploitation of African labour in the United States in the same period. In these instances important sections of the dominant class justified their economic and political activity by labelling those whose labour they exploited in various ways as belonging to an inferior 'race'. The political application of the 'race' label was explicitly accompanied by the employment of racist ideology: Africans, both in Africa and the United States, were defined as belonging to the 'Negro race' which was held to be inferior, biologically and culturally, when compared with the 'race' to which their exploiters allegedly belonged.

The fact that this racism was used to justify mass murder in the heartland of a European continent which various national ruling classes defined as the epitome of 'civilization' and 'democracy' was one of the reasons why the manner in which politics were racialized change in Europe after 1945. Another, equally important, factor was the process of decolonization that was well under way by the 1950s. Although direct political control over colonies was conceded, often after direct armed struggle, European and North American capital wished to retain economic control as far as was possible and this necessitated no longer defining the emerging ruling classes as members of an inferior 'race'. For this same reason, European and North American policy toward South Africa changed to the extent that political opposition towards the manner and content of its ruling class means of domination was expressed while trade and investment continued relatively unhindered. The necessary desire to maintain the international domination of capital was not the sole determinant of this changing ideological content of ruling-class ideology, but it provided the parameters for such a change. It also had major repercussions within European and, particularly, American societies. The contradiction between political legitimation of the American ruling class in terms of 'freedom' and 'equality', when combined with changing world political relationships in the 1950s and 1960s, was clearly contradicted by the position and experience of the African-descended population within the United States. The result was the rebellion and revolt of those who were the object of that contradiction, and as a longer-term consequence, a redefinition by the exploited of what 'race' meant to them.

This general process was neither uniform nor universal. Moreover, it did not mean that the idea of 'race' was removed from political discourse. Rather, although the language of biological racism was removed from bourgeois politics, the language of 'race' remained and was accompanied by assertions of cultural inferiority. Only the neo-fascist right retained the 'old' racism: parliamentary politicians articulated the 'new' racism. The process is particularly clear within western Europe (in Britain the process is evident in the extreme form) where, since 1945, the racialization of politics has become an internal issue.

Before the major labour migrations beginning in the 1940s, the racialization of politics occurred primarily in connection with colonial affairs. The political reaction to these migrations was at first out of step with the economic reaction: capitalists required labour power and so welcomed migrant labour as a solution to their problem. But there was a hostile political reaction from the start and this gained in strength through the 1960s. The hostility was expressed by drawing attention to cultural differences and linking them with the idea of 'race' (in that the migrants were identified primarily by certain phenotypical features). On the basis of this new form of racialization, a wide range of racist legislation was passed in different European countries to confine the migrants to a marginal legal/ideological position. In some instances, the legislation preceded and directly structured the entry to the migrants.

As a result of this process, 'race' is widely defined as a political problem requiring attention and policy decisions in western Europe. This is so irrespective of the fact that not only has the language of the nineteenth-century scientific racism been largely absent from official political discourse but also that elected governments have consistently denied being motivated by, or having institutionalized in law, racism. The official, explicitly defined object and problem is 'immigrants', but the language and imagery used by all classes to discuss this 'problem' draws directly, yet separately, upon that store of late eighteenth and nineteenth century racism.

Read:

Race, Conflict and the International Order, by H. Tinker (Macmillan, 1977), for an account of the political and economic effects of decolonization on a world scale.

A Different Hunger, by A. Sivananden (Pluto, 1982), for a challenging account of the racialization of British domestic politics since 1945.

The New Racism, by Martin Barker (Junction Books, 1981), for an analysis of the changing form of racism in British politics.

See *Apartheid; Colonialism; Migration; Racialization; Racism*

Robert Miles

Positive discrimination See *Affirmative action*

Powell, Enoch (1912-) 'Numbers are of the essence,' insisted Enoch Powell, Conservative MP for Wolverhampton in a speech to local party members in Birmingham on 20 April 1968. 'We must be mad', he continued, 'literally mad, as a nation to be permitting the annual inflow of some 50,000 dependants, who are for the most part the material of the future growth of the immigrant-descended population.' On immigration, or more precisely, nonwhite immigration, he was clear: he wanted it stopped. If not, he prophesied that the UK would experience the same 'tragic and intractable phenomenon' witnessed in Watts, Detroit, Newark and elsewhere in the USA. The difference, according to Powell, was that in the UK 'rivers of blood' would flow 'by our own volition and our own neglect'.

The far-reaching effects of Powell's 'earthquake', as he and others later referred to it, were generated not entirely by the content of his speech, nor by his insidious use of personal anecdote to sustain and endorse his assertions. In fact, he had covered similar ground and invoked the same emotive imagery in a speech delivered in nearby Walsall only two months before. The difference, however, was that he had deliberately contrived to ensure that his Birmingham speech would receive saturated media coverage; and it did. For the following couple of weeks, the speech and the discussion it generated dominated the news media. That some of the editorial comments were opposed to his inflammatory opinions and the emotive way in which he had presented them, was largely irrelevant. The fact remained that a survey poll taken a few days after the speech revealed that 96 per cent of the sample had heard or read about the speech.

Powell's thrust was to challenge what he considered a false impression of consensus on the immigration issue as conveyed by politicians and the media. Surveys of the time revealed that somewhere between two-thirds and three-quarters of the UK population were opposed to immigration: Powell was the first prominent politician to articulate and lend credibility to these views, though Paul Foot has argued that Powell's decision to enter the immigration debate at such a controversial level – a debate from which he had previously remained firmly detached – was stimulated largely by his failure to secure leadership of the Conservative party in 1964.

The immediate effect of Powell's 'earthquake' was his dismissal from the Conservative party shadow cabinet and, following this, a 'We Back Powell' strike, augmented by a protest march for dockers (traditionally Labour party voters). In the following weeks, Powell received over 110,000 letters, only a small number of which expressed disapproval at his speech.

The 'earthquake' was to have far-reaching effects on the immigration debate and related policy interventions. The introduction of restrictive immigration control in 1962 had already placed 'a question of numbers' on the agenda for debate; Powellism ensured that it would be the focal point of debate. In short, numbers became the name of the game and not the dimensions of racial disadvantage or the racist and divisive nature of the UK's immigration laws. Even those politicians and commentators who rejected the tenets of Powellism were compelled to subscribe implicitly to the view that numbers constituted the main agenda item for debate. Ever since the 1968 'earthquake' the starting point for political and popular debate on immigration has, for Powell's opponents, been to appease the anxieties of the white indigenous population that it will not be overrun by colonial migrants and their children. Statistics on the size and proportion of nonwhites in the UK, projections on the birth-rate and so on comprise the debate's defining features.

The legacy of Powellism can also be discerned in 'the new racism' which has flourished under the political leadership of Margaret Thatcher, according to Martin Barker (1981). This is geared to the notion of the 'British way of life' which is threatened by the infusion of aliens with different beliefs, customs and languages. Thatcher's insistence in 1978 that immigration control was necessary to avert the possibility of this way of life being 'swamped' by nonwhite immigrants concurred exactly with Powell's prognosis ten years earlier.

Whether or not Powell's views could be legitimately described as racist depends largely on how one defines the concept. John Rex believes they were; Michael Banton disagrees. Whatever the view, it is clear that such semantic niceties are of secondary importance in an appraisal of Powell's impact on UK politics. Though he is now confined to the margins of the body politic, having resigned from the Conservative party and taken his seat as an Ulster Unionist MP, his version of the reality of race relations has now been firmly appropriated as the basis for intervention on this issue by many leading politicians.

Read:

The Rise of Enoch Powell by Paul Foot (Penguin, 1969), a detailed and critical account of Powell's political career with particular reference to the factors which encouraged him to enter the 'race' debate, the legitimacy of his views on the subject, and the reactions they generated.

The Political Impact of Mass Media by Colin Seymour Ure (Constable, 1974), chapter 4 provides an illuminating insight into the way in which Powell contrived to ensure maximum media coverage for his 'earthquake'; the political effects of the speech are also considered.

The New Racism by Martin Barker (Junction Books, 1981), considers the emergence of sociobiology in mainstream political debate on race relations and immigration. He reveals the extent to which this spurious 'scientific theory' informed the arguments of Powell and many of his supporters.

See *Immigration laws; Politics and 'race'; Racism*

Barry Troyna

Power This is a crucial concept in race and ethnic relations for it refers to the ability to exact a degree of compliance or obedience of others in accordance with one's own will.

Power may be rested in individuals, in groups, whole societies or even blocs of societies; the distinguishing feature is the capacity to influence others into performing and maybe, thinking in accordance with one's own requirements.

There has been great debate over the exact nature of power and there are many different forms of power. For example, slavery is an extreme example of what might be called 'raw power' – an unmitigated coercion based on physical might. It entails one group exercising its will over another through almost total control of circumstances; conformity is enforced through the application of negative sanctions to undesirable behaviour. But, as the French philosopher Jean-Jacques Rousseau noticed: 'The strongest man is never strong enough to be always master unless he transforms his power into right and obedience into duty.'

Sheer compulsion works effectively under some conditions, particularly where there is a large disparity in material resources, but modern race relations usually have more complex power relationships entailing a recognition by the power*less* group of the powerholding group's right to exercise its will. For instance, in many situations, a group will retain its power because other groups accept the *legitimacy* of its position and so never challenge the unequal relationship. It would be plausibly argued that blacks in the USA, for many years, did not seriously question the legitimacy of the power relationship of which they were part: they acknowledged the right of whites to rule and so accepted their own subordinate position. So the threat of force that lay behind the whites' power in slave days was not necessary to the maintenance of the power relationship.

Power is sometimes operationalized through a unified framework of rules, such as the laws existing in the States up till the civil rights legislation. These institutionalized whites' power and ensured blacks were kept powerless through legal means. The extreme example of this is the law relating to apartheid: this effectively denies nonwhites access to power. This type of arrangement was characterized by the sociologist Max Weber as 'rational-legal', but there are alternatives. There may be a 'traditional' mode of legitimation in which authority has been vested with one group for a long period of time. On occasions, there may emerge a 'charismatic' leader who is attributed with power because his followers believe him or her to be endowed with some special gifts, perhaps from some supernatural agency. In these situations, the ultimate legitimating power may be the 'will of God' and they often engender forces for changes in power relationships rather than those securing existing arrangements. Gandhi's successful campaign against British power over India is an obvious example.

The Gandhi case is an illustration of the loss of plausibility of the legitimacy of one power relationship and the gain in plausibility of an alternative. Once legitimacy is lost, then forms of resistance to it are likely to proliferate. Basically, all ethnic struggles are about power relationships. Where there is a diversity of groups with divergent interests and no absolute attribution of legitimacy to a power relationship, a perpetual resistance is likely to take place.

Read:

Sociology: a biographical approach by Peter and Brigitte Berger (Penguin, 1976), has a clear chapter 13 called 'Power' that deals with the various issues about the nature and exercise of power, giving plenty of emphasis to Weber's important analysis.

Power, Racism and Privilege by William J. Wilson (Free Press, 1973), an analysis of race relations, particularly in the American context, using a power framework and some good comparative material.

Modern Sociology edited by Peter Worsley (Penguin, 1980), contains a chapter on 'Social Stratification' in which race, ethnicity and nation as divisions of power relationships are discussed.

See *Colonialism; Gandhi; Hegemony; Riots (UK and USA); Slavery*

Ellis Cashmore

Prejudice This may be defined as learned beliefs and values that lead an individual or group of inviduals to be biased for or against members of particular groups. Technically then, there is a positive and negative prejudice, though, in race and ethic relations, the term usually refers to the negative aspect when a group inherits or generates hostile views about a distinguishable group based on generalizations. These generalizations are invariably derived from inaccurate or incomplete informations about the other group.

For example, we might say a person (or group) is

prejudiced against Asians; we mean that they are oriented towards behaving with some hostility towards Asians (that behaviour is called discrimination). The person believes that, with the odd exception, all Asians are pretty much the same – much of a muchness. But the general characteristics they attribute to Asians are faulty. The generalization is called stereotyping and means assigning properties to any person in a group regardless of the actual variation among members of the group. In a recent piece of research it was found that many white residents of housing estates were prejudiced against Asians, believing them all to be, amongst other things, 'unhygienic, crafty and antiwhite'. The views were not gleaned from valid experience, but from hearsay or secondhand images.

Such prejudices might not be restricted to ethnic groups, but to virtually any group (including whole nations or continents) to which generalized characteristics can be applied. Thus individual members of those groups are denied the right to be recognized and treated as individuals with individual characteristics.

Examples of this process are rife in history, though the antisemitism of the Second World War stands out: millions were identified as sharing alleged characteristics because of their Jewish background. Gross generalizations were made about Jews and these were used as the basis of all manner of atrocities.

In the aftermath of the war, a large-scale study of prejudice was made by Theodor Adorno and his colleagues. Published in 1950, *The Authoritarian Personality* concluded that certain people are prejudiced because their prejudices meet certain needs associated with their personality. Further, those who were highly prejudiced were likely to have authoritarian personalities; they tended to be submissive and obedient to authority and to reject 'out-groups' in a punitive way. They also saw people in dichotomous terms – 'either you're with us or against us.'

The upshot of this was that, if prejudice was bound up with a fundamental type of personality, people with this type of personality would be prejudiced not just against one particular 'out-group' but against all people and groups who were considered different in some way.

This general and complex form of prejudice, the researchers called 'ethnocentrism' as contrasted to the more one-dimensional antisemitism (prejudice against Jews). This ethnocentrism referred to a tendency to regard one's own group as the standard and all other, different groups as strange and, usually, inferior. One's own ways of thinking and behaving were seen as normal, the natural way of doing things. The main finding of the research was that there was a strong relationship between this consistently high degree of prejudice against all 'out-groups' and a personality with the following features: possession of 'conventional values'; intolerance of weakness; rigidity of beliefs and views; tendency to be punitive and suspicious; respectful of authority to an extreme degree. Hence the 'authoritarian personality'.

Adorno *et al.* traced the development of this personality complex and prejudice to early childhood experiences in families tending to be harshly disciplinarian. As a child, the possessor of an authoritarian personality was insecure, dependent on, fearful of parents and unconsciously hostile towards parents. As an adult he or she has a high amount of pent-up anger which, because of basic insecurity, manifests itself in a displaced aggression against powerless groups. At the same time, the individual remains respectful of and obedient towards those in authority.

Though *The Authoritarian Personality* has become a classic study of the causes of prejudices, modern psychologists and sociologists have tended to lay the emphasis off unconscious childhood conflicts and on the pressures and influences in the social context. In particular, many have pointed to prejudice as a matter of learning: people simply pick up prejudices against groups from others with whom they identify. Those others may be parents or they may be peers. Either way the individual feels a pressure to conform, so adjusts his views accordingly. This helps explain why prejudices seem to pass from one generation to the next. Thomas Pettigrew has argued that although personality features may account for some prejudice, the greater proportion of it stems from a straightforward conformity to prevalent standards. So that if one grows up in an environment in which all those with Spanish-sounding names are regarded as imbeciles fit only for menial work, then one strongly feels a pressure to align one's own negative prejudices to conform with this generalization.

Other explanations also invoke social factors. For example, the phenomenon known as scapegoating implicates minority groups in situations that are not of their own making, yet produces high amounts of prejudice against them. A general social decline might lead to sharp contraction of the job market and a general deterioration in material conditions. The underlying causes of decline may be complex, so people may look for something more immediate and locate it in the form of a minority group. So an immigrant or minority group might be made into a scapegoat and negative prejudices against that group can be created.

Prejudice, then, can be explained as a result of childhood experiences, pressure to conform or scapegoating. There are many other explanations; it can be approached as an individual or a social phenomenon. But, however it is explained, one must consider it as an important factor in race and ethnic relations. For being aware of another group's presence and holding negative values and beliefs about that group bears a crucially strong influence on how behaviour towards that group will be organized and, therefore, on the general pattern of race relations.

Read:

The Authoritarian Personality by T.S. Adorno, E. Frenkel-Brunswick, D.J. Levinson and R.N. Sanforo (Harper & Row, 1950), the most influential study of prejudice since the war.

The Social Animal by Elliot Aronson, 3rd edition (Harper & Row, 1980), has a clearly written chapter on 'Prejudice' that summarizes the main arguments.

The Nature of Prejudice by Gordon Allport (Addison-Wesley, 1954), in its day, a major statement on the psychology of race relations; still an impressive, scholarly account of the causes of and solutions to prejudice.

See *Discrimination; Dollard; Scapegoat; Sterotype; Xenophobia*

Ellis Cashmore

Pruitt-Igoe The name of two areas in St Louis that were designated by city planners the sites of a large-scale housing project. In the early 1950s, big, high-rise apartment blocks situated in grounds intentionally left open for the use of both the resident and surrounding community, were erected in the two areas.

The project was developed in the spirit of good ethnic

relations, the idea being that blacks would live more harmoniously together and away from whites. Originally, the plan was to house whites in one estate and blacks in the other, but the US Supreme Court considered this unconstitutional, and the two areas were eventually occupied by some 10,000 mostly black residents. The first families moved in during 1954; by 1959, the project had become a total scandal, not only because of the unusual architecture but because of the high incidence of crime, vandalism and prostitution. Its unattractiveness was reflected in its vacancy rate which exceeded that of any housing complex in the States.

In total contrast to the concept of dispersal, the basic philosophy informing the project was to herd 'problem' families, those for which there were no other places to live in. Lee Rainwater studied the area and noted: 'The original tenants were drawn very heavily from several land clearance areas in the inner city. . . . Only those Negroes who are desperate for housing are willing to live in Pruitt-Igoe.'

Many of the families were very large and over half were one-parent arrangements. For the 'average family', life in Pruitt-Igoe proved 'particularly unappealing', as Rainwater puts it. The place became a 'dumping ground' for poor blacks. Street violence became an everyday occurrence, robbery was commonplace and buildings were allowed to deteriorate. Families left as quickly as possible: a vacancy rate of 65 per cent attested to the ultimate failure of the project. Twelve years after its construction, Pruitt-Igoe was quite literally blown up.

The 'public housing monstrosity,' as Oscar Newman called it, served as a reminder of the negative effects of projects based on *de facto* segregation. It posed one half of the housing policy dilemma in regard to ethnic groups: if you don't deliberately disperse and attempt to integrate ethnic minorities, you can herd them together in public housing – possibly with dire consequences.

A similar policy almost materialized in the UK in 1978 when the Greater London Council announced its proposal for a 'racially segregated' area for Bengalis in the Tower Hamlets borough. Its divisiveness was, however, noted and it came to nothing. Herding is a simple 'response' to problems of the inner cities, but is in no sense a solution to them; it submits to people's prejudices and fears and can lead to the artificial creation of vast ghettoes – as Pruitt-Igoe demonstrates.

Read:

Behind Ghetto Walls by Lee Rainwater (Penguin, 1973), a study of life as lived by the residents of Pruitt-Igoe with an assessment of the effects.

Defensible Space by Oscar Newman (Architectural Press, 1972), an analysis of how people's physical environments can affect their social behaviour, with particular attention taken of Pruitt-Igoe.

Racial Harassment on Local Authority Housing Estates by the London Race and Housing Forum (Commission for Racial Equality, 1981), a short study of tensions on inner city housing estates.

See *Busing; Dispersal; Ghetto; Inner city*

Ellis Cashmore

Puerto Ricans in the USA About a third of the total Puerto Rican population live in the United States with over half of that migrant group domiciled in New York City. Between 800,000 and 900,000 Puerto Ricans live in New York and that is around twice as many as in San Juan, the capital city of Puerto Rico.

Puerto Rico itself is a Caribbean island about 1,000 miles southeast of Florida. It was conquered by the Spanish and made into a slave colony with the introduction of African labour in the early sixteenth century. The dominant cultural influence remains Spanish. After the Spanish-American War, Puerto Rico was given to the USA under the terms of the Treaty of Paris, 1898, and was granted a measure of local government until 1917 when Puerto Ricans were declared citizens of the United States. This precipitated a migration to the mainland.

Improvements in health and sanitation produced a decline in the deathrate, thus swelling Puerto Rico's population and putting pressure on the economy. This hastened migration in the pursuit of employment; access to the States was simplified by the availability of citizenship and migration grew rapidly in the 1920s.

Natural disasters in 1928 and 1932 devastated coffee planations (the major source of income for the island) and stimulated more migration. The Second World War curtailed the movement, but the development of inexpensive air travel after the war (e.g. to New York in six hours for about $50) resulted in a mass migration. By 1973, almost 5 million people were travelling to and from the States, in search of work they could not find in their homeland.

New York became the centre of gravity for migrants, particularly the area of East Harlem called *El Barrio* (the neighbourhood), which is still the prototype Puerto Rican ghetto. Like most other immigrants, Puerto Ricans faced the problems of family fragmentation, inadequate living conditions, poor health, exploitation at work, the handicaps of language and education and the underlying obstacles of racialism. These had the effect of binding them together and the perception of sharing common problems produced a vigorous ethnicity.

With little improvement, ethnicity was sustained and had the perhaps unwanted consequence of compounding the deprivation. Oscar Lewis, in his study of Puerto Ricans in New York, describes a 'culture of poverty' in which Puerto Ricans grow up in a tightly bonded community and assimilate poverty as a way of life instead of trying to break away from it. Catholicism is all-pervasive and enhances the sense of group identity, and family solidarity has worked as a kind of fetter to social and geographical mobility. Often, educational and occupational advancement necessitates moving away from the community and therefore from the family unit (which is rather large – about four people – compared to the New York average). Adherence to this culture alone vitiates any prospect of betterment and locks the Puerto Rican into a world of fatalism and the kind of street violence portrayed in *West Side Story*.

The indications are that modern Puerto Ricans are trying to advance in both education and occupations, but at the expense of the family solidarity and, ultimately, Puerto Rican ethnicity. Marrying outside the ethnic group will also work to weaken the sense of community and identity Puerto Ricans have displayed since the war.

Despite the visibility of Puerto Ricans in film and literature and the celebration of their ethnicity, they form only a small minority compared to other Hispanic groups like Chicanos and Cubans.

Read:

La Vida: A Puerto Rican Family in the Culture of Poverty – San Juan and New York by Oscar Lewis (Secker & Warburg, 1967), a detailed study of Puerto Rican life, rich illustrations and theoretically strung together by the author's 'culture of poverty' thesis.

Puerto Rican Americans by Joseph P. Fitzpatrick (Prentice Hall, 1971), a fairly comprehensive account of Puerto Rican migration to and life on the mainland.

Puerto Rico and the Puerto Ricans by Clifford A. Hauberg (Twayne Publishers, 1974), an account of the island and its people; an alternative is Kal Wagenheim's *Puerto Rico, A Profile* (Pall Mall, 1970).

See *Chicanos; Ethnicity; Minorities*

Ellis Cashmore

R

Race: Perspective one A group or category of persons connected by common origin. The word entered the English language at the beginning of the sixteenth century; from then until early in the nineteenth century it was used primarily to refer to common features present because of shared descent. But it was also used more loosely, as when John Bunyan in 1678 wrote 'of the Way and Race of Saints', or, a little over 100 years later, Robert Burns addressed the haggis as 'the chieftain o' the pudding race'. The literary usage to designate the descendants of an ancestral figure, or as a synonym for nation, continues to the present day, although it now appears archaic. Since the beginning of the nineteenth century the word has been used in several other distinct senses. It is important to notice these changes because there is an assumption that there is one scientifically valid way of using the word. Physical differences catch people's attention so readily that they are less quick to appreciate that the validity of race as a concept depends upon its use as an aid in explanation. From this standpoint, the main issue is not what 'race' is but the way it is used. People draw upon beliefs about race, as they draw upon beliefs about nationality, ethnicity and class, as resources for cultivating group identities.

The changes in the way the word race has been used reflect changes in the popular understanding of the causes of physical and cultural differences. Up to the eighteenth century at least, the chief paradigm for explaining such differences was provided by the Old Testament. This furnished a series of genealogies by which it seemed possible to trace the peopling of the world and the relations which different groups bore to one another. Differences of outward appearances could then be interpreted in one of three ways: firstly as part of God's design for the universe; secondly, as caused by environmental differences irrelevant to moral issues; thirdly as arising from different original ancestors. In any event, the dominant meaning attaching to the word race was that of descent. In the early nineteenth century increased knowledge about the differences between the world's peoples suggested to many people that they were part of a more general pattern of natural differences encompassing the animal and vegetable kingdoms. Under the influence of Georges Cuvier, the French comparative anatomist, such differences were seen as expressing distinctive types. 'Type' was defined as a primitive or original form independent of climatic or other physical differences. Types were thought to be permanent (for this was a pre-Darwinian view of nature). Race came to be used in the sense of type as designating species of men distinct both in physical constitution and mental capacities. This conception survives to the present and forms the core of the doctrines often designated 'scientific racism'.

Darwin showed that no forms in nature were permanent. His work led to a new interpretation according to which the physical differences between people stem from their inheriting different genes. Race (or geographical race in Darwin's vocabulary) became a synonym for subspecies, i.e. a subdivision of a species which is distinctive only because its members are isolated from other individuals belonging to the same species. If their isolation did not reduce opportunities for mating between these populations, the distinctiveness of their gene pools would be reduced. The theory of natural selection and the establishment of genetics as a field of experimental research had revolutionary implications for the study of racial differences, but it took some two generations for these implications to be properly appreciated. For half a century after the publication of Darwin's *Origin* in 1859, anthropologists continued to propose racial classifications of *Homo sapiens* in the belief that in this way the nature of the differences could be better understood. Subsequent research suggests, to the contrary, that classifications based upon phenotypical variation are of very limited value and that it is of more use to ascertain the frequency with which various genes occur in different populations.

'Race' has to be defined in other ways for social purposes.

RACE: PERSPECTIVE ONE

When the law penalizes the unfavourable treatment of persons 'on racial grounds' it becomes necessary to elaborate a legal definition of a racial group which may differ from a definition suited to zoological purposes. When someone registering the birth of a baby or completing a census form is required to list an individual's 'race' a definition must be agreed which can be reliably utilized in that context. In those countries which classify people racially, social rules for assignment are recognized that often run counter to any calculation of genetic inheritance. In the United States, anyone with an ascertainable degree of African ancestry has been counted as Negro or black, whereas in much of Latin America a person of only partially African ancestry can be counted with the white population. One reason for the concern about the use of 'race' as a classification in a population census and in other official documents is that it appears to give goverment sanction to a classification which is no longer of explanatory value in zoology, and to imply that it is important to the understanding of differences which are of a social, cultural and economic character.

Read:

The Race Concept by Michael Banton and Johathan Harwood (David & Charles, 1975), an elementary history combined with a simple scientific exposition of the concept.

The Concept of Race edited by Ashley Montagu (Free Press, 1964), a useful collection of essays.

Evolution and Human Behaviour by Alexander Alland (Tavistock, 1967), can be commended as an introduction to evolutionary theory and genetics.

See *Genotype; Phenotype; Race: perspective two; Racism; UNESCO statements on race*

Michael Banton

Race: perspective two As applied to groups of living organisms, the term 'race' has been used in at least four different senses. The most common use of the term in biology has referred to a subspecies, that is, a variety of a species that has developed distinguishing characteristics through isolation, but has not yet lost the ability to interbreed and to produce fertile hybrids with other subspecies of the same species. Today, biologists prefer the term subspecies or breed (in the case of a domesticated species) to 'race,' and thus avoid the confusion associated with the latter term.

Physical anthropologists used to speak of human 'races' in the sense of subspecies, the most common scheme being the great tripartite division of mankind into Negroid, Mongoloid, and Caucasoid. Over the last forty to fifty years, however, it became increasingly clear that no meaningful taxonomy of human races was possible. Not only were numerous groups not classifiable as belonging to any of the three main groups, but physical anthropologists could not agree with each other as to where the genetic boundaries between human groups were to be drawn, or even on how many such groups there were. The essential condition for subspeciation is breeding isolation, often maintained by ecological barriers. Humans, on the contrary, have migrated over large distances and interbred extensively for thousands of years. Especially with the maritime expansion of Europe starting five centuries ago, this process of interbreeding has greatly accelerated, thereby blurring 'racial' boundaries, and contributing more than ever to the genetic homogenization of our species.

A second usage of 'race' is as a synonym for species, as in the phrase 'the human race'. That usage is often deliberately antithetical to the first one, when the stress is put on the unity of mankind (or 'humankind' as feminists would have us say).

A third meaning of 'race' is as a synonym for what we usually call a nation or an ethnic group, as, for example, 'the French race' or 'the German race'. This third usage has become obsolete, but it was common in the nineteenth and early twentieth centuries.

Finally, a 'race' can mean a group of people who are *socially* defined in a given society as belonging together because of *physical markers* such as skin pigmentation, hair texture, facial features, stature, and the like. To avoid the confusion, some people specify 'social race' when they use 'race' in this fourth meaning. Nearly all social scientists *only* use 'race' in this fourth sense of a *social* group defined by somatic visibility. It is important to stress here that any resemblance with the first usage is little more than coincidental. For example, 'blacks' in South Africa and in Australia, although they occupy somewhat similar *social* positions in their respective societies, are no more closely related genetically to each other than each of them is to the 'whites'. Even where there is some shared ancestry in broad parental stocks (as, for instance, between the Afro-American populations of Brazil and the United States, both of which came predominantly from West Africa and interbred with Europeans), the same social label may cover very different blends of ancestry. In Brazil, a 'black' is a person of predominantly African ancestry, while, in the United States, the term often refers to persons of predominantly European stock who would be called 'white' in Brazil.

The significance of racial labels is thus purely a function of the specific content attached to racial terms at a particular time and place. Social races are *not* genetically bounded subspecies. In fact, members of different social races are frequently close kin of each other in many multiracial societies, particularly those with a history of slavery.

It is also important to note that not all societies recognize social races. In fact, the great majority of human societies have not used physical phenotypes as the basis of group distinctions. Where social races exist, there is invariably an attribution of social and behavioural importance to physical markers. Societies that recognize social races are invariably *racist* societies, in the sense that people, especially members of the dominant racial group, believe that physical phenotype is linked with intellectual, moral, and behavioural characteristics. Race and racism thus go hand in hand.

Read:

The Idea of Race, by Michael Banton (Tavistock, 1977), a thorough investigation of the development of western racism.

Race and Racism, by Pierre L. van den Berghe (Wiley, 1978), a comparison of four societies (Brazil, Mexico, South Africa, and the United States), attributing different degrees of importance to 'race'.

See *Apartheid; Eugenics; Phenotype; Pluralism; Race: perspective one; Race relations; Racism; UNESCO statements on race*

Pierre L. van den Berghe

Race relations: perspective one A term used in academic writing and in the everyday world to refer to a particular category of social relations. There is an academic tradition which focuses upon these relations and this has come to be known as the sociology of 'race relations', a now distinctive and institutionalized subdiscipline within sociological analysis. However, within and outside that subdiscipline, there is a controversy about what characterizes this apparently distinct category of social relations, a controversy which arises from the recognition that *homo sapiens* is one species. The biological sciences take account of genetic variation, but this does not correspond to what, in the everyday world, is regarded as a difference of 'race', founded as it is on phenotypical variation. Hence, 'race relations' cannot be naturally occurring relations between discrete, biological groups but have come to be seen as relations between groups which employ the idea of 'race' in structuring their action and reaction to each other.

This latter notion of 'race relations' links together the pioneering work of Robert Park, John Dollard, Lloyd Warner, Gunnar Myrdal and Oliver C. Cox in the United States, all of whom were concerned in one way or another with 'race relations'. A large proportion of the work in the United States in the 1950s and 1960s refracted the new political definitions that arose out of the renewed struggle against racism and discrimination but agreed that 'race relations' were a real and distinct category of social relations. Hence, for them the idea of 'race' was employed with a new positive content as a collective characteristic of the Afro-American population, one which set it apart from the majority American population of European origin. But they agreed that the relations between these two defined groups were 'race relations'.

This American-derived conception influenced political, media and academic reaction to the labour migration from the New Commonwealth to Britain in the 1950s, although this reaction also drew upon that deep reservoir of imperialist thought about the inferior 'races' of the empire. The consequence was that 'race relations' 'appeared' within Britain in the 1950s, displaced as it were from the colonies or, more particularly, from Africa (especially the ill-fated Central African Federation). Most writers and commentators took this definition, and its history, for granted. Some academics went further and attempted to explicitly and analytically classify 'race relations', not only as a discrete category of social relations, but also as having a specific place within sociological theory. The project was defined as setting out the defining features of a 'race relations' situation and the classifying different types of such a situation.

RACE RELATIONS: PERSPECTIVE ONE

The sociology of 'race relations' that has developed from these analytical concerns has been preoccupied with two main themes, first with assessing the extent and effects of racism and discrimination upon those who have been its object, and second with the political struggle against racism and discrimination. It is thereby a sociology of conflict which reflects everyday conceptions of what 'race relations' are, although it offers a quite different explanation for that conflict from that employed in the everyday world.

More recently, a new line of enquiry has developed which is critical of this tradition of work and which moves towards a rejection of 'race relations' as a legitimate form of study. This emerging position is firmly grounded in historical analysis of both the idea of 'race' and the academic study of relations between groups who utilize the idea of 'race' to organize their social relations. It is concluded from this analysis that because 'race' is no more than a socially constructed phenomenon, then so are relations between the groups that are constituted through this social construction. Consequently, there is nothing distinctive about the resulting relations between the groups party to such a social construction. Put another way, what are called 'race relations' are quantitatively no different from other forms of social relations.

There remains the problem of determining how such historically and socially constructed relations are, therefore, to be analysed. To this problem, one can currently distinguish two solutions. The first sees 'race and ethnic relations' as a subdivision of a sociology of intergroup relations. This is premised on the observations that a tradition of enquiry has been established and that any new development should be contained within the tradition established by earlier contributors. But, more significantly, it is argued that the circumstances under which individuals are ascribed, or ascribe themselves, to membership of a 'race' (together with the varied and various consequences of such ascription) warrant explanation in terms of a theory of intergroup relations. The second position, developed using marxist categories of analysis, claims that this process of social ascription should be analysed as an ideological and political process and, for that reason, it cannot employ everyday conceptions of 'race' and 'race relations' as either descriptive or analytical categories. This leads to the conclusion that there can be no theory of race relations because this only serves to reify what is a historically specific political and ideological process.

Read:

Race Relations in Sociological Theory by John Rex (Weidenfeld & Nicolson, 1970), for an analysis which claims a theoretical status for the sociological analysis of race relations.

'Analytical and folk concepts of race and ethnicity' by Michael Banton in *Ethnic and Racial Studies* (1979, vol. 2, No. 2, pp. 127–38), for a critical reflection on what counts as the subject matter of race relations studies, but which continues to assert the need for a theory of 'race (and ethnic) relations'.

Racism and Migrant Labour by R. Miles (Routledge & Kegan Paul, 1982), for an elaboration of the latter critique but within a marxist frame of reference which concludes that the analytical task is not to develop a theory of 'race relations' but to explain, historically, why certain forms of social relations are racialized.

See *Race: perspective two; Racism; Racialization; UNESCO statements on race*

Robert Miles

Race relations: perspective two An alternative approach is the one advocated in *Introduction to Race Relations* where it is argued that the term race relations can and, indeed, must be applied to a specific form of social relationship. This approach fully recognizes and endorses the hollowness of the concept of race itself, but, at the same time, insists that, in many situations, people believe in the existence of race and so organize their relationships with others on the basis of that belief. In other words, people fashion their relationships with others on the basis of what they believe about those others. If they believe those others belong to a group that is genetically and permanently different (and possibly inferior in some respect) then we have a situation of race relations. And this is the object of enquiry.

The exact nature of race is not at issue, though, in *Introduction*, the biological conception is refuted and evidence to support this refutation is offered. The point is, however, that people, rightly or wrongly, accept it as a reality and so act in accordance with their belief. This makes race subjectively real: no matter how offensive we may find race and how unimpressed we are by the (largely spurious) scientific research on it, it remains a powerful motivating force behind people's thoughts and behaviour. It is as real as people want it to be and cannot simply be wished away. Recognition of this is the starting point of the study of race relations in this perspective.

This allows for the acceptance of Michael Banton's advice that 'the student who wishes to understand the nature of the field of race relations study . . . should approach it from the standpoint of the growth of knowledge.' Believing in race is tantamount to holding a form of knowledge (even if that knowledge is built on uncertain foundations). This in no way denies the huge influences on race relations which lie outside people's minds and quite beyond their control. In fact, the approach stresses that the study of race relations should proceed at two levels: (1) to discover the reasons why people might believe others are so different, culturally or biologically; and (2) to find out how this belief effects their actions towards others – this usually takes the form of maintaining social (and often geographical) distance in the attempt to keep unequal relationships.

A narrow conception of this programme of study might locate the answer to these types of questions in the individual, suggesting for example why certain groups are prejudiced and examining how this has impact on their behaviour and relationships over a period of time. The classic study in this vein is *The Authoritarian Personality* by Theodor Adorno and his colleagues (which is covered elsewhere in this book). The preferred approach would be much wider in scope, seeking to integrate historical analyses of the colonial conditions underlying most contemporary race relations situations with an examination of how capitalist economies mediate these situations. The capitalist system is seen to foster race relations situations. Certainly, in many instances, race relations situations are highly complementary to the perpetuation of capitalism (through, for example, widening divisions between black and white workers and thus undermining working-class solidarity). But, it is proposed that this does not prove that race relations cannot exist independently of capitalism; so there is a very close, but not direct, relationship between the two. The present form racism takes and the form it has taken in recent history does indicate that it is intimately related to the development of modern capitalism.

There are many historical and modern processes crucially affecting what people believe and often, therefore, what they do, so it is necessary to analyse those processes as carefully as possible rather than simply at the level of the individual (or group) doing the believing, or, at the other extreme, the capitalist system seeming to generate the race divisions.

The effects that these processes have on individual and group behaviour is also central to the study of race relations: it should not only be a historical-analytical discipline, but also an empirical one. Race relations situations are not a perfectly defined series of events, but rather an evolving complex. A mature race relations study should be able to incorporate the investigation of changing events and interpret these in the context of historical, political and social conditions. In this way, it is possible to acknowledge that race as a concept is analytically redundant, yet still identify race relations situations as the focus of study.

Read:

Introduction to Race Relations by E. Cashmore and B. Troyna (Routledge & Kegan Paul, 1983), an elaborated version of this approach to the study of race relations which argues strongly for the retention of this distinct area of study.

Statement on Race by Ashley Montagu (Oxford University Press, 1972), a summary of the scientific research on the subject of race.

Report on the Experts' Meeting on Racism and Race Prejudice (UNESCO, Paris, 1967), the statement which rejected the concept of race as having any values for scientific purposes.

See *Colonialism; Prejudice; Race: perspective one; Racism; Slavery*

Ellis Cashmore
Barry Troyna

Racialization A term which has emerged in analysis in the 1970s to refer to a political and ideological process by which particular populations are identified by direct or indirect reference to their real or imagined phenotypical characteristics in such a way as to suggest that the population can only be understood as a supposedly biological unity. This process usually involved the direct utilization of the idea of 'race' to describe or refer to the population in question.

The use and meaning of the term emerges from historical analysis. This work demonstrates that the idea of 'race' is not a universal idea, but, rather, emerges at a particular point in western European history, and, over time, comes to be used to refer to supposedly fixed and discrete biological categories of the world's population. This shows that 'race' is not a biological fact but a social construction. The first use of the notion of racialization arose in the course of establishing these claims and was used to refer specifically to the development of the idea of 'race', first in historical writing and, later, in European 'scientific' writing of the late eighteenth and nineteenth centuries.

The term's usage has been developed and widened in time with the fact that the process of identifying particular populations as 'races' is not confined to the level of 'intellectual' activity. By a process not yet adequately understood and analysed, this social construction of 'race' was passed down to the level of everyday categorization and action. In recognition of this, the notion of racialization has been used in a broader sense to refer to any process or situation wherein the idea of 'race' is introduced to define and give meaning to some particular population, its characteristics and actions. Hence, the fact that the public and political reaction to the Irish migration and presence in Britain in the nineteenth century employed the idea of 'race' to refer to the Irish can be understood, analytically, as an instance of racialization. Similarly, when the political and ideological consequences of New Commonwealth migration to Britain in the 1950s began to be defined by politicians by reference to the idea of 'race', one can refer to this process as the racialization of British politics.

In the narrower usage, the ideological content of the process of racialization will warrant description as racism, or more specifically, scientific racism. In the wider usage, referring in addition to the attribution of social significance and meaning to phenotypical/genetic variation in all dimensions of social life, the ideological content of the identified process is not necessarily racist. Before that can be determined, it is necessary to analyse the content of the attributed significance and the populations party to the attribution (both object and subject). In this way we can take account of the fact that those who have historically been the 'victims' of racialization may employ the idea of 'race' in turn to refer to those who so label them without necessarily concluding that their response is racist in content. This, therefore, requires that the concepts of racism and racialization be kept analytically distinct.

Read:

The Idea of Race by Michael Banton (Tavistock 1967), for one of the first uses of the term to refer to historical and scientific writing in the eighteenth and nineteenth centuries.

Racism and Migrant Labour by Robert Miles (Routledge & Kegan Paul, 1982), for an example of the utilization of the term in a wider sense.

See *Ideology; Race; Race relations; Racism*

Robert Miles

Racialism A term more evident in everyday discourse than in academic analysis. Where used in the latter, it is rarely explicitly defined, but tends to be used to denote the practices which embody or express racism. These practices are more commonly referred to by the concept of racial discrimination.

See *Racism*

Robert Miles

Racism A word used in several senses. Up to the late 1960s most dictionaries and textbooks defined it as a doctrine, dogma, ideology or set of beliefs. The core element in this doctrine was that 'race' determined culture, and from this were derived claims to racial superiority. In the 1960s the word was used in an expanded sense to incorporate practices and attitudes as well as beliefs and in this sense racism denotes the whole complex of factors which produce racial discrimination, and sometimes, more loosely, designates also those which produce racial disadvantage. Early in 1983, the Greater London Council announced plans 'to tackle the problems of racism and racial disadvantage in the capital' including the declaration of London as 'an Anti-Racist Zone'.

A third usage is to be found in some academic writing. It is said that the expansion of capitalism in the New World required the exploitative use of African labour. This could be achieved more effectively if black labour could be treated simply as a commodity, so a whole complex was created to facilitate this. Beliefs about black inferiority can be adequately understood only as part of a new historical creation which in subsequent centuries has been modified as the economic structure has changed. Racism is the name for this historical complex.

There is no reason why the word racism should not be used in different senses for different purposes. Within sociology, however, it is certain that there will continue to be at least two kinds of definition corresponding to two contrasting theories of knowledge. Those writers who stand within the Kantian philosophical tradition believe their definitions have to be elaborated by the observer in the attempt to formulate theories that will explain as many observations as possible. Those writers who stand within the Hegelian tradition believe that the observer is part of the world which he studies. The observer has to understand the principles underlying the development of the world and first work out definitions which grasp the essence of historical relationships.

The implications of this distinction can be better appreciated if the definition of racism is compared with that of antisemitism. Social scientists who use a Kantian epistemology will start from common elements in the prejudice against black people and Jews. Those who use a Hegelian epistemology may, like Oliver C. Cox, assert that racism and antisemitism are different phenomena serving different functions in the social system (although it should be noted that not all who write within this epistemology would accept a functionalist analysis). The same opposition of views can be seen in discussions of the attitudes and practices of minority groups. Writers in the first tradition can point to evidence of what they define as racial prejudice expressed by black people just as much as by white, and may call it racism. In Britain, for example, Afro-Caribbeans and Asians can speak as harshly about one another as white people speak about them. For writers in the second tradition, the ideological reaction of those subject to ('white') racism cannot be immediately so defined, not only because of differences in ideological content, but also because explanatory significance is attached to the structural position of the respective groups. From this perspective, hostility between Afro-Caribbeans and Asians will be traced to their historical experience within British imperialism and/or to conflicts arising out of their structural positions within Britain. It is in the context of such an analysis that the ideological content of hostility will be assessed to ascertain whether it can be considered racist.

In recent years, the word has been used in so many ways that there is a danger of its losing any value as a concept. How restricted a definition is to be preferred? Some writers have wished to limit its use to refer to an ideology tied to the development of racial thought in western Europe. The observation that it was only in the nineteenth century that the idea of 'race' came to mean a typological classification of the human species (one which asserted that biological characteristics determined cultural and psychological characteristics) has suggested to them that racism be the name for identifying the doctrine which was first advanced in the mid-nineteenth century and which claimed scientific status. As a concept, therefore, racism would distinguish those claims and arguments which explicitly assert that people's biological characteristics are signs of their cultural and psychological characteristics. Since 1945, such claims have been increasingly less common, from which it has been concluded that the expression of racism is declining. Some writers prefer to name this body of arguments scientific racism, while others call them racial typology.

From another direction, it is maintained that the examination of the content of the ideological form which is called racism should be subordinated to consideration of its structure. While biological arguments are less frequently advanced, new ones have taken their place which justify by other means the unequal treatment of the same groups of people. Hence, it is argued that what distinguishes racism as an ideology is that it asserts a deterministic relationship between a group and supposed characteristics of that group. Such a definition of racism broadens its application, but to the point where its generality renders it analytically meaningless. The ideological process of deterministic attribution of characteristics to particular groups is widespread, with many different types of group being its object. For example, the exclusion of women from a wide range of activities is often justified by the deterministic attribution of such supposed characteristics as physical weakness, emotionalism and irrationalism. A definition of racism which refers solely to the structural features of the ideological process must encompass such claims, thus denying any possibility of distinguishing between racism and sexism.

The deterministic ascription of real or supposed negative characteristics to a particular group is generally seen as a central characteristic of racism as ideology. This constitutes common ground for the present authors. However, one of us (MB) believes that what he sees as racial relations can be analysed quite adequately without employing any concept of racism, provided that there is some way of identifying the nineteenth-century theories that 'race' determines culture. The other (RM) wishes to continue to employ the term, but with a specific meaning. Thus, it is the attribution of social significance (meaning) to particular patterns of phenotypical and/or genetic difference which, along with the characteristic of additional deterministic ascription of real or supposed other characteristics to a group constituted by descent, is the defining feature of racism as an ideology. But, additionally, those characteristics must, in turn, be negatively evaluated and/or be designated as the reason to justify unequal treatment of the defined group.

This definition of racism does not presuppose or reify the (real or attributed) biological characteristics which become the identifying feature of the group which is the object of racism. Thus, racism is not an ideology which only has 'black' people as its object. This allows us to take account of the observation that, for example, Jewish and Irish people have been the object of racist ideology because they have been identified by reference to real or supposed biological characteristics and, additionally, have been negatively evaluated and treated. It is also a definition which specifically allows for the way that racism takes different empirical forms in different societies at different points in time. It encourages an historical analysis of the emergence of sets of meanings and evaluations about particular populations in conjunction with the expansion of economic and political activity of European merchants (and, later, European capitalists) and of the changes in those meanings and evaluations in relation to changes in the nature and activity of capitalism based in western Europe and North America. However, the specific relationship between the generation and reproduction of racism and the development of capitalism, dependent as it was upon imperialism, remains the object of a continuing debate.

There is little likelihood that the intellectual gulf between the two philosophical traditions will be bridged in the present generation since they generate different criteria for the definition of racism (and for other concepts too). Each has its attractions and weaknesses. Scholarly progress will be assisted if those who write about these matters appreciate the nature of the gulf and different concepts and empirical emphases that are thereby generated.

Read:

The Idea of Race, by Michael Banton (Tavistock, 1977), for a historical account of the development and influence of the theory of racial typology (scientific racism) and for an analysis of some of the conceptual problems.

Racism and Migrant Labour, by Robert Miles (Routledge & Kegan Paul, 1982), for a more general overview of the conceptual problems surrounding particular definitions of racism and for an attempt at a resolution of some of the difficulties within a marxist frame of reference.

Portraits of White Racism, by David Wellman (Cambridge University Press, 1977), for an example of a text which proposes a much wider definition of racism, one which refers to structural subordination of particular groups of people. It is a good example of a definition of racism which is so wide that it loses analytical precision.

A Dangerous Place, by D.P. Moynihan (New York, 1975; London, Secker & Warburg, 1979), discusses the use of 'racism' in resolutions at the United Nations.

See *Institutional racism; Race; Race relations; Racialization*

Michael Banton
Robert Miles

Rampton/Swann committee The UK's national policy vacuum on race-related matters in education has often been adduced as the most significant of the factors inhibiting the development of multiracial education. According to this line of argument, Local Education authorities and their individual schools have been reluctant to initiate programmes and practices along multiracial lines in the continued absence of a coherent policy and directives from the Department of Education and Science (DES).

Against this background, the publication of the interim report of the committee of enquiry into the education of children from ethnic minority groups had been eagerly awaited. The enquiry had been established by the Labour government in March 1979, although the subsequent general election meant that the committee members were selected by the Conservative Secretary of State for Education, Mark Carlisle. The initial function of the committee, according to its terms of reference, was to give 'attention to the educational needs and attainments of pupils of West Indian origin' and to present government with 'definite and positive recommendations'. Carlisle made it clear to the Chairman of the Committee, Anthony Rampton, however, that any recommendations which called into question the existing educational structure or which involved increased government spending would be routinely dismissed. The imposition of such constraints, the social, political and ethnic composition of the committee and its chairman, and the ideological framework in which it functioned did nothing to undermine claims from radical critics of the enquiry that it was, to all intents and purposes, a public relations exercise designed mainly to appease the anxieties of black parents. At the same time, however, many educationists saw the impending report as a means to an end: a document which would precipitate the development of multiracial education both at central and local government level.

But, as John Rex has argued, the most significant point about the report was not its content but 'the whole political drama' which surrounded its publication in June 1981. Not long before the interim report was published, Rampton had been asked to resign as chairman by the Secretary of State and was replaced by Lord Swann, Provost of Oriel College, Oxford. The reason? Administrative incompetence, although it was more commonly assumed that Carlisle had been annoyed about Rampton's inability to prevent the black militant committee members from identifying racism as the pre-eminent cause of black 'underachievement'.

However, as Rex points out, the facts simply do not support this interpretation. First, none of the black members could legitimately be described as militant, however broadly that term might be defined. All had been drawn from the higher echelons of their respective professions. Second, if the thrust and content of the report had been determined solely by this caucus of black militants, then it is unlikely that they would have permitted the title, 'West Indian

Children in *Our* Schools' (emphasis added), a deeply insensitive and Anglocentric title which offended many black and white people. Finally, while the Rampton Report did recognize racism in schools as a cause of black 'underachievement' this constituted only one of the ten contributory factors they pinpointed. At least as much space was devoted to what was popularly referred to as 'pathological' conceptions of underachievement: poor family background, lack of parental support and understanding, and so on.

The report also suffered from a lack of sophisticated or persuasive use of empirical data. For instance, claims that black pupils were 'underachieving' in relation to white and South Asian children were based on an impoverished analysis of data taken from the DES. On the face of it, these data did reveal stark differences in the performance of black, white and South Asian pupils in public examinations. What they failed to take into account, however, was the class and educational background of the pupils' parents. It has since been argued that if these variables had been considered they would have shown that class background rather than ethnic background exerted the most important influence on performance. In other words, looked at from a class perspective, black pupils are performing no better or worse than other pupils of the same (working) class background.

Nor did the report lead to the implementation of policy by central government. Despite the number of recommendations directed at the DES, the response of the Department had been little less than dismissive: it simply circulated the report, without comment, to Local Education Authorities and, organized a one-day conference!

The final report of the Swann Committee was published in the summer of 1983. Its theme was: the education of pupils of south Asian origin. The controversy and disquiet aroused by the interim report, however, undermined the credibility of the Swann Committee. It was generally accepted, then, that neither report would be able to facilitate, let alone ensure, any significant improvement in the education of minority groups in the UK.

Read:

'Culture clashes' by John Rex in *Times Educational Supplement*, (7 August 1981), a detailed account of the superficiality of the

'Rampton Report' and an agenda of issues to be considered in the subsequent enquiry chaired by Lord Swann.

'The "underachievement" of Rampton' by Frank Reeves and Mel Chevannes in *Multiracial Education* (vol. 10, no. 1, 1981), re-analyses the data along class lines which had been adduced by the committee as evidence of the differentially lower academic performance of black pupils.

'Multiracial education and the politics of decision-making' by Andrew Dorn and Barry Troyna in *Oxford Review of Education* (vol. 8, no. 2, 1982), argues that the national policy vacuum on multicultural education constitutes an explicit ideological position by the DES.

See *Institutional racism; Multiracial education; Underachievement*

Barry Troyna

Rastafarian movement Arguably the fastest-growing black movement of the 1970s/80s, it first appeared in Jamaica in 1930 just after the decline in fortunes of the leader Marcus Garvey, who organized his Universal Negro Improvement Association around the ambition to return to Africa. 'Africa for the Africans' was Garvey's basic philosophy and he worked at mass migration programmes, buying steamship lines and negotiating with African governments.

Garvey had some success in the West Indies (he was born in Jamaica), but was more influential after his demise, for he was reputed to have prophesied: 'Look to Africa when a black king shall be crowned, for the day of deliverance is near.' Around this prediction a whole movement was mobilized. In 1930, Ras Tafari was crowned Emperor of Ethiopia and took his official title of Haile Selassie I. Garvey, at this stage, had slipped from prominence, but at least some black Jamaicans remembered his prophecy and made the connection between 'the black king' – Haile Selassie – and 'the day of deliverance' – the return to Africa. The connection was reinforced by a new element added by new adherents of Garvey. They made the conclusion that Haile Selassie was not just a king but also their God and Messiah who would miraculously organize a black exodus to Africa (used synonymously with Ethiopia) and simultaneously dissolve the imperial domination of western powers – 'Babylon' to the new Garveyites.

It's worth noting that in no way did Garvey endorse this new interpretation of his philosophy. Indeed, he assailed

Haile Selassie as 'a great coward' and 'the leader of a country where blackmen are chained and flogged'. Further, Garvey insisted on practical organization and de-emphasized the value of spiritual salvation; his new followers went in the other direction, making no provision for returning to Africa, simply awaiting the intervention of their Messiah, Ras Tafari.

However, what Garvey actually said was less important that what he was reputed to have said and, quickly, the new movement gained followers amongst the socially deprived black Jamaicans, hopeful of any kind of change in their impoverished lives and willing to cling to the flimsiest of theories of how they might escape their condition. They adopted the Garvey movement's colours of red, black and green (from the Ethiopian flag) and twisted their hair into long matted coils called dreadlocks as if to exaggerate their primitiveness in contrast to western appearances. Some made use of ganja, a type of cannabis found in Jamaica, and even endowed this 'weed' with religious properties. They used it in ritual worship of *Jah* (the form of 'Jehovah' used in bibles before the King James version). Many took to the hilly inner regions of the island and set up their own communes, one celebrated one being led by Leonard Howell, who, with Joseph Hibbert and H. Archibald Dunkley, is popularly attributed as one of the original formulators of the new Garveyism.

Garvey remained a reluctant prophet, though a careful reading of his speeches and published comments reveals his great interest in Ethiopian royalty and his repeated use of biblical, often apocalyptic, imagery to strengthen his beliefs. 'We Negroes believe in the God of Ethiopia, the everlasting God,' wrote Garvey in volume one of his *Philosophy and Opinions*. His conception of a black god was also significant; he implored his followers to destroy pictures of white Christs and Madonnas and replace them with black versions. 'No one knows when the hour of Africa's Redemption cometh,' he once warned his followers. 'It is in the wind – It is coming. One day like a storm, it will be here.'

Periodically, the Rastas, as they came to be called, gathered at ports to await the ships to take them to Africa and, at one stage, a faction of the movement resorted to guerrilla tactics in a vain effort to assist the destruction of Babylon. More recently, the movement in Jamaica has gained a more respectable status and, nowadays, has become a vital cultural force on the island.

In the middle of the 1970s, the Rastafarian movement manifested itself in such places as the USA, England, Holland, France, New Zealand and Australia. Its growth was stimulated by the rise in popularity of Rasta-inspired reggae music which was given a personal focus by the almost prototype Rasta Bob Marley (1945–1981). It seems that the vision of a united African continent and a black god was a potent one. It was used in sharp counterposition to the imperial dominance of the west. Blacks feeling disaffected with society and searching for alternatives found in the movement a new force which upgraded blackness and instilled in them a sense of identity belonging to unity.

Despite an infinite variation in interpretation of Garvey's philosophy, two themes remained central to Rastafarian beliefs: the divinity of Haile Selassie (whose death in 1975 did little to dissuade Rastas of his potency in instigating the transformation) and the impulse to return to Africa – if not physically then in consciousness (as the Rasta reggae musician, Peter Tosh, sang: 'Don't care where you come from, as long as you're a black man, you're an African').

Read:

Rastaman by E. Cashmore (Unwin Paperbacks, 1983), a study of the English movement based on two years' research, but with chapters on the Jamaican Rastas.

The Rastafarians by Leonard Barrett (Heinemann, 1977), an account of the movement in Jamaica up to the late 1970s with interesting observations on the new Rastas who came from the middle class.

Rastas! by E. Cashmore (Minority Rights Group, 1984) is the most recent statement on the history and present condition of the movement and its role in changing the consciousness of young blacks.

See *Africa; Ethiopianism; Garvey; Nation of Islam; Negritude; Reggae*

Ellis Cashmore

Reggae Probably the most influential musical form to emerge since the 1950s, reggae transcended conventional barriers by being both a reflection of the inequality and impoverishment of blacks and a catalyst of a new political consciousness amongst blacks. Reggae was the music of the Rastas and was pivotal in the growth of the Rastafarian movement in such places as the USA, Canada, England and Europe. Thus the music of reggae has been inspiration to tens of thousands of blacks in the 1970s and 1980s.

Essentially a music of protest, reggae fused several different elements of popular music in Jamaica where it originated. Indeed, Sebastian Clarke has traced its origins way back to the hybrid music that was born out of slave days. But, it seems that the significant stage in the development of reggae was in the 1950s when the sound of black American rhythm and blues and soul music filtered across to the Caribbean via radio stations and West Indians who migrated temporarily to the United States to look for work. Early attempts to imitate the American music foundered, but inadvertently gave rise to a unique style which came to be called 'blue beat' and, later, 'ska'. This was popularized in the West Indies, particularly in Jamaica, by peripatetic disc jockeys who operated a 'sound system'. The DJs stamped their own identity on the music by 'dubbing' over the music, literally speaking into the microphone while the records were playing, in efforts to urge the dancers; this became known as 'toasting' and many DJs established more prestigious reputations than the musicians they dubbed over.

In the 1960s, ska was introduced into the UK and was received enthusiastically by sections of white youth without ever growing into a popular music. Occasionally, ska records would become commercial successes, 'Long shot kick the bucket,' and 'The return of Django' being examples.

Late in the 1960s, however, ska underwent mutations and the flavour of its lyrics became altogether more political. Musicians, either adhering to or being sympathetic with Rastafarian ideals, began expressing statements on the condition of black people through their music. The themes of the music included exploitation, poverty, inequality, liberation and the critical experience of 'suffering'. They were articulated through Rastafarian imagery, the system of control being Babylon, as contrasted with the liberty of Zion. Predictions of 'war in a Babylon' and 'Catch a Fire, the wheel will turn, slavedriver you gonna get burn' were incorporated into the music.

Without doubt, the most popular contemporary musician of this *genre* was Bob Marley (1945–81) who presented the image of the archetypal Rastaman. Marley provided a personal focus for reggae and, with his band the Wailers, elevated reggae to a musical and social force. His tours of the UK and USA, brought recognition not only for him, but for his ideals. Although he didn't claim any divine status, Marley was identified as someone akin to a prophet by many black youths who structured their own lives around his and immersed themselves in the Rastafarian movement.

The popularity of reggae in general and Marley in particular spread to the third world and reggae became an instrument for stimulating new perspectives on the conditions besetting all black peoples. Many British-based bands such as Aswad and Steel Pulse gained recognition through their own self-styled reggae based on the Jamaican original. More recently, reggae has been divided into variants such as dub, heavy reggae and lovers' rock.

Its importance parallels that of American blues in conveying the messages of despair and despondency of blacks. But, more than this, reggae actually forced a recognition of these issues and prompted a new response to them. Reggae was a necessary condition for the rapid growth of the Rastafarian movement in the 1970s and was, therefore, vital to the emergence of the type of critical consciousness that proliferated amongst urban black youth, particularly in the UK.

Read:

Jah Music by Sebastian Clarke (Heinemann, 1980), easily the most thorough and carefully researched account of the historical development of reggae.

Catch a Fire by Timothy White (Elm Tree Books, 1983), the best and most comprehensive biography of Bob Marley based on interviews with Marley and members of an 'inner circle' of friends in a seven-year period before the artist's death in 1981; chronicles Marley's childhood and early involvement with reggae and shows how he was promoted to the position of 'superstar' in the 1970s; also contains full 'discography' of Marley, the Wailers and his backing singers, the I Threes.

'Differential commitment to ethnic identity by black youths in Britain' by Barry Troyna in *New Community* (vol. 7, no. 3, 1979), a study of the various ways in which black schoolchildren responded to the affects of reggae in the 1970s.

See *Blues; Ethiopianism; Rastafarian movement*

Ellis Cashmore

Riots: UK, 1981 The term 'race riot' was used in both popular and political discourse to describe and define the wave of violent disturbances which erupted first in Brixton, London, in April 1981 and subsequently in a range of the UK's other major cities during the 'long, hot summer' of that year. The typification of these incidents as 'race riots' not only helped to shape ensuing political debate on the matter but also helped to determine the nature of subsequent policy interventions.

In fact, careful scrutiny of what took place at Brixton, Southall, Toxteth, Moss Side, and elsewhere in 1981 reveals that 'race riot' is a wholly inappropriate mode of classification: not only is it a factually incorrect description, it also denudes the incidents of any political complexion and the participants of any political edge to their protest.

Of the various and often disparate violent episodes of 1981 only the confrontation in the Southall district of London could be labelled legitimately as 'racial' insofar as the clashes were primarily between white youth, on the one hand, and the young local Asian residents, on the other. A concert in a local public house by the 4-Skins – a group which constantly made reference to Nazi slogans – had attracted a large following of Skinhead youths into the district; a contingent of this group abused an Asian shopkeeper, smashed a few windows and had set off down the main street of Southall intent on more malicious damage. Local Asian youth reacted strongly and despite (or because of) police intervention; the scene outside the concert venue degenerated into a battle. Molotov cocktails were thrown and the public house was eventually petrol-bombed and gutted.

The violence which had erupted three months earlier in Brixton and which was soon to engulf Toxteth, Moss Side, and other districts was of an entirely different nature. Here, hostilities were directed, first and foremost, at the police and like the Watts outbreak in Los Angeles in 1965, were precipitated largely by what the residents perceived as racial harassment and intimidation by police officers. What is more, though these disturbances took place in districts containing relatively large black populations, they were not simply black youth v. police confrontations; a substantial number of white youngsters participated. In fact, of the 3,074 people arrested during the disturbances, over 2,400 were white, according to Home Office figures.

Historically, and in its current usage, the term 'riot' popularly connotes an image of widespread mindless violence, perpetrated by people who are intent, purely and simply, on creating havoc and inflicting malicious damage on people and property. What came to be called the 'burnin' and lootin' ' episodes of 1981 were presented via media and political debate largely in these terms. Indeed, the media assumed a major role in this process of 'depoliticizing' the incidents; first, by including under the riot heading a whole series of events which on other occasions might never have been reported or which would simply have been recorded as normal crime. The media were also accused of producing a 'copycat effect'; by showing graphic and dramatic scenes of the Brixton disturbances, the media were said to have encouraged youths in other parts of the country to imitate their Brixton counterparts. This interpretation of the 'burnin' and lootin' ' episodes was in part supported by Lord Scarman in his official report. But, there is no evidence to sustain this view, nor does it explain why the youths in Toxteth, Moss Side and elsewhere waited almost three months after the Brixton disturbances before deciding to imitate those scenes. Most importantly, however, the 'copycat' interpretation plays a significant ideological role in undermining the notion that the disturbances were inspired by real and substantive political grievances. As one youth in Handsworth, Birmingham, explained: 'We're fighting for our rights – against the police – it's not copycat.'

If the disturbances were neither 'race riots' nor 'copycat riots' but forms of protest against specific conditions, one has to establish what these conditions actually were. Clearly, the dramatic rise in unemployment, especially among the young, locally and nationally constituted one of the most significant of the underlying causes. Though as the studies of the 'burn, baby, burn' incidents in the USA revealed, unemployment does not directly and inevitably provoke social unrest. What is more, unemployment levels in parts of Scotland and the northeast of England exceeded those in Brixton, Toxteth and Moss Side but were not scenes of disorder.

When they took to the streets, the youths made it clear that their hostility was directed towards the police: in all the major districts affected in 1981, relations between the police and the local community had reached a low ebb; mutual distrust, suspicion and resentment characterized this relationship. On the one hand, the communities insisted they were maltreated by the police, subjected to racial harassment and to an intensification of police control such as the Swamp 81 exercise in Brixton in which the Metropolitan Police had saturated the district with extra police, including the Special Patrol Group. The police, on the other hand, justified these modes of action by pointing to the disproportionately high crime rates in Brixton and other multiracial areas.

The characterization of the Brixton and July 1981 episodes as 'riots' ensured that the thrust of political debate and policy prescriptions would be firmly within a 'law and order' framework. The imperative for action, in other words, has been to ensure that there is no repetition. An intensification of policing in the affected areas and more generally, a broadening of police powers have been the most significant of the subsequent initiatives. But, while the incidents of 1981 may have included some wanton acts of destruction and thieving, the participants in general were remarkably selective in their choice of targets. To have responded to these episodes purely and simply in terms of a law and order crisis degrades and disparages the communities' sense of grievance. Worse still, it is myopic because it leaves untouched the underlying causes of these incidents and increases the possibility of further, perhaps even more severe, rebellions.

Read:

Uprising by Martin Kettle and Lucy Hodges (Pan, 1982), a detailed account of the 1981 disturbances which discusses the various explanations adduced and identifies policing as the main catalyst of what took place.

Race and Class (Special double issue, 'Rebellion and Repression' vol. 23, nos 2/3, 1982), presents an account of the disturbances with due regard to historical and contemporary factors.

Public Disorder by Simon Field and Peter Southgate (Home Office Research Study no. 72, 1982), comprises two reports: the first considers the 'burn, baby, burn' episodes in the USA and the relevance of the studies to the UK 1981 incidents. The second is a survey of the views and experiences of male residents in Handsworth, Birmingham – scene of one of the 1981 disturbances.

RIOTS: USA, 1965–67

See *Kerner Report; Media and race relations; Police and race relations; Riots (USA); Scarman Report; Skinheads*

Barry Troyna

Riots: USA, 1965–67 The south Los Angeles area contains the largest concentration of blacks in the city. It includes the district called Watts. On 11 August 1965, blacks took to the streets and for six days engaged in what became known as the 'Watts riots'. Some whites were attacked, but mostly the destruction was aimed at property: cars were overturned, stores were looted and buildings set afire. The watchword of the riots summed up the imperative: 'Burn, baby, burn.' The burning continued for two years, ravaging ghetto areas in such places as Detroit and New York City.

The actual incident that precipitated the Watts riots involved a white police officer's attempted arrest of a black youth (a similar episode started the Brixton riot, see above). More and more people became involved and police reinforcements were brought in. Five arrests were made before the police withdrew under a hail of stones from an angry mob. Instead of dispersing, the crowd grew and began assailing whites. Over the next few hours, there were periodic bursts of rockthrowing and gasoline bombing.

Then came a lull: police called in the National Guard and the situation seemed under control. This tactic, however, served to aggravate matters and the rioting escalated: buildings were burnt and looting was rife. 'One of the most ravaging outbursts of Blacks in the history of this nation,' is how Douglas Glasgow described the event. 'Their rage was directed at white society's structure, its repressive institutions and their symbols of exploitation in the ghetto: the chain stores, the oligopolies that control the distribution of goods; the lenders, those who hold the indebtedness of the ghetto bound; the absentee landlords; and the agents who control the underclass while safeguarding the rights of those who exploit it.'

One estimate placed the total number of participants as over 30,000 or 15 per cent of the adult black population of the area. Of the 3,927 people arrested, most were black, but only 556 were under eighteen, while 2,111 were over twenty-five; 602 were over forty. It was not a youth riot as such.

All manner of explanation was invoked to determine the

causes of the Watts riots; they ranged from the excessively warm weather (the 'long, hot summer theory') to the influence of outside agitators. Glasgow is probably the most plausible when he cites the conditions: 'Poverty, racial discrimination, long-term isolation from the broader society.' Added to this was the sense of frustration elicited by the failure of the civil rights movement to instigate any immediate, tangible changes after years of campaigning for social reform.

Clearly, there was a frustration that was not just confined to blacks in Los Angeles, but which existed throughout the USA; for over the next two years, similar outbursts occurred at other American cities. They reached a virtual climax in July 1967 when a Detroit vice squad conducted raids on gambling clubs frequented by blacks. There were several arrests (there is an uncanny parallel here with the incident in Bristol, England, in 1980 when police raided a café used by blacks; this sparked a mass disturbance with police eventually withdrawing to leave a virtual 'no go area'). By the following morning, some 200 blacks had gathered on the streets; a bottle hurled from the crowd smashed through the window of a leaving police car. The crowd grew to about 3,000 by 8.00 a.m. and the police mobilized for action. As in Watts, rocks were thrown and buildings were burnt, prompting a police withdrawal. Reports of gunfiring filtered back to the police, who, in midweek, when the initial outburst had died down, started a series of raids on residents' homes. Once more, the services of the National Guard were invoked. The efforts to restore order and re-establish control only exacerbated the situation and violence erupted again, so that by the end of the week, 7,200 people had been arrested. Forty-three people were killed, thirty or more by the police. Property damage exceeded 22 million dollars.

The middle 1960s were a period of severe black discontent. Rioting may not have been an effective method for overthrowing the social order, but it certainly enlisted the attention of the American population and forced the problems unique to blacks into public visibility. In this sense, the riots were spectacularly successful. As one observer put it: 'Reporters and cameramen rushed into the ghettoes; elected and appointed officials followed behind; sociologists and other scholars arrived shortly after. The

President established a riot commission; so did the governors.' That commission was to conclude that the cause of the riots lay in racism and the resulting poverty suffered by blacks, leading to their being undernourished, underpaid, badly clothed and poorly housed. The civil rights movement had complained about precisely these features of blacks' life, but it is arguable that the violent pressure of rioting in two years achieved more than ten years of peaceful protest.

Read:

The Black Underclass by Douglas Glasgow (Jossey-Bass, 1980), a reflective summary of the reasons behind and the aftermath of Watts and an appraisal of blacks in modern America.

Report of the National Advisory Commission on Civil Disorders (Kerner Report, 1968), with an introduction by Tom Whicker, the study document resulting from the investigation of the Watts riots.

'Violence and grievances: reflections on the 1960s riots' by Robert M. Fogelson in *Journal of Social Issues* (vol. 26, winter, 1970), an interesting perspective on the whole complex of events.

See *Black Power; Civil rights movement; Ghetto; Kerner Report; Media and race relations; Riots (UK, 1981)*

Ellis Cashmore

Riots: USA (Miami) 1980 The disorder that centered on the district of Liberty City signalled a slight variation on the pattern established by the urban disturbances of the 1960s. The earlier riots tended to be precipitated by blacks in response to what they perceived to be police provocation. Also, the violence was more frequently directed at property rather than persons. The grievances of blacks were about poverty and racialism, particularly that practised by the police.

Liberty City was slightly different. The first incident started in court. Four police officers who had been accused of beating to death a black Miami businessman were acquitted. Many suspected a miscarriage of justice with underlying racist themes. In addition to this, there was a feeling amongst blacks that the needs of migrant Cubans in the area were being given priority over their own.

Like the 1960s riots, conflict with the police proved to be a catalyst for violence, but, unlike the 1960s version, the violence was concentrated on white people. As one eyewitness, quoted by Leonard Broom, described it: ' . . . the anger is so intense, the feelings are so rampant now, that the attacks have been aimed at white people with intent to do great bodily harm to people.'

Whites were attacked as they walked the streets, they were dragged out of cars and chased through the city. Property was vandalized too, but the Liberty City riots were distinguished by the gross violence done to people. Eighteen people were killed and the cost of the destruction was put in hundreds of millions of dollars.

Read:

Sociology, 7th edition, by L. Broom, P. Selznick and D. Darroch (Harper & Row, 1981), has a chapter on 'Law and disorder' that compares the different modes of 'black riot' this century.

See *Ghetto; Kerner Report; Riots (UK, 1981; USA, 1965–7); Scarman Report*

Ellis Cashmore

S

Scapegoat The term originated in the Hebrew ritual described in the Book of Leviticus: 'Aaron shall lay both hands upon the head of the live goat, and confess over him all the iniquities of the children of Israel, and all their transgressions, even all their sins; and he shall put them on the head of the goat' (16:20–22). In other words, the sins of the people were symbolically transferred to the goat which was then let go into the wilderness taking with it the guilt of the people.

At a different level, a schoolgirl may be humiliated by a teacher at school; she can't hit back at the teacher, so she gets frustrated. When she gets home, she might take it out on her younger brother or sister, who is a more accessible target.

In race and ethnic relations, similar processes often take place: people shift the responsibilities for their misfortunes and frustrations on to other groups and those groups are usually visibly identifiable minorities, such as blacks, Orientals or Mexicans, who have little power. These groups can be singled out and attributed with blame for all manner of evil, whether unemployment, housing scarcity, or literally anything else.

Jews and blacks have been the most popular scapegoats in modern times; they have had to shoulder the blame for almost everything from the economic decline of whole societies to the escalation of crime rates. Political groups, like communists, and religious denominations, like Roman Catholics, have historically been used as convenient scapegoats. It is, of course, no accident that the scapegoated groups are invariably powerless; they can be blamed and picked on without the possibility that they might hit back and resist the attribution. Lynchings and pogroms were carried out against blacks and Jews, when it was reasonably certain that those groups didn't have the power to fight back with any effectiveness.

One important feature of the scapegoating process is the failure of the group doing the blaming to analyse fully the circumstances producing the apparent misfortunes. Economic decline, for example, may be caused by a complex of factors, some rather obscure and difficult to comprehend. Yet scapegoating removes the need to analyse: it provides readymade explanations; 'the blacks caused it' is simple and comprehensive – but wrong.

For the scapegoating to work best, there must be an available stereotype, so that the blame can be transferred with a minimum of ambiguity. If people have a fairly well-defined stereotyped conception of Asians as people who work too hard, make too much money and engage in less-than-conventional business dealings, then they have a convenient group to scapegoat. If there is widespread recognition that a great many Asians work in bad conditions for poor wages and are overcrowded in rundown homes, then this complicates the stereotype and makes the scapegoating more difficult – depending, of course, on what problems Asians are meant to be blamed for. The abiding rule seems to be not to analyse in any depth the group to be scapegoated.

A final point about the scapegoat should be borne in mind: the image of the group identified and blamed may be created anew for the purposes of scapegoating, but, more frequently, it exists as a stereotype in the popular imagination; the scapegoating adds new dimensions to the image.

Read:

The Nature of Prejudice by Gordon Allport (Addison-Wesley, 1954), an important, comprehensive textbook on the social psychological aspects of race relations, with a whole chapter on 'The choice of scapegoats'.

The Social Animal by Elliot Aronson (Freeman, 1980), a clear and well-illustrated textbook on social psychology with a chapter on 'prejudice'.

'The ultimate attribution error' by Thomas F. Pettigrew in *Readings About the Social Animal* (Freeman, 1981), designed to test some of Allport's theories about prejudice.

See *Discrimination; Prejudice; Racism; Stereotype*

Ellis Cashmore

Scarman Report Four days after the outbreak of violent disorders in Brixton, London, the Home Secretary, William Whitelaw, appointed the Right Honourable Lord Scarman to enquire into the causes of the disturbances and 'to report, with the power to make recommendations'. During the course of the enquiry, violence erupted in the streets of Toxteth, Southall, Moss Side and Handsworth (in July 1981) and in his subsequent report to parliament, Scarman made passing reference to these disorders, focusing particularly on the ways they shared with or differed from prevailing social and economic conditions in Brixton. Scarman also considered the claim that there had been an imitative, or 'copycat' element, to the July outbreaks, stimulated by media portrayals of the Brixton disorders.

The Scarman enquiry differed in at least two significant ways from its US counterpart, the Kerner Commission's report on the 'burn, baby, burn' disorders in the 1960s. First, the gathering of evidence by the US Commission was completed by a team of researchers; in the UK, this role was undertaken solely by Lord Scarman. The result: Scarman collected a less detailed and comprehensive account of the extent of racial disadvantage and the grievances of the black communities than his US counterparts. Second, Scarman presided over a quasi-judicial enquiry, established under Section 32 of the 1964 Police Act. The nature of the enquiry, then, enhanced already existing scepticism about its function and relevance and deterred a number of members of the black communities from submitting either oral or written evidence. This further underlined the contention that the report, published in November 1981, presented only a partial view of what actually happened.

Scarman's appraisal of the Brixton district highlighted the social and economic privations experienced by the local black and, though to a lesser extent, white communities. Poor-quality housing, the paucity of recreational and leisure facilities and the almost obscene levels of unemployment especially amongst black youngsters constituted some of the most important of the underlying causes of the disorders, wrote Scarman. But, the evidence received indicated unequivocally that oppressive – some might say repressive – policing procedures in the locality provided the spark which ignited the flames in April 1981. Scarman was extremely critical of the decision taken by the local police chief,

Commander Fairbairn, to inaugurate Swamp 81 on 6 April. The essence of the operation was to 'swamp' certain areas of the district with police officers who were empowered to stop and search suspected criminals. Despite the notoriously poor police-community relations in Brixton – especially in the Railton Road/Mayall Road area, the 'Front Line' as it is often called – the decision was taken independently of discussions with local community leaders. As Scarman pointed out: 'I am . . . certain that "Swamp 81" was a factor which contributed to the great increase in tension . . . in the days immediately preceding the disorders' (para 4.43).

Amongst the various criticisms of the police received by the enquiry – harassment, unimaginative/inflexible policing, overreactions, etc. – Scarman was informed that certain police officers were racists. With some circumspection, Scarman conceded that this might have been a legitimate appraisal of a small caucus of police officers in Brixton and elsewhere. He was insistent, however, in his denunciation of accusations that the police force, and the UK in general, were characterized by institutional racism (see paras 2.21 and 9.1). His remarks on this issue have subsequently attracted considerable and widespread dissent and, as David Mason has argued, are based on an inchoate understanding of this concept.

Scarman's tendency to divide policing into 'hard' and 'soft' methods and to advocate the latter – in the form of community policing, or putting 'bobbys back on the beat' – he also attracted criticisms, largely from within the police force. The argument here, then, is that 'soft' policing is not a cure-all for crime and is simply not appropriate for all circumstances. Others, outside of the police force, are also critical of community policing, though for distinctly different reasons: they argue that it is a more subtle, though no less invidious, form of ensuring repressive control over the communities.

The notion of 'police accountability' figures prominently in the report: 'Accountability' wrote Scarman, 'is, I have no doubt, the key to successful consultation and socially reponsive policing' (para. 5.57). His recommendation that accountability be statutory has met with little enthusiasm from most police forces, however, who maintain that it would undermine the operational independence of their forces. A contrast view is that policing can only take place, effectively, with the consent of the public; therefore, a new police act is necessary to provide the statutory framework for consultation at the local level.

Scarman's emphasis on the role of the police both in the context of the disorders and in general, was not surprising in view of the fact that the enquiry was set up under a section of the 1964 Police Act. He did, however, engage in wider questions of social policy both in the substantive sections of the report and in his subsequent recommendations. As he pointed out, issues such as housing, education, local community relations councils and the media, and their specific relation to the needs of ethnic minority communities, 'must be kept constantly in view if the social context in which the police operate is not to continue to breed the conditions of future disorder' (para. 6.42).

The Scarman enquiry was designed to function within a liberal-reformist framework; the aim was to identify those factors which precipitated the disorders in Brixton in April 1981 and elsewhere in the UK, three months later, and to recommend those policies and practices necessary to restabilize the foundations and structures of the society. Consequently, those who perceived the disorders as exercises in mindless violence, as a further indication of the erosion of traditional values and mores, criticized the report for its liberal orientation. On the other hand, those who viewed the disorders in terms of an uprising or rebellion against repressive state institutions and who advocate the eradication of those institutions, rejected the report as conservative, myopic and largely irrelevant. Either way, Scarman was bound to disappoint and antagonize – and he did!

Read:

The Brixton Disorders, 10–12 April 1981, by Lord Scarman (HMSO, Cmnd. 8427, 1981. Also published by Penguin, 1982).

Scarman and After, edited by John Benyon (Pergamon, 1984), a set of readings reflecting on the disturbances, the report and their aftermath.

Policing the Riots, edited by David Cowell, Trevor Jones and Jock Young (Junction Books, 1982), a series of essays by academics, politicians and libertarians which take issue with Scarman's analysis and recommendations.

See *Institutional racism; Kerner Report; Police and race relations; Politics and 'race'; Riots (UK and USA)*

Barry Troyna

Segregation Segregation in the field of race and ethnic relations means spatial separation between groups who share a common society. This separation can be *de facto* (as, for instance, school or residential segregation by race in US or British cities), or *de jure* (as with apartheid in South Africa, and many forms of racial separation in the US south until the 1950s). The degree of separation may also vary widely. It can range from attempts to create and maintain large racially or ethnically homogeneous territories, as in the 'Bantustan' policy of the South African government, to more symbolic segregation of contiguous facilities, like park benches, building entrances, drinking fountains, and toilets labelled by race, as once were prevalent in the US south and as are still common sights in South Africa. (In South Africa, this 'micro-segregation' is often labelled 'petty apartheid', as if all apartheid were not petty!)

A distinction is often made between voluntary and imposed segregation. Presumably, segregation imposed on a group from the outside is always invidious in intent, and, therefore, resented. However, some groups, especially small groups who want to maintain a distinct way of life incompatible with that of the dominant society, may wish to maintain a degree of voluntary self-segregation. Hassidic Jews in New York City, for instance, would find it very difficult to practise their strictly orthodox Judaism if they did not segregate themselves. Indeed, even in Israel, the ultra-orthodox segregate themselves by residence. Frequently, it is no simple matter to determine to what extent segregation is voluntary or imposed. Often, dominant groups claim that imposed segregation is voluntary. Some pariah groups find in segregation a measure of protection against hostility and discrimination even though that segregation may have been externally imposed. Thus, around 1968, there was a seeming shift in emphasis in the Afro-American leadership in the United States from integration to a measure of self-segregation.

Imposed segregation is only one form of racial or ethnic discrimination. Indeed, in pre-industrial societies, highly rigid and unequal relationships (as between master and slave or landowner and serf) can be maintained in the nearly total absence of segregation. Spacial, physical, and even emotional intimacy are not incompatible with a high measure of inequality and discrimination. In more traditional, paternalistic types of relationship, inequality is often symbolized through an etiquette of dominance and servility which permits physical intimacy without reducing gaping status differences. In industrial settings, however, the perpetuation of a rigid ethnic, racial, or caste hierarchy is often accompanied by some degree of segregation. Segregation in those plural societies with more 'competitive' types of race and ethnic relations is both a mechanism for the perpetuation of group inequality and a symbolic reminder thereof.

Read:

Patterns of Dominance, by Philip Mason (Oxford University Press, 1971), a sophisticated comparative history of systems of inequality, both traditional and modern.

South Africa, A Study in Conflict, by Pierre L. van den Berghe (University of California Press, 1967), an account of South African apartheid.

The Strange Career of Jim Crow, by C. Vann Woodward (Oxford University Press, 1955), a history of the development of racial segregation in the American South after the abolition of slavery.

See *Apartheid; Discrimination; Jim Crow; Racism*

Pierre L. van den Berghe

Skinheads A British youth subculture that had two distinct phases: 1969–72, when it first surfaced as a working-class reaction to the (culturally) revolutionary hippie movement; and 1977-82 when it reappeared to form an alliance with neo-fascist political organizations like the National Front (NF) and the British Movement (BM). In both manifestations, the skinheads were explicitly hostile to what they perceived to be 'outsiders', like blacks and, most particularly, South Asians – in their terms, 'pakis'.

Skinheads proliferated in the early 1970s, when gangs of white youths cropped their hair and dressed in what has been described as the uniform of the 'model workers': denim jeans, braces and working boots. The appearance was to emphasize their close affinity to white working-class traditions and this was reflected in their desire to protect their own territories, or communities, and traditions by repelling the 'threats' of outsiders. Indians and Pakistanis fell into this category and were subjected to almost ritualistic beatings by skinheads, abbreviated to just 'skins'.

The skinhead revival coincided with the rise of the NF and its strategy to recruit urban youth. Recruitment campaigns were mounted in football stadia, leisure centres, rock concerts and virtually anywhere young people could be found. In 1978, the NF even brought out its own youth-oriented publication, *Bulldog,* which was distributed around schools. The other main organization to attract the mark of skinheads was the BM which actually encouraged attacks on 'outsiders'.

Although some thought the political connections of the skins exaggerated, the NF and BM certainly prospered from the membership of skinheads, and, in turn, provided the youths with some kind of theoretical justification for their street-level racism. This comes across in Trevor Griffith's play *Oi! for England,* the title of which derives from the skinheads' preferred music called 'Oi!' One of the characters in the play, a skin, talks of his attack on an Asian: 'I'm WHITE. I'm proud of it. I think it's the best thing ter be . . . I ain't tekn' second place to no nigger 'n' Yids in me own country.'

Although the skinheads have been variously depicted as 'folk devils' and social menaces, writers of very different political persuasions have seen them as little more than caricatures of older working-class generations. They can be seen as standing for values, traditions and attitudes that existed before the Second World War when the British empire and nationalism were both strong.

It's possible to see the skinheads as a kind of white ethnicity in an atmosphere of imminent threat – especially from the accelerating unemployment amongst youth in the early 1980s. Such conditions can engender a hostility and resentment that is directed against specific groups designated as outsiders and possible causes of the worsening conditions. Asians fitted the bill and were thus scapegoated.

After 1982, skinheads were less prevalent; at least, fewer and fewer youths wore their hair shorn, and the links with the NF/BM were broken. Yet the type of racist mentality informing the skinhead posture remained amongst white urban youth. Social conditions failed to improve and scapegoating continued.

The skinheads as a distinct subcultural form gave shape and clarity to a fusion of racism and nationalism and this was given political expression through its connection with neo-fascist organizations. It is doubtful, however, whether the disappearance of the skins spelled any significant diminution of the racism of white youth in the 1980s.

Read:

No Future by E. Cashmore (Heinemann, 1984), an assessment of youth subcultures in the 1980s with particular attention paid to the mark 2 skinheads and the legacy they left in the form of 'skinhead mentality'.

'Skinheads and the search for white working class identity' by Dick Hebdige in *New Socialist* (September/October, 1981). in many ways, a sympathetic study of an area of London skinheads.

'Recruiting racists' by G. Murdock and B. Troyna in *Youth in Society* (no. 60, November, 1981), an examination of the strategies employed by racist organizations to mobilize the support of youths.

See *British Movement; Fascism; National Front; Racism; Scapegoat*

Ellis Cashmore

Slavery One of the frequent protests of modern blacks in the western world is that they are never allowed totally to throw off the shackles their ancestors wore during slave days. Not literally, of course, but in a metaphorical sense; black leaders believe that the failure of black people to press vigorously for and achieve greater equality in all social spheres is the result of a kind of slave mentality. In this view, blacks have, over the generations since 1865 (the year of full emancipation), failed to confront basic issues surrounding their continued subordination. The critique holds that whites have maintained the position of dominance they established in slave days and blacks, for a variety of reasons, have not been allowed effectively to challenge that position. Slavery, then, is a source of many modern inequalities and, for this reason, merits careful attention when considering race and ethnic relations.

'Slavery is the status or condition of a person over whom any or all of the powers attaching to the right of ownership are exercised,' according to the United Nations Slavery Convention (I (1), Geneva, 1926). The condition invariably involves the forced, unremunerated labour of the person held as property and his or her exclusion from any kind of participation in politics or civil rights.

The process by which this condition comes about is the 'slave trade', defined by the United Nations as: 'all acts involved in the capture, acquisition of a slave with a view to selling or exchanging him; all acts of disposal by sale or exchange of a slave acquired with a view to being sold or exchanged and, in general, every act of trade or transport in slaves' (I (2), Geneva, 1926).

Pierre van den Berghe adds the further important point that: 'Slavery is a form of unfreedom and disability that is largely restricted to ethnic strangers – to people who are defined as outside the solidary group.' Types of unfreedom have been institutionalized in imperial Rome, in China and in some quarters of West Africa, though the particular type of interest here is that operated by European powers when expanding and maintaining their colonies between the sixteenth and nineteenth centuries. The especially virulent form of racism that lies at the root of race relations issues was, in large part, born out of the desire and need to justify this slavery.

The conditions for this slavery were quite basic: the conquest of a territory, followed by the capture of its people and their sale to traders, then their transportation to a distant country where they were forced to work. Most of the Europeans' attentions were concentrated on Africa, so the native peoples underwent what Stanley Elkins calls a series of 'shocks' in the process of enslavement: 'We may suppose that every African who became a slave underwent an experience whose crude psychic impact must have been staggering and whose consequences superseded anything that had ever happened to him.' Before the trade in slaves ended in the mid-nineteenth century, between twelve and fifteen million Africans were transported to North, Central and South American countries to work as slaves (about 60 per cent of them were taken in the eighteenth century when the slave trade peaked). Most came from a narrow strip of the West African coast with a significant majority coming from Central Africa. The areas now known as Angola and southern Nigeria were fertile grounds for slave traders. The native peoples' robustness and acclimatization to tropical conditions were thought to make them suitable for cotton or sugar plantation work in such places as Brazil, the Caribbean and the southern states of America. The physical environments were harsh and demanding, but the first slaves had come from lands rife with diseases and subject to droughts and famines.

Slaves were made to labour on plantations, in mines (especially in Brazil) or in houses (as domestic servants or artisans). The motivation for keeping them working in this way and depriving them of any sort of freedom was, in most cases (but not all) profit-maximization. Productivity was paramount and slave-owners and traders were unaffected by moral considerations. Racist ideologists served useful purposes in several contexts, for clearly it was morally wrong and unchristian to subject a fellow human being to all manner of atrocity in the pursuit of wealth. If all men were equal before God, then it was simply not right to hold another in bondage and deprive them of all basic human rights.

Racism provided a legitimation of sorts, however, for it proposed a theory of human types in which some races were superior to others. In this instance, whites were thought to be obviously superior: their military and technological advancement demonstrated that. Blacks were considered a race apart, inferior and even subhuman. So, if they were not equal, there was no reason to treat them equally.

The problem with racist ideologies is that, unlike chalk marks on a blackboard, they cannot be rubbed away when no longer needed. After the abolition of slavery, racism did not disappear. Rather, it endured in the popular imagination and continued to affect relationships between whites and the descendants of slaves most substantially. Racism permanently stigmatized the succeeding generations of those who had previously been enslaved.

In 1872, 10,000 slaves were freed in Britain and, in 1807, the legal slave trade ended after a period of antislavery pressure, mostly from religious groups. The following fifty years saw some small improvements in slaves' conditions, such as housing, clothing, and diet, though the average life expectancy of slaves was at least 12 per cent below that of whites by 1850. In 1833, some 800,000 slaves in British territories were freed and ten years later slavery was abolished in British colonial India; one year later it was abolished in Ceylon (now Sri Lanka). Full emancipation came in 1865, though a system of indentured labour in some areas ensured that ex-slaves in the Americas remained tied to plantations.

Technically, emancipation meant that slaves were released from their bondage and relieved of their status as chattel (that is, someone's possession). Yet, various pieces of legislation and other developments made sure that, for the next hundred years, their progress towards some form of equality would be painfully slow. The upsurge of Black Power in the 1960s was to accentuate this. Similarly, members of the Rastafarian movement in the 1980s would cite 'mental enslavement' as one of the principal causes behind blacks' persistent subordination to whites. In other words, they argued that the majority of blacks were still labouring with a slave's mentality in the sense that they regarded themselves as inferior. Conversely, it has been argued that modern whites work with a 'colonial mentality' and still hold images of blacks as modified slaves. When modern blacks speak of '400 years' they refer to the fact that slavery has operated in some (perhaps disguised) form from the sixteenth century to the present day.

The particular combination of slavery and racism was a potent one and one which was to have far-reaching effects. There are, however, instances of slavery without racism and it seems that some system of unfreedom can be imposed wherever conditions facilitate slavery; the prime condition being where human labour can be profitably exploited. This is attested to by the endurance of various forms of chattel slavery. The ownership of one human by another persists in the modern world, particularly in India where a system of debt bondage ensures that an estimated 6.5 million people are held in a slavelike state. The absence of bankruptcy laws in India means that a creditor can claim back money or goods owed by acquiring his debtor as his property. Another type of slavery in Asia is the kidnapping of women from Bangladeshi villages, followed by their transportation and sale as servants in the Gulf states.

In South America, there are various types of labour that come very near to slavery, such as in Peru where certain tribes are classed as 'savages' and denied citizenship, or Brazil where the 'yoke' keeps unpaid labourers working the plantations while in bondage.

There is evidence to suggest that slavery exists in such unlikely places as the People's Republic of China, the Soviet Union and even the United States. As recently as 1982 arrests were made involving the sale of illegal Indonesian immigrants to wealthy Los Angeles homes as domestic servants. The number of illegally held Haitians, Mexicans and Salvadoreans in the USA is speculated to be in the tens of thousands.

The most visible state of slavery in the modern world is that practised in the Islamic republic of Mauritania in West Africa. Although technically outlawed, a system of chattel slavery is an integral part of the economy and continues to thrive with about 100,000 held in bondage. Having reviewed the relevant research, Russ Vallance, the Development Secretary of the Anti-Slavery Society (to whom I am grateful for the information on modern slavery), concludes that there are 'probably more slaves in the world today than were freed by the great reformers of the 19th century' (personal communication, 13 April 1983). Such a view reinforces the idea that slavery surfaces in virtually any social situation where human labour can be forced and exploited.

Read:

Slavery and Social Death by Orlando Patterson (Harvard University Press, 1983), an original treatment of slavery, tracing its many historical forms and theorizing why this form of domination and exploitation occurs even when it is economically useless; slavery is seen as a form of 'social death' and slaves' membership of society is totally negated; the author's earlier work was *The Sociology of Slavery* (MacGibbon & Kee, 1961).

Roll, Jordan, Roll by Eugene D. Genovese (Pantheon, 1974), something of a classic text on slavery, complemented by *Race and Slavery in the Western Hemisphere* edited by Genovese with Stanley L. Engerman (Princeton University Press, 1975); *Slavery* by Stanley Elkins (University of Chicago Press, 1968), provides the contrast to these.

The White Man's Burden by Winthrop Jordan (Oxford University Press, 1974), an historical analysis which argues that English explorers in the eighteenth and nineteenth centuries conceived of Africans as heathen savage beasts which were in need of severe discipline; in this way, the adventurers were able to be consistent with the moral tone of the Protestant reformation.

See *Africa; Black Power; Brazil; Colonialism; Ideology; Native peoples; Racism*

Ellis Cashmore

Smuts, Jan Christiaan (1870–1950) 'It ought to be the policy of all parties to do justice to the Native and to take wise and prudent measures for their civilization and improvement. But I don't believe in politics for them.' So spoke Jan Smuts who exerted some of the influences shaping South Africa's internal and foreign policy this century.

Born in Riebeck West, the son of a wealthy farmer, Smuts was a brilliant scholar at Stellenbosch and Cambridge where he studied law. He was made State Attorney of Transvaal in 1898. After serving in the Anglo-Boer war, 1899–1902, he joined Louis Botha to form the political movement called *Het Volk* (the people). His parliamentary career took off after 1906 when responsible government was granted the Transvaal.

After serving in a variety of ministerial capacities under Botha, he took office as Premier in 1919 after Botha's death. In his first years, he was made to suppress many violent disturbances involving disaffected blacks. He also antagonized poor whites when, in an attempt to save ailing mines, he agreed to replacing 2,000 unskilled white labourers with cheaper black labourers in 1922. He lost office in 1924 after his indelicate handling of a series of disputes in which he lost the support of the white working class.

Returning to command at the start of the Second World War, Smuts for a while declared himself against segregation. In 1945, however, he asserted that 'it is fixed policy to maintain white supremacy in South Africa.' Nonwhites suffered badly in the 1940s and 1950s, living in slave-like conditions, and thousands of Indians were imprisoned under the 'Ghetto Act' which removed their already limited franchise and property rights.

When the system of apartheid was being established in 1946–8, amidst widespread turmoil, Smuts came out in favour of the system, though, it seems, with some misgivings. His political career ended in 1948 and he died two years later.

Read:

Smuts, two volumes, by W.K. Hancock (Cambridge University Press, 1962), the definitive biography based on letters and papers assembled in Cape Town by the author; volume 1 sees Smuts as a student, attorney and statesman; volume 2 details his life after 1919 when he became the Prime Minister of the Union of South Africa.

Smuts edited by Zelda Friedlander (Allan Wingate, 1970). a set of essays in the form of a tribute.

South Africa by Alex Hepple (Pall Mall Press, 1966), a political and economic history tracing the arrangement of white masters and black servants back to the seventeenth century.

See *Apartheid; Segregation; Verwoert*

Ellis Cashmore

Social Darwinism Widely, but misguidedly, regarded as a distinctive school of thought which flourished at the end of the nineteenth and beginning of the twentieth centuries. Authors commonly said to be members of this school include Herbert Spencer, Walter Bagehot, Ludwig Gumplowicz, William Graham Sumner, Gustav Ratzenhofer, Franklin H. Giddings and Benjamin Kidd. Some textbooks identify a separate, and contemporaneous, school of 'anthropo-sociology' led by Otto Ammon and Georges Vacher de Lapouge, writers who showed similarities of approach with some of the authors in the first list.

The Origin of Species was published in 1859. Within twenty years Bagehot and Gumplowicz were consciously attempting to apply in the study of society principles they believed to have been established by Darwin, but the expression 'social Darwinism' did not make an appearance for almost another thirty years when it was employed by critics to designate a political philosophy which they considered pernicious. Social Darwinism came to be seen as a doctrine defending free-market economics and opposing state intervention. This was far removed from a literal interpretation of the name, which could with greater justification have been applied to the argument that social evolution results from the natural and sexual selection of favourable inherited variations.

Within the early twentieth-century debate about social evolution, several contending schools can be distinguished. As described by R.J. Halliday, the Oxford idealists explained it in terms of the dominance of rational mind over instinct. The Spencerian individualists represented human evolution as primarily a genetic or hereditarian process with a stress upon man's biological make-up rather than his rational mind. A third group, the civics movement, presented evolution as an adaptive process resulting from the interaction between man and his environment. Man was unique because of his ability to plan and to influence his own evolution. A fourth group, identified with the Eugenics Society, was closer to Darwin's conception of natural selection as resting upon a theory of population. Spencer disagreed with almost all the components of the eugenic doctrine and retained in his biology a strong environmental emphasis, insisting in particular upon the inheritance of acquired characteristics. The Eugenists can be seen as the true Darwinians in that they interpreted the social problem of reproduction in terms of the biological problem of competition for resources. On such a view, the conventional definition of social Darwinism as a laissez-faire economic ideology is misleading: the economic theory presupposed an ability rationally to allocate scarce means to competing ends, whereas those who started from biological principles saw human rationality as relatively unimportant. It is also misleading to label particular authors as social Darwinists without allowing for changes in their positions. Gumplowicz and Sumner each at one stage of their careers advanced Darwinist arguments but then moved on to write in quite other ways. Spencer's arguments were so special to himself that nothing is gained by classing him as a social Darwinist.

Arguments appealing to Darwinian principles had a significant influence upon racial relations in the early twentieth century. They introduced an element of ruthlessness and immorality into the justification of European expansion into overseas territories. They gave additional force to the anti-immigration campaign in the United States that resulted in the exclusion act of 1924 establishing quotas for different national groups. They produced a theory which represented racial prejudice as a positive element in human evolution (most elegantly expressed by Sir Arthur Keith). This theory reappeared in the 1970s in connection with the approach known as sociobiology and it has been applied to racial and ethnic relations by Pierre L. van den Berghe. Whether sociobiology is properly described as a new version of social Darwinism is disputable. I have maintained that for the study of racial relations the best resolution is to isolate what is called the selectionist theory. This holds that: (1) evolution may be assisted if interbreeding populations are kept separate so that they can develop their special capacities (as in animal breeding); (2) racial prejudice serves this function and in so doing reinforces racial categories in social life; (3) therefore racial categories are determined by evolutionary processes of inheritance and selection. Where the pre-Darwinian racial typologists inferred that pure races must have existed in the past, the selectionists see racial purity as something constantly advanced as humans adapt to new circumstances and cause their groups to evolve. Sociobiologists often advance some version of the selectionist theory; this enables their arguments to be classified without entering upon the dispute as to whether or not they are social Darwinists.

Read:

'Social Darwinism: a definition' by R.J. Halliday (*Victorian Studies*, vol. 4, 1971). a review of the definitional problem.

Social Darwinism in American Thought by Richard Hofstadter (Beacon Press, 1975), for a more conventional history.

Racial and Ethnic Competition by Michael Banton (Cambridge University Press, 1983, pp. 47–50), on the selectionist theory.

See *Darwin; Darwinism; Environmentalism; Eugenics; Hereditarianism; Sociobiology*

Michael Banton

Sociobiology Since the popularization of the term by Edward O. Wilson in 1975, sociobiology has referred to the study of animal behaviour from the perspective of Darwinian evolutionary theory. The approach goes back to the work of William D. Hamilton and John Maynard Smith in the mid-1960s, however. An older label is ethology, and others prefer behavioural biology or population ecology. Applied to other animals, the subject is relatively uncontroversial, but human sociobiology has been energetically attacked as racist, sexist, hereditarian, social Darwinist, and so on. The core proposition of sociobiology, namely that behaviour, like anatomy, has evolved by natural selection, and therefore has a genetic basis, should hardly be controversial.

The sociobiological model is *not* hereditarian; on the contrary, it is premised on the theorem that any phenotype is the product of the interaction of a genotype and an environment. Furthermore, it takes no *a priori* position on the relative importance of each, which is highly variable from species to species, and behaviour to behaviour within a species. Nor does sociobiology deny or minimize the importance of symbolic language and culture in humans.

Human sociobiologists merely insist that human language and culture themselves evolved biologically, and hence are under some genetic influence, however remote, indirect, and flexible that influence might be. They only reject the extreme environmentalism holding that humans are equally likely to learn anything with equal facility, and that cultural evolution is entirely unrelated to biological evolution.

A central tenet of sociobiology (as distinguished from the earlier ethology) is the emphasis on individual-level selection as against group selection. Organisms act to maximize their individual fitness (measured in terms of reproductive success), not to benefit the group or species, except insofar as group fitness coincides with individual fitness. Ultimately, the unit of natural selection is the gene rather than the organism, which is, evolutionarily speaking, a gene's way of making copies of itself, an idea popularized by Richard Dawkins.

What seems like altruistic behaviour is explained in sociobiology as ultimate genetic selfishness. Beneficient behaviour can increase an individual's fitness in two principal ways: through *nepotism* or kin selection, and through *reciprocity*. By helping kin reproduce (nepotism), an organism can maximize its own inclusive fitness, because kin share a certain percentage of their genes by common descent with ego (one-half between siblings and offspring; one-fourth between grandparents and grandchildren, uncles, and nephews; one-eighth between first cousins, etc.). Helping kin reproduce is thus an indirect way of reproducing one's own genes. Between kin, nepotism can be fitness-maximizing even if the behaviour is not reciprocated, and indeed many forms of nepotism are highly asymmetrical (for example, between parents and offspring). Nepotism has been found to be a powerful explanatory principle of animal sociality, and is obviously also universal in human societies.

Between unrelated individuals, beneficient behaviour can only increase fitness if it is reciprocated, though systems of reciprocity are always vulnerable to cheaters and freeloaders (who seek to avoid reciprocation). In nature, sexual reproduction is a widespread form of reciprocity between males and females: each sex benefits by being 'nice' to the other, but nature will not select for unrequited love! Many of the most successful applications of sociobiology have been in the field of male and female strategies of reproduction and 'parental investment', and in the resulting mating systems of different species. In humans, systems of reciprocity can be extremely complex and sophisticated, because human intelligence allows for extensive deceit, and hence the need to develop complex counterstrategies of foiling cheaters. The conditions for the evolution of reciprocal altruism in humans and other animals have been specified by Robert Trivers.

A neglected aspect of human sociality in sociobiology has been the role of coercion to promote intraspecific and intrasocietal parasitism. Clearly, with the rise of states in the last seven to eight thousand years of human evolution, many relationships are asymmetrical, in that some individuals use coercive means to appropriating resources to maximize their own fitness at the expense of others. Indeed, human societies have become increasingly coercive as they have grown in size and complexity.

Sociobiology should not be seen as a threat to the humanities and social sciences, but as an invitation to incorporate the study of human behaviour in the theoretical mainstream of the neo-Darwinism synthesis, the dominant theory of biology for over a century. Its insights complement, specify, and enrich what we have long known about ourselves: that we are a product of both heredity and environment, and that nature and nurture are but the two sides of the same evolving coin.

Read:

Sociobiology and Behaviour, by David Barash (Elsevier, 1981), a lucid, nontechnical summary of the ideas of the main theoreticians of sociobiology.

Sociobiology, Sense or Nonsense, by Michael Ruse (Reidel, 1979), a thorough review of the scientific, ethical and ideological arguments pro and con sociobiology, and of their human implications.

On Human Nature, by Edward O. Wilson (Harvard, 1978), a statement written for a lay audience, about the relationship between genes and culture, by the man who gave sociobiology its name.

See *Darwinism; Environmentalism; Genotype; Hereditarianism; Phenotype; Social Darwinism*

Pierre L. van den Berghe

South Africa See *Apartheid; Smuts; Verwoerd*

Stereotype A stereotype is defined by Gordon Allport as: 'an exaggerated belief associated with a category. Its function is to justify (rationalize) our conduct in relation to that category.' This definition implies a discrepancy between an objectively ascertainable reality and a subjective perception of that reality.

In the field of race and ethnic relations, a stereotype is often defined as an overgeneralization about the behaviour or other characteristics of members of particular groups. Ethnic and racial stereotypes can be positive or negative, although they are more frequently negative. Even ostensibly positive stereotypes can often imply a negative evaluation. Thus, to say that blacks are musical and have a good sense of rhythm comes close to the more openly negative stereotypes that they are childish, and happy-go-lucky. Similarly, there is not much difference between saying that Jews show group solidarity and accusing them of being clannish.

It is, of course, a difficult empirical question to determine where a generalization about a group ceases to be an objective description of reality and becomes a stereotype. At the limit, almost any statement of group differences can be termed stereotypic, unless it is precisely stated in statistical terms and leaves the issue of causality open. Let us take the example of differential rates of violent crimes between racial groups. Afro-Americans in the United States have conviction rates for crimes of violence that are five to ten times those of whites; they are greatly overrepresented in the prison population; and they also fall disproportionately victim to crimes of violence, frequently committed by other blacks. An unqualified statement such as 'blacks are criminals', or 'blacks are prone to violence' would generally be labelled a stereotype. 'Blacks are more violent than whites', although somewhat qualified, could still be called stereotypic, as the statement implies an intrinsic racial difference in proneness to violence.

The more careful formulations above would probably escape the label of stereotype, because, even though they state the existence of statistical differences between racial groups, they leave open the question of causality. For example, the higher conviction rate of blacks could be due to hidden class differences rather than to racial differences, or to racial bias in the predominantly white police and courts in arresting and convicting blacks. Indeed, probably all of these factors are at work in producing the statistical outcome.

The relationship between stereotypes and prejudice is also of interest to social scientists. Racial or ethnic stereotypes are generally expressions of prejudice against the groups in question, but insofar as they often have a grain of truth, they may also have a measure of statistical validity, and, therefore, be moderately useful guides for predicting behaviour. Since we benefit by trying to predict the behaviour of others, and since we all have to rely, for simplicity's sake on rough and ready categories such as ego, sex, class, ethnic group, religion, and the like, implicit stereotypes form the basis of much social life. Such stereotypes do not necessarily reflect deeply ingrained prejudices.

Thus, for example, we know that crimes of violence in the United States are statistically correlated not only with race, but also with age, class, sex, time of day, and urban residence. The old lady who walks past a group of young, black, working-class men, late at night, in a street of Harlem is not necessarily a racial bigot if she feels a twitch of apprehension. She merely applies pragmatic formulae for survival. She probably *is* more at risk in such a situation than say, at a church picnic. That she is aware of the difference is a testimony to her common sense, not to her racism, though she *may* be a racist.

Because of the difficulty of ascertaining the gap between the objective reality and the subjective perception thereof, the concept of stereotype is not a useful scientific tool in the analysis of behaviour, nor has it been used much in the last twenty years.

Read:

The Nature of Prejudice, by Gordon W. Allport (Addison-Wesley, 1954), a standard text on problems of prejudice, discrimination, and stereotypes by an American social psychologist.

See *Discrimination; Prejudice; Scapegoat; Xenophobia*

Pierre L. van den Berghe

Supplementary schools The supplementary school movement indicates that minority-group parents lack confidence in the state schools either to meet their particular needs or to reform themselves to accommodate these aspirations. The nature of this dissatisfaction differs from group to group, however; consequently, the function of supplementary schools also varies both within and between minority communities.

For instance, those schools which have developed within the UK's black population are principally academically oriented. The publication of Bernard Coard's pamphlet, *How the West Indian Child is made Educationally Sub-Normal in the British School System* (1971) underlined the conviction of many black parents that the relatively low academic performance of their children was, in a sense, manufactured by the racist structure and operation of the state education system. The emergence of black supplementary schools, then, has been stimulated by the belief that state schools do not provide equality of educational opportunity for all pupils. Their aim has been to develop basic intellectual skills and competences complemented by an apppreciation of the students' ethnic and cultural identity. In so far as these schools represent black parents' protests about the outcomes rather than the aims of the state system, they may be said to constitute a supplement rather than alternative form of education.

In contrast, the supplementary education service provided by the Chinese, Polish, Greek and various south Asian communities is directly concerned with mother-tongue maintenance, cultural continuity and religious instruction. In short, they provide the students with a formal education in the mother culture. Whether or not this function could, or indeed should, be entirely appropriated by the state system remains open to argument, not least within the ethnic communities themselves. Whatever the view taken, it is clear that the presence of these forms of supplementary education do not represent such a severe indictment of state schools as those which have been established by the UK's black communities.

The state response to these community initiatives has been ambivalent. Some education officials and teachers have been highly critical about the quality of teaching, the divisive nature of recruitment procedures and of the strain which an extra day's schooling imposes on the student. On the other hand, some Local Education Authorities have agreed to support these initiatives, either through direct funding or, more commonly, by providing the schools with facilities and equipment, free of charge or at a reduced rate.

SUPPLEMENTARY SCHOOLS

Without doubt, the supplementary school movement has highlighted many of the issues relating to educational services in multi-ethnic contexts. For instance, fears that the movement represents a trend towards separatist education have stimulated demands for a reappraisal of traditional curricular, pedagogic and organizational practices along multicultural lines. Similarly, issues such as the maintenance and teaching of the mother-tongue of minority group students have now been placed firmly on the agenda. It remains to be seen whether the state system will modify and expand its provision to ensure that such community initiatives will soon become redundant. Whatever the outcome, the signs are that the very presence of supplementary schools is ensuring that those teachers and educationists in the state system are seriously scrutinizing their provision and their insistence that they provide equality of educational opportunity to all pupils.

Read:

The Education of the Black Child in Britain by Maureen Stone (Fontana, 1981), provides an insight into the functions and successes of supplementary schools within the UK's black communities.

'Dachwyng Saturday School' by Nel Clark in *Community Work and Racism* (Routledge & Kegan Paul, 1982), edited by Ashok Oshri, Basil Manning and Paul Curno, a detailed account of the rationale, objectives and effectiveness of one supplementary school set up in London in 1975 by black parents.

Why Ethnic Schools? by Paul Kringas and Frank Lewins (Australian National University Press, 1982), an interesting account of the Greek, Italian, Ukranian and Slovenian supplementary schools in Sydney, Melbourne and New South Wales.

See *Ethnicity; Multiracial education; Rampton/Swann Committee; Underachievement*

Barry Troyna

T

Third World Derived from the French *le Tiers-monde,* used to describe collectively those countries that are no longer politically affiliated with either of the two power blocs, soviet and western-capitalist. In a great many instances, third-world countries have been colonized by imperialist powers and have had their material and human resources exploited. The colonial system ensured that much of the natural wealth of the countries was drawn off and appropriated elsewhere. A legacy of this is the heavy investment of European and American companies (multinationals) in third-world countries. Many states in Africa, Asia and South America are still very economically dependent on ex-colonial powers' support via overseas aid or in the form of financial grants or loans.

Since the Second World War, the trend has been for previously colonized countries to strive for political independence, and the old colonial empires have virtually been dissolved. In some cases, colonies were relinquished and independence granted voluntarily; in others, independence was grudgingly given after periods of internal warfare. In the majority of cases, the third-world countries have had great difficulty in actually operating as independent powers. The examples of the Thieu regime in Vietnam and the Shah monarchy in Iran show how the US government actively supported and, indeed, protected pseudocolonial arrangements. Both regimes were overthrown.

The persistence of former colonial powers in influencing third-world countries economically and politically has resulted in a state of underdevelopment despite rapid urbanization, industrialization and a massive shift to the cities. Even predominantly rural countries have large industrial cities where most of their population is concentrated. These centres have sprung up mainly since the war with the attainment of independence and with the advent of overseas investment. In the short period of time after the war, agrarian, feudal economic systems have been supplanted by modern economic systems (either capitalist, soviet or mixed-capitalist), financed by ex-colonial or soviet sources.

The majority of independent countries of Africa, Asia and Central and South America suffer from underdevelopment and have had their general poverty compounded by their vulnerability to natural disasters. American countries whose economies depend on such things as coffee or cocoa have their raw materials severely affected by natural conditions; these are also affected by price fluctuations in the world market for the commodities they supply. The United Nations Organization and the World Bank recognize many underdeveloped countries and support them with special policies connected with aid and trade.

In the main, third-word countries tend to have their development undermined further by their lack of educational institutions, their absence of health systems and the continual emigration of skilled workers to more advanced industrialized countries.

Exceptions to the general trend are the countries affiliated to the Organization of Petroleum Exporting Countries (OPEC): these (mostly) middle-eastern states (plus Nigeria) are rich in natural oil resources and have organized themselves in such a way as to control the production, price and availability of their valuable mineral.

Read:

The Third World, 2nd edition by Peter Worsley (Weidenfeld & Nicolson, 1977), an influential examination of the issues in a sociological perspective.

The Third World by M.E. Willard and R.M. Millar (Vance Bibliographies, 1981), an up-to-date assessment of the natural resources, economics, politics and social conditions of third-world countries.

The Third World Coalition in Inernational Politics by Robert A. Mortimer (Praeger, 1980), a study of the political relations between third-world countries and former colonial powers.

See *Africa; Brazil; Colonialism; Power*

Ellis Cashmore

Trade Unions and racism The ideology of trade unionism includes a commitment to the international solidarity of the working class throughout the world, from which is derived a principled opposition to racism and racial discrimination. This principle is embodied in resolutions at trade union conferences, which are usually passed with unanimous support. However, the actual policy and practice of trade unions within western Europe and North America tells a rather different story. One can find considerable evidence to show that trade unions have discriminated against particular groups of workers and have expressed opinions about them which are implicitly or explicitly racist.

One useful example to illustrate the point is the recent history of the policy and practice of the British Trades Union Congress (TUC) towards New Commonwealth migration to Britain since 1945. Although this policy and practice was not as explicitly hostile and extreme as that of the American trade union movement towards Asian workers on the west coast of the USA at the turn of the present century or towards black workers in the interwar decades, it was nevertheless equally racist in character. The migration from the New Commonwealth was prompted directly by labour shortages in certain sectors of the British economy, and those who came to fill those jobs thereby became part of the British working class. Indeed, all the evidence collected since then shows that these migrants showed explicit recognition of this by joining the relevant trade unions and, in some sectors, showed a higher rate of union membership than indigenous workers. However, their commitment to trade unionism was not matched by a commitment by the unions to their problems and concerns, particularly those arising out of racism and discrimination.

By the mid-1950s, soon after the migration began, certain elements of the leadership of the TUC were expressing support for a policy of immigration control, and the support for this position grew after the attacks on West Indian property and people in London and Nottingham in 1958. For the TUC, these events were not indicative of the extent and political significance of racism in Britain, but, rather, proved a need to reduce the number of 'immigrants' entering the country. In other words, the TUC was willing to express the demands of the racists. In addition, it began to argue that the problem was also one of ensuring that the migrants adapt to 'our' way of life, a view which came to constitute the core of TUC policy in the 1960s. Thus, although the TUC was not making explicit claims about the supposed biological inferiority of West Indian and Asian workers, it was willing to call for their entry into Britain to be controlled and it was willing to claim that the migrants' behaviour in Britain was causing problems. The problems were, therefore, defined as 'their' presence and 'their' characteristics, rather than as the hostile (and racist) response of sections of the British working class as well as the media and politicians. Thereby, the voice of trade unionism was added to the growing racist clamour that eventually led to the 1962 Commonwealth Immigrants Act.

In the course of the 1960s, the TUC remained discreetly silent about racist immigration control and continued to insist that its major concern was with the culture and behaviour of the migrants. With the development of state institutions to encourage integration, it was, therefore, no surprise to find that the TUC willingly involved itself with the local and national bureaucracies, although it initially resolutely opposed the plans of the Labour government to extend the provisions of the 1965 Race Relations Act to cover racial discrimination in employment. Thus, for the decade of the 1960s, the TUC took its place amongst the forces of the state which was then arguing that 'integration' and immigration control were inseparable.

The tacit alliance between the TUC and the British state in support of racist policies began to break down in the 1970s. In 1973, the TUC belatedly agreed that the 1971 Immigration Act passed by the Conservative government was racist and should be repealed. In addition, it was finally faced with explicit and substantial evidence that the British working class was not, by tradition, characterized by tolerance and understanding. A series of industrial disputes in the early 1970s clearly showed that workers, trade union representatives and employers were willingly collaborating to pursue racist policies to exclude Asian and West Indian workers from access to skilled and higher paid jobs. The then Commission on Industrial Relations warned of the possibility of independent trade unions being set up in response to such an alliance. The final event that forced a change in TUC policy was the growth of support in the 1970s for neo-fascist politics, a growth that was clearly premised on racism. This combination of developments allowed that group of rank-and-file activists who had been consistently opposing the policy and practice of the leadership to successfully press for internal changes within the TUC, for a positive commitment to 'equal opportunity' policies, for opposition to racist immigration policies and for a campaign within the labour movement against racism. Most of these developments were agreed in the 1976 Congress.

Although the TUC did organize a campaign in conjunction with the Labour Party, and although a number of its policies did exhibit a more explicit antiracist position, its practice since the late 1970s leads to the conclusion that it regards the issue of racism as only of limited significance. Certainly, a number of investigations conducted by the Commission on Racial Equality have shown that trade unions and management at local level remain willing to collaborate in the practice of excluding West Indian and Asian workers from certain sectors of the labour market. The policy and practice of the TUC shows that it remains unwilling to act in a determined way to eliminate racist practices within the workplace.

This evidence is not to be explained solely as the product of racist beliefs held by trade union members and leaders, although such beliefs are widely held and do have an effect on policy and practice. It is also important to recall the nature and role of trade unionism in a capitalist society. Trade unions are predominantly defensive organizations which protect and attempt to advance the interests of their members at the workplace. In practice, they take for granted the institutions of capitalism and attempt to obtain the best available deal from the employer and the state within the limits set by those institutions in any given set of historical circumstances. Additionally, the context for this relationship between labour and capital is a national one, so that the TUC, for example, views its responsibilities first within the context of Britain as a nation-state. Consequently, its essentially defensive activities and strategies have as their explicit object the British working class. The outcome is that any labour migration from outside the national boundary tends to be viewed as an unwelcome addition to the labour market, carrying with it the possibility that its presence will have the effect of reducing wages or serving as a source of labour for strike-breaking. Indeed, historically, the migration of some groups of workers has led to such outcomes.

However, this was not the case with respect to the New Commonwealth migration of the 1950s and 1960s because, at the outset at least, the migrants were entering the economy to do the jobs that the British workers did not want to do. Nevertheless, the evidence shows that the activity of the trade union movement has played a part in keeping workers in that position, despite the opposition of those trade unions who have consistently argued for the implementation of an internationalist position and despite the commitment of West Indian and Asian workers to the trade union movement. Although the historical context and details differ, the evidence for other trade unions in other countries demonstrates a similar combination of racist attitudes with the defensive role of unions to produce an outcome which ensures that migrant labour becomes the object of racism within the labour movement. This is a result of both the existence of racism within the trade union movement and of the defensive role of trade unionism which accepts as legitimate parameters for action, both capitalism and the nation-state.

Read:

The TUC, Black Workers and New Commonwealth Immigration, 1954–1973 by R. Miles and A. Phizacklea (RUER Working Paper in Ethnic Relations, No. 6, 1977), for a detailed account of British TUC policy and practice from the early 1950s.

Discrimination and Disadvantage in Employment, edited by P. Braham, E. Rhodes and M. Pearn (Harper & Row, 1981), for a useful selection of articles in Section 3 on trade union policy and practice towards racism.

Labour and Immigration in Industrial America by R.D. Parmet (Twayne Publishers, 1981), for an historical account of American trade union opposition to migrants in the late nineteenth and early twentieth century.

See *Capitalism; Integration; Migration*

Robert Miles

U

Underachievement The ideological notion of schooling as a good thing derives from the liberal-democratic assumption that education is the main instrument of occupational and social mobility. Underpinning this is the conviction that the possession of formal educational credentials plays a determining role in the distribution of future life chances. Without these credentials it is commonly assumed that a school-leaver is unlikely to find the sort of job to which he or she aspires, or indeed any job.

In the UK, concern about the relatively low academic performance of working-class pupils (compared to their middle-class counterparts) led to the dissolution of the tripartite system of secondary education and the establishment of comprehensive secondary schools. The imperative for this action was clear: to repair the meritocratic credibility of schools by ensuring that all pupils, irrespective of background, be given an equal opportunity to develop their intellectual potential to the full through unimpaired access to educational institutions and the credentials they offer. In western capitalist societies, then, equality of opportunity is the organizing principle of state education.

Despite the introduction of comprehensive schooling and related initiatives, there remains a significant difference in the academic achievement levels of pupils from working-class and middle-class backgrounds. Now, insofar as this pattern is rarely explained in terms of innate intellectual differences between these two social groups, working-class pupils are considered to be formally underachieving; that is to say, unlike their middle-class peers, they are not realizing their full intellectual potential. A group cannot underachieve if their intellectual and attainment levels have been genetically determined; the causes of this relatively lower academic performance lie elsewhere. Some have argued that working-class pupils come from culturally deprived backgrounds and that schools must provide a compensating environment in order to increase their academic performance: hence, compensatory education initiatives. Marxists, on the other hand, locate the causes of underachievement in the institutional structures of society and their relationship to the education system. Different again is the view that teachers perpetuate these differential patterns of achievement through their expectations and treatment of working-class pupils. These pupils are stereotyped as low achievers and are offered educational opportunities in accordance with these assessments.

A similar range of explanations has been adduced to account for the underachievement of pupils of West Indian origin in UK schools. Ever since the early 1960s, research has reported a strong trend towards the lower academic performance of these pupils compared to their white and south Asian peers. The early and optimistic prognosis that this was a transient phenomenon which derived largely from the pupils' newness in the UK educational system and would therefore diminish with the passage of time was no longer tenable in the late 1970s and early 1980s. In her 1980 review of 33 studies, ranging from large-scale group tests to small-scale individual tests, Sally Tomlinson found that in 25 instances the average scores of ethnic minority pupils, especially young blacks, were lower than those obtained by white pupils.

Of course, certain educationists and psychologists such as Arthur Jensen and Hans Eysenck argue for the lower innate intellect of black pupils; but, for reasons already spelt out, those who adhere to this 'scientific racism' argument cannot legitimately typify these pupils as 'underachievers'. What is more, these arguments have been thoroughly demoralized and discredited by evidence which shows that the difference in IQ within populations is greater than the difference in average between populations.

What the specific causes are of this trend is a question which has tantalized educationists for many years, and the answer remains elusive. At the same time, many researchers have been so overwhelmingly concerned with establishing differences, or otherwise, along ethnic lines that they have tended to overlook the significant influence of social class background on performance levels. Black pupils in the UK come largely from working-class families and it has been clearly established that family background has a profound moderating effect on school performance levels. Could it be that 'West Indian underachievement' is a misnomer and that if the research data were standardized to take into account class backgrounds the results would show few significant differencs between black pupils and their white working-class counterparts?

Perhaps the emphasis on differential levels of academic performance is largely misplaced, anyway. Research into the experiences of black and white school-leavers has conclusively shown that job-seekers of equal merit (as measured by formal educational credentials) do not have equal access to the labour market and that skin colour has more significance than qualifications in the determination of adult opportunities. If black pupils are underachieving at school, in relation to white pupils, it could be because they recognize the futility of the academic paperchase in a society suffused with racism.

Read:

Caught Between: A Review of Research into the Education of Pupils of West Indian Origin by Monica Taylor (NFER-Nelson, 1981), a detailed, though largely uncritical, account of 'underachievement' by black pupils in the UK education system.

Racism, School and the Labour Market, edited by Barry Troyna and Douglas Smith (National Youth Bureau, 1983), demolishes the myth that the underachievement of black youth in the UK labour market is attributable primarily to their relatively poor performance in school.

'The educational performance of ethnic minority children' by Sally Tomlinson (*New Community*, vol. 8, no. 3, 1980), a summary of all the research in this area.

'The ideological construction of black underachievement' by Frank Reeves and Mel Chevannes (*Multiracial Education*, vol. 12, no. 4, 1983), throws up doubts about the validity of the whole debate.

'Fact or Artefact: the educational underachievement of black pupils', by Barry Troyna (*British Journal of the Sociology of Education*, vol. 5, no. 2, 1984), states the cases for and against the argument on underachievement.

See *Intelligence and race; Multiracial education; Rampton/Swann Committee; Stereotype; Supplementary schools*

Barry Troyna

Underclass The concept of underclass has been used by sociologists to describe the bottom stratum of complex societies, especially in the urban context. Underclass refers to a heterogeneous group, below the stably-employed working class, which is regarded as beyond the pale of 'respectable' society. It includes such social categories as the chronically unemployed, vagrants or transients, the criminal 'underground,' some occupational groups considered defiling or immoral (e.g. prostitutes), and sometimes, some despised outcaste groups which may be either ethnically or racially defined (e.g. gypsies in Europe, untouchables in India, the Burakumin of Japan, or 'ghetto blacks' in the United States).

Near synonyms for underclass are *Lumpenproletariat*, subproletariat, pariahs, and outcaste groups. Each of these terms has special connotations, and tends to be used by social scientists of different ideological persuasions. Thus, *Lumpenproletariat* is generally used by marxists, and refers more to the economic dimensions of status, while pariahs refers more to the moral devaluation of the status group and is used more by liberal scholars. Underclass is probably the most neutral term.

A key feature of the underclass in modern post-industrial societies is its marginality to the system of production, and its relative redundancy to it. In previous periods of industrialization the bulk of the urban working class consisted of lowly trained and, therefore, interchangeable factory operatives, and the unemployed were a reserve army of the proletariat used to break strikes, keep wages low, and perpetuate the exploitation of the working class as a whole. With the emergence of the postindustrial, social democratic welfare states of western Europe, Australia and North America, an increasingly sharp line has been drawn between a stable, secure, working-class protected by trade unionism and increasingly employed in skilled service occupations, and an unstable, underemployed underclass subsisting from a mixture of welfare payments and an extralegal underground economy (drug traffic, gambling, prostitution, illegal sweat-shop labour, and so on).

The low skill level of the modern underclass in relation to the increasingly high demands for skilled labour in the mainstream economy combined with the dependency syndrome created by the welfare system to perpetuate the marginality and the superfluity of the underclass. In societies like Britain and the United States, where a substantial sector of the underclass is also racially stigmatized and discriminated against, the self-perpetution of the urban underclass is further aggravated by racism.

Illegal immigration, as among Hispanics and Asians in the United States, complicates the problem yet more, by favouring the superexploitation of workers whose illegality excludes them from normal legal protection in wages, employment, and social benefits. An additional factor is the rising number of urban children raised by single parents (overwhelmingly mothers) who, in addition to handicaps of race and lack of skills, are further marginalized in the system of production by sexual discrimination and their parental responsibilities. For example, an estimated 50 per cent of black children in the United States are raised in single-parent families. Many of them inherit underclass status, and are condemned to forming the hardcore of the unemployed ghetto youth. Currently some 40 per cent of young urban blacks are chronically unemployed, four times the national average, and subsist largely on welfare and on illegal or fringe activities. The economic dependency of the single mother is often in part the *creation* of the welfare system. The absence of a resident adult male is often a necessary test of qualification for welfare; this, in turn, encourages male desertion and perpetuates the welfare mother syndrome in the underclass.

Read:

Social Inequality, edited by André Béteille (Penguin, 1969), a collection of classic articles, both theoretical and empirical, covering many parts of the world.

The Other America, by Michael Harrington (Macmillan, 1962), the book most influential in the 'discovery' of the American underclass.

See *Caste; Disadvantage; Exploitation; Oppression*

Pierre L. van den Berghe

UNESCO statements on race The fact that the German government of the 1930s and the 1940s (up to 1945) conducted its policy partly with regard to a theory of history, which postulated that 'race' was a central determinant of human capacity and action, led to mass murder of over 6 million persons. For the German fascists, the supposedly superior Aryan/German 'race' had to physically eliminate the inferior Jewish race to ensure its own survival. The inhumane consequences of this theory of history and politics was the object of both political and scientific attention after the end of the Second World War. The United Nations Educational, Scientific and Cultural Organization (UNESCO) was particularly concerned with this theory and, in 1949, it set up a committee of experts with the task of drawing up a scientific statement about the nature of 'race'. Their conclusions were publised in Paris in July 1950.

What has since become known as UNESCOs 'First statement on race problems' made the following main claims. First, it concluded that all men and women belong to the same species and are derived from common stock. Biological differences between groups of people were acknowledged to exist, but these were identified as being the product of evolutionary factors and not as permanently fixed attitudes. Second, it was concluded that what distinguishes different populations biologically is differences in the frequency of occurrence of a small number of particular genes, but that genetic similarities were greater than genetic differences between groups. Hence, and third, they defined a 'race' as a population group with a distinct but changing gene pattern. Fourth, they concluded that these genetic differences have no causal relation to cultural differences or to intelligence. They argued that there is no proof that different populations differ in their innate characteristics and that IQ tests are incapable of differentiating between what might be innate capacity and environmental factors in the determination of intelligence. Finally, they concluded that 'race' was more of a social myth than a biological fact, noting that when most people use the term in daily life, they do not refer to different patterns of gene occurrence.

The UNESCO statement was followed by the publication of three further statements in the 1950s and 1960s. These involved elaboration on the themes and omissions of the first statement, but also in one instance a significant difference of opinion. The latter was made evident in the second UNESCO statement, published in Paris in July 1951, a statement which originated in the reaction to the first by a group of physical anthropologists and geneticists who objected to some of its formulations. Although this group of scientists did not object in principle or substance to any of the claims listed above, they did want to broaden the formal definition of 'race' to include more than statistical differences in population gene profiles. For this group 'race' referred to population groups distinguished by heritable physical differences. In this way, they were giving scientific credibility to the everyday, commonsense notion of 'race' which is premised upon such differences as skin colour, hair type, etc., a notion which the first statement implicitly rejects.

The third 'UNESCO statement on race' was drawn up in Moscow in August 1964 and represented a re-examination of the first two statements. It accepted and reiterated the main conclusions of the first statement and outlined a major qualification to the central claim of the second. In the latter connection, the Third statement argued that classification based on hereditary physical characteristics is unable to produce discrete categories and is of limited scientific interest or utility.

The Fourth UNESCO statement was drafted in Paris in September 1967 and was concerned with the historical, social and political causes of racism (not race) and made a series of recommendations about the means by which racism might be more effectively combated.

Read:

Statement on Race, by Ashley Montagu (Oxford University Press, 1972), for a complete reprinting of these four statements and a detailed exposition of two of them.

The Concept of Race, edited by Ashley Montagu (Free Press, 1964), for further analysis of the evidence concerning the supposed biological reality of 'race', in which the editor argues that the term has no scientific validity whatsoever.

The Idea of Race, by Michael Banton (Tavistock, 1967), for a historical analysis of the meanings attributed to 'race'.

See *Race; Race relations; Racism*

Robert Miles

V

Verwoerd, Hendrik Freutsch (1901–1966) One of the most important architects of the legal structure of South African apartheid, Verwoerd regarded his mission as divinely inspired. On his rise to national leader in 1958, he announced: 'I believe the will of God was revealed in the ballot. I do not have the nagging doubt of ever wondering whether perhaps I am wrong.'

In consolidating the political, legal and economic division of South Africa, Verwoerd saw himself enacting the will of God; he merely served as an instrument. He was a Nazi sympathizer and reigned for eight years as the autocratic Premier of South Africa.

Verwoerd was born in Amsterdam and spent the first part of his career as an academic before moving into politics. He became vice-chairman of the National Party of the Transvaal and then moved on to positions as senator (in 1946) and minister of native affairs (in 1948). After his election as national leader in 1958, he introduced legislation designed to realize his ideal of 'separate development' or what he euphemistically called 'separate freedom', the complete differentiation of whites and nonwhites.

The 1959 Bantu Self-Government Act set up provisions for eight separate 'homelands' where the various native African peoples could have their independent states which were ultimately under the control of the Union Parliament. Black Africans were allowed to enter urban 'white areas' as migratory labourers and only for specific periods of time.

Verwoerd's justification for (or rationalization of) this was: (1) whites were in a majority *if* the rest of the South African population was seen as a fractionalized series of subgroups split by tribal or religious differences; and (2) it was whites' duties as 'guardians' to look after all others. There were 3 million whites and some 15 million nonwhites, a ratio of 1:5.

World opinion swung away from Verwoerd's extreme policies and he declared that: 'It appears to me that the white nations are prepared to abandon the whites in Africa. . . . We do not accept that the white inhabitants must be satisfied as a minority in a multiracial country to compete with the black masses on an equal basis.' He insisted that blacks 'be rooted in the areas inhabited by their forefathers'. Campaigns by blacks against their subordination and deprivation were suppressed: Verwoerd outlawed the African National Congress and the Pan-Africanist Congress and, at one stage, declared a state of martial law in 1960.

Verwoerd's recognition of the need to keep South Africa divided influenced his decision to withdraw the country's application for continued membership in the Commonwealth. In 1961, South Africa became a republic. Thereafter, Verwoerd pursued his apartheid policy even more vigorously with Bantu Laws Amendments Acts in 1963 and 1964; these eliminated any semblance of blacks' employment security remaining after 1961 and effectively reduced them to the status of chattel.

Rising black protest was dealt with harshly as was demonstrated at Sharpeville in 1963 when police opened fire on a tense but not hostile crowd, killing 67 and wounding 186, mostly as they fled. Verwoerd survived one assassination attempt, but, in 1966, at the height of his political popularity amongst whites, he was stabbed to death by Demetrio Tsafendas, who was conveniently declared insane – as if to negate any political comment in his act.

Read:

South Africa: An Historical Introduction by Freda Troup (Penguin, 1975), a concise account of the political developments in South Africa from the seventeenth century with a chapter on 'The Republic (1958–74)' which deals with the Verwoerd era.

The Oxford Study of South Africa, volume 2, edited by Monica Wilson and Leonard Thompson (Clarendon Press, 1978), part of a comprehensive analysis of the country in all aspects; this volume deals with the period 1870–1966, and so covers Verwoerd's spell in office.

South Africa by A. Kepple-Jones (Hutchinson, 1975), a clear historical account, particularly of the black–white conflicts.

VOLK

See *Africa; Apartheid; Slavery; Smuts; Zimbabwe*

Ellis Cashmore

Volk The word corresponding to 'people', which in German and related languages is applied to cultural groups and would-be nations. In German, it applies much more than 'people' does in English. Since the growth of the romantic movement from the late eighteenth century, it has signified the union of a group of people with a transcendent 'essence'. The essence was given different names, like 'nature', 'cosmos', 'mythos', but in each instance it represented the source of the individual's creativity and his unity with other members of the Volk. From it there stemmed a strain in German thought which diverged from traditional western nationalism and religion. The Volk mediated between the isolated individual, alienated by the forces of modern society, and the universe. In *Mein Kampf*, Adolf Hitler criticized the naiveté of the Volkists but made use of their ideas to describe his vision of a racially powerful and united Germany.

A derived word, Herrenvolk, means a 'master-people' and has been used by Pierre van den Berghe to characterize 'herrenvolk egalitarianism' and 'herrenvolk democracy'. In white supremacist societies such as those of southern Africa after European conquest, a white minority have been the masters of a larger black population. To preserve their privileged position the white needed to maintain a front of solidarity, and this required the cultivation of trust and sentiments of equality within their own group. These attitudes contrasted with the assumption of inequality in their dealings with blacks. To a considerable extent this pattern repeated that prevailing in the southern region of the United States, although blacks were a numerical majority in only a small part of that region. Over much of the region there was a substantial poor white population but, since they had the vote, the master class had to cater to their racial prejudices in order to maintain their economic position. Equality for whites went together with inequality for blacks.

Read:

The Scientific Origins of National Socialism by Daniel Gasman (Macdonald, London and Elsevier, New York, 1971).

South Africa: A Study in Conflict by Pierre van den Berghe (Wesleyan University Press, 1965).

Introduction to Race Relations by E. Cashmore and B Troyna (Routledge & Kegan Paul, 1983), looks at the interpenetration of concepts such as *Volk* and *Germanen* in the development of national socialist philosophy.

See *Aryan; Chamberlain; Gobineau; Haeckel; Race; Racism*

Michael Banton

Xenophobia A somewhat vague psychological concept describing a person's disposition to fear (or abhor) other persons or groups perceived as outsiders. The xenophobia may have a rational basis to it, such as when it refers to a worker whose job is threatened by the intrusions of migrants whom he labels outsiders and therefore fears. It may also take an irrational form, for example when someone fears Sikhs because he believes (mistakenly) that they carry knives for use as potential weapons. But, to call a person xenophobic does not necessarily say anything about the rationality of that condition. Nor does it entail examining the underlying causes of their disposition. And for this reason, xenophobia has only a very limited analytical value and has fallen from the contemporary race and ethnic relations vocabulary.

Read:

'Hostility and fear in social life' by John Dollard (*in Social Forces*, vol. 17, 1938), an early theoretical statement on fears and prejudices.

The Nature of Prejudice by Gordon Allport (Addison-Wesley, 1954), a classic social psychological text exploring the roots of prejudice.

See *Dollard; Prejudice; Scapegoat*

Ellis Cashmore

Z

Zimbabwe (Rhodesia) This country ranks with South Africa as having one of the most legally oppressive political systems designed to subordinate blacks. This was once a British colony called Southern Rhodesia, which had been self-governing on the basis of a white electorate since 1922. Although its inequality between whites and blacks was not as rigid or as formalized as in South Africa, the ownership of land and capital and the control of politics were almost entirely in white lands.

It was isolated by the dissolution of the Central African Federation and by Britain's granting of independence to Northern Rhodesia, now Zambia, and Nyasaland, now Malawi, in 1964. In these two countries, electoral franchises conferred political power on black African leaderships.

Resisting this trend and quite unwilling to grant the black majority an extension of franchise, the Rhodesian Front, under the leadership of Ian Smith, in 1965, made a unilateral declaration of independence (UDI). In world diplomatic terms, this was an illegal move and the United Nations imposed economic sanctions. But to alter the system of white supremacy was anathema to the rulers of Rhodesia. In a situation where the near total dominance of one group by another had been established, as it was originally by conquest and institutionalized by centuries of colonialism, only an intense guerilla war (or freedom fight) plus international pressure would stimulate change. And this is what happened.

Negotiations between Britain and South Africa centred on the crucial question of how to provide political participation and representation for black Africans. In the absence of this, there grew African freedom-fighting resistance movements which received military support from neighbouring African states. With the increasing pressure, South Africa, which had previously supported the Smith regime, withdrew its support.

Continued pressure and protracted negotiations eventually produced a scheme of transition and the establishment of an independent African state taking the name Zimbabwe in 1979. The first president under majority rule elections was Robert Mugabe. His assumption of leadership came after seven years of conflict which claimed over 20,000 lives.

Read:

Rhodesia: White Racism and Imperial Response by Martin Loney (Penguin, 1975).

The Rhodesian Election Campaign by Claire Palley (Catholic Institute for International Relations, 1979).

Rhodesia: Background to Conflict by B.V. Mtshali (Frewin, 1968).

See *Africa; Apartheid; Verwoerd*

Ellis Cashmore

Zionism Zionism, in its modern form, developed from a late nineteenth-century belief in the need to establish an autonomous Jewish homeland in Palestine. Theodor Herzl (1860-1904), a Hungarian journalist who lived in Vienna, was eventually persuaded by the events of the Dreyfus case in France and the 'pogroms' (i.e. the organized massacre of Jews in Russia) to conclude in his book *Der Judenstaat* that the only way the Jewish people could practise their religion and culture in safety was by having their own nation-state. In 1897, at the 1st World Zionist Congress in Basle, Chaim Weizmann (1874-1952) insisted that this had to be recreated in Palestine, even though there had been no significant Jewish settlement there after the conquest of Jerusalem in AD70.

Nevertheless, it was argued that Jews had always considered Palestine their spiritual home, citing that Jews throughout the Diaspora prayed for 'next year in Jerusalem'. It is, however, equally arguable that Orthodox Jews thought of this sentiment in a philosophical way: a means of affirming old beliefs, not of recommending the formation of a Jewish state with Jerusalem as its capital.

Herzl and Weizmann faced opposition to their ideas from both Orthodox Jews and those Jews who felt themselves to belong to the countries where they and their families had settled. Even after the Balfour declaration of 1917, expressing the British government's sympathy with Zionist aspirations, favouring 'the establishment in Palestine of a National Home for the Jewish people,' there was not a large migration of Jews to Palestine, which, for hundreds of years, had been predominantly Arab.

Up to the Second World War, Zionist claims that Jews throughout the world were persistently longing and striving to return to a homeland from which they saw themselves exiled, has very little foundation in fact. Not until after the genocidal antisemitism of the Nazi party had murdered 6 million Jews between 1939 and 1945 did the classical Zionist theories of Herzl, Achad, and Ha'am, come to mean anything to the Holocaust survivors and Jews throughout the Diaspora.

Just as the Pogroms had convinced Herzl, so the Holocaust convinced millions. The majority of Jews now believed that they were a separate people who had suffered unending discrimination and persecution. The only way they could be safe to practise the Jewish way of life was in a Jewish state, controlled and run by Jews where they constituted the majority. The major theoretical aspiration of Zionism became reality when the Jewish state of Israel was proclaimed in 1948.

Whilst the fundamental demand for the creation of a Jewish state in Palestine had been met, contemporary Zionism means more than pro-Israel support in the Diaspora and more than Israeli patriotism in Israel. Although it includes both of these ideologically, it claims to represent an all-encompassing approach to the problems of the Jewish people. The essential constituents of a Zionist programme are contained to a large extent (although not completely) in the resolutions of the 27th Zionist Congress held in Jerusalem in 1978:

1 The unity of the Jewish people and the centrality of Israel in Jewish life.
2 The ingathering of the Jewish people into their historic homeland, the land of Israel.
3 The strengthening of the state of Israel.
4 The presentation of the identity of the Jewish people through the fostering of Jewish and Hebrew education and Jewish spiritual and cultural values.
5 The protection of Jewish rights everywhere.

ZIONISM

The encouragement of 'aliya' (immigration to Israel) is the primary task of the Zionist movement.

Contemporary Zionism has not been without its critics; most notably in November 1975 a majority in the General Assembly of the United Nations passed a resolution defining Zionism as 'racist'. Not surprisingly, Zionists refute such definitions, stating that Zionism is only concerned with stimulating the cultural distinction of the Jewish community. However, when this cultural distinction manifests itself in the functioning of Israeli social institutions and related organizations in favour of Jews over the Arabs (by favouring one group over another, we refer not only to intentions but consequences), the link between Zionism and racism becomes more apparent. For example, in 1983 the World Zionist Organization (WZO) announced its intention for another 57 West Bank settlements over the next few years. The consequences of this would be that Arabs who had lived on the West Bank for generations would be forced to move as they were dispossessed of their land. Zionism on paper may not read as racist, but when such theories are open to practical implementation in Israel, then the result is both ideologically and institutionally racist.

Read:

The Idea of the Jewish State by B. Halpern (Harvard University Press, 1969), outlines the political developments.

Jewish Identity by S.N. Herman (Sage, 1977) an historical analysis.

The Origins of Zionism by P. Vital (Clarendon Press, 1975), a comprehensive guide to Zionism and its roots.

See *Ethnicity; Holocaust; Racism*

Carl A. Bagley

Index

INDEX

INDEX